Talking to Trees

A chronicle of one coach's journey into a new coaching paradigm

Talking to Trees

A chronicle of one coach's journey into a new coaching paradigm

Kim Krisco

La Peñita Press

Amado Nervo #37, La Penita Jaltemba, Nayarit, Mexico

La Penita Press

ISBN: 0984813500
ISBN-13: 9780984813506

To Sara and missamissachickapea

Acknowledgements

Neither the completion of our home and center, nor the publication of this book, would have been possible without **Sara Rose Ferguson**. Most of the time, it is Sara who is breaking the trail when we are on "developmental expeditions." In particular Sara's remarkable editing and writing skills made a ten-fold improvement in what I thought was the final draft of my manuscript. Her love and ever-present faith in me are woven deeply into every word on these pages.

As a father, I was a late-bloomer, so I need to give thanks for my daughter – **Jennifer Krisco** – for loving me for who I am, rather than *in spite* of who I am. Jennifer has grown into a beautiful woman who can manifest anything she imagines.

The beautiful home and center Sara and I created was far from two-person effort. Dozens of people toiled along side us over the years, but I need to acknowledge and give special thanks to **Bob and Bobby Hernandez**, **Manny Montoya**, **Dave Morgan**, and the **Turner clan**.

I also need to thank **Marilyn and Bill Veltrop** for supporting me, and saving the letters that sparked the idea for this book. And also, thanks to Bill for allowing me to use two of his groundbreaking models and concepts.

I have been blessed with talented and generous friends like Frank LaLumia – a renowned painter who created the artwork on the cover of this book. And I also wish to acknowledge Ron Lagerman whose creativity and talents can be seen in the design and layout of the book. Thanks guys.

This book evolves and advances ideas and concepts that germinated in the minds of many great thinkers. I single out these pioneers within the body of the book, but I would be remiss if I did not give a *special thanks* to Father Anthony DeMello S.J., John L. Austin, Abraham Maslow, John Searle, Rene Dubois,

Fernando Flores, Mihaly Csikszentmihalyi, Henry David Thoreau, and David Lesser.

Finally I wish to thank the Emissaries of Divine Light, and Sunrise Ranch in Loveland Colorado for providing the fertile soil in which my heart and spirit is able to take root and grow.

TABLE OF CONTENTS

THE SECOND YEAR

CHAPTER SUMMARIES

Domain:	Eukaryota
Kingdom:	Animalia
Phylum:	Chordata
Subphylum:	Vertebrata
Class:	Mammalia
Subclass:	Theria
Order:	Primates
Superfamily:	Hominoidea
Family:	Hominidae
Subfamily:	Homininae
Tribe:	Hominini
Subtribe:	Hominina
Genus:	Homo
Species:	Homo sapiens
Subspecies:	*Homo sapiens sapiens*

Trinomial name: Homo sapiens sapiens
Linnaeus, 1758

Human being — (Origin: 1590–1600; < L homō man; OL hemō earthly being, also Homo sapiens — Latin: "**wise human**" or "**knowing human**")

FORWARD

If you are reading this book, you have probably already dedicated yourself to making a difference. You recognize that helping people discover the aliveness and potency of who they are helps create a safer and more nourishing world for all. You know also that you cannot take others where you have not been yourself. You want to show the way ahead by going there first.

Those of us who have made such a commitment understand this is too much to do alone. The companionship, wisdom and inspiration of fellow wayfarers are vital.

I invite you to enjoy *Talking To Trees* in the way you might benefit from the support of trusted friend. When we reach out and share our quandaries or our accomplishments with a trusted friend, we get the benefit of being seen by someone who understands our journey. We feel understood in this way because we can tell they too are traveling a similar journey.

The specific events of Kim Krisco's journey will of course be different from yours and mine. Yet he is making available the essence of his learnings. I would be surprised if you do not find that you have faced and do face similar experiences, in yourself and in those with whom you work. As you bring your own experiences to your reading of this book, you might find, as I did, that the essence of what has been and is being discovered is mutual. What Kim learned from his experience enriches my understanding of my own life and work. And, although in reading there is no direct dialogue with the author, in a funny way there is the feeling that as we bring our experience to the book this also enriches Kim. Like speaking with a trusted friend.

Through the body of his story, Kim mines the insights, models and techniques that have become helpful in his coaching practice. Such a gift to have these distilled and laid out in a useable way. No doubt you will find things you can use to help others or help yourself. Have a care here.

I will venture to suggest that efficacy of these things comes not just from the insight, model or technique itself but from the substance of lived experience from which it arose. There are many coaching manuals on the market crowding for attention. Too often easy-to-apply fixes have only superficial effect leaving lasting change and authentic self-emergence still illusive. Few are the writings which make available the underlying experience in as personal and raw a way. To fully benefit from the gift that *Talking To Trees* offers, you will want to calibrate its insights, models and techniques with your own experience. Kim links his own story so clearly to the practices he proposes, so it is easy and natural to do likewise.

Finally, there is the opportunity for those of us perhaps who seek to be an inspiration to be inspired. We won't be giving what we cannot receive. For those who have been around the block a few times, however, it is sometimes hard to be genuinely and lastingly inspired. The kind of charismatic heart-lift or blasts of new insight that might have done it for us once don't apply now in the same way. What inspires and empowers now is the confidence that it is possible. The journey you have chosen is shared by fellow wayfarers.

My request to you is to let yourself be inspired in this way. As you read this book, yes. More importantly, as you live your life. I know this what Kim wants for you. If his telling of his discoveries helps you, great. If it helps you help others, also great. Let it also open you to the many sources of inspiration that abound all around. What your neighbor does, let that instill confidence that a new range of the fulfillment of who you are is available in your life. Also, you can make what you do, the experiences of your life available to show the way ahead for anyone who may care to look.

David Lesser
ExecutiveConfidant.com

INTRODUCTION

We are constantly being invited to be ourselves.

Henry David Thoreau

I used to think I was special. But my special-ness rubbed off over a period of ten years while building a home and coaching center in the foothills of the Sangre de Cristo Mountains of Colorado. The construction process is complete now, and enough of my defensive, ego-based armor has sloughed off for me to see my journey and myself more clearly.

I will share my decade long journey with you as a vehicle for gaining deeper insights into human evolution – which, for me, is what coaching is about. Coaches are the midwives of personal growth and transformation – accelerating a natural, universal process toward higher consciousness. If this is true, then it would seem to follow that **a coach's skill and ability grows in proportion to their own personal growth and level of consciousness.**

The term "higher consciousness" was a vague concept for me until I became deeply immersed in my coaching practice. I had previously made *consciousness* analogous with greater awareness. While there is certainly truth in this, I was confusing the process with the goal. That is, greater awareness is the primary *means* to understanding and living our true Nature as human beings. After we have shed our erroneous notions about the "nature of mankind," we will arrive at our reason for being – personally, and as a species.

While it may not appear overtly, there is a sense of urgency underlying my message. I believe we human beings are currently in a crucial race. The planet earth, and our species, is being endangered by our own lack of consciousness and integrity. While neither the precise means, nor the exact timing is known, there is little doubt in the minds of many people, myself included, that unless we as a species are to accelerate and elevate our consciousness, we will go the way of the dinosaur.

Dinosaurs dominated the earth for 200 million years. In that sense, it is ironic that the dinosaur has become an almost universal symbol for extinction. In actuality, dinosaurs are one of the more successful species that has ever inhabited this planet.

On the other hand, human beings – homo sapiens – have been around for only about 25,000 years. The spark of consciousness that enabled us to amble out of the primordial swamp has grown and allowed our species to create amazing things. However, human consciousness has not grown collectively, and in a manner that enables us to see and address the true impact, and long-term consequences, of what we create. And so today we find ourselves dancing with the dinosaurs on the edge of extinction.

One at a Time

One of my favorite places to be is Mexico. Over the years, I have enjoyed the beauty and hospitality of my neighbor to the south. In more recent years, I've had the time to begin exploring Mexico's arts, crafts and literature. One particularly amazing art form is created by the Huichol Indians, an indigenous group from the Sierra Madre Mountains in west-central Mexico. Objects and animals are fashioned from thousands of tiny colored beads, each the size of a pinhead. Each bead is meticulously placed on a sculpted form, *one bead at time*, using an adhesive made from beeswax and pine resin.

The designs and subject matter that cover these beaded forms have their genesis in shamanic visions, and they burst with color and mystical symbolism. These creations are relatively expensive, in part because they represent, not just hours of painstaking hand work, but days or weeks of effort. No one has been able to speed up the process or automate the creation of these singular art forms. And so it is with efforts to elevate human consciousness.

Just as Huichol artisans cannot create their art work by taking a handful of beads, glue and a carved object and shake them up in a bag; there is no way to mass produce human consciousness. It happens *one person at a time*. However, there are processes that facilitate, support and accelerate the growth of human consciousness. One of these is coaching.

The coaching discipline is focused on clients in a way that ultimately leads them to discover their true Nature and innate purpose. And while coaching is performed in service to another, the *act* of coaching also serves as a catalyst for the transformation of the coach as well.

As in any chemical reaction, a catalyst alone is not enough. Other ingredients are required. The ingredients for "transformation stew" are familiar to you – a commitment to change, compassion for self and others, time for reflection, and big challenges or breakdowns. All of this inevitably leading to creative action. We intentionally use and work with these ingredients when coaching others. But what happens when we intentionally use these same ingredients with ourselves – to accelerate our own evolution?

What follows in future chapters is what I have more recently discovered about myself, and the discipline of coaching. It is constructed around a series of letters I wrote to friends, family and colleagues when I first moved to Colorado and began my "building process." Since my letter writing became sporadic as time progressed, I will also share a few journal entries and stories.

When I moved onto a 35-acre parcel of land in the spring of 1997, I set myself up in a camping trailer that had no electricity, water, sewer, radio or TV. When my workday ended, I had a handful of great choices regarding how to spend my evenings. I could eat, sleep, read, listen to music, or write. On many occasions, I wrote letters to friends and family, mailing my letters when I went into town on the weekends.

I tossed my letters in the mailbox and their relevance vanished for me. I never expected to see them again. But years later, when some of them came back to me, I was able to take a rare and wonderful look back to reflect on my past actions, thoughts and attitudes. I became an observer of the observer. And, from this vantage point I was able plumb the depths of my evolution and gain valuable insights into coaching via my experiences and observations of people and Nature. More importantly, I was able to clearly see for the first time how my own evolution, and evolving consciousness, had changed and improved my coaching skills.

Rereading my letters was, at the same time, terrifying and wonderful. I was able to relive the sweet moments with my dog Phantom, who is gone now. I was able to embrace the scared man who, at times, was literally talking to the trees and crying out at midnight into the dark forest for help. More importantly, I was able to observe my inner and outer awareness grow with each letter written and sent.

I am compelled to share this new awareness. I do so, in part, as a way to validate my experience, but also with the hope that it might help others who share my passion for coaching.

I don't hold myself up as a teacher. I would expect that some of my insights and perspectives are not be new to you at all. However, I hope that, at a minimum, I will be able to deepen some of your distinctions around coaching. I also offer what I believe are some unique models and coaching techniques.

I make this offering with a caveat: Please treat this book as an *exploration* of the coaching discipline. I don't wish to add to the burden of programming that we all encounter when we are presented with new or different ideas. I simply ask that you "try them on" for yourself.

How It All Began

A while back I reconnected with a couple I had written to over the years. Bill and Marilyn are coaches, colleagues and dear friends (and angels) who seem a bit farther down the road than myself. When Marilyn visited for the first time, and saw the place Sara and I were building, my ego swelled a bit as she appreciated and complimented our efforts. However, the "me-bubble" burst when Marilyn recalled the letters I had sent to them over the years. I was transported back to the camper trailer where I initially passed countless quiet nights reading and writing in the dim light of a lantern, and laying awake to chat with the ponderosa pines next to my trailer.

Marilyn recalled how she and Bill eagerly received and read my missives. And, almost as an afterthought, said that she thought they had kept my letters. I was surprised and curious. Marilyn didn't have a ready explanation for why they saved the letters, but then remarked, "Maybe we saved them for you."

A week later my letters arrived, tied with a gold ribbon. I began reading one letter each dawn during my morning quiet time. As I did, I became reacquainted with a fifty-one year old man who came to Colorado fourteen years ago with a pick-up truck, a couple of suitcases, and a dog.

I had set out to find land and build my home and coaching center. At that time I had about $34,000 in total assets. I estimated it would cost about $180,000 and take twenty months to complete the project. While both estimates turned out to be off by a factor of three, the gap between my resources and my dream was large enough to create the psychological breakdown I was seeking for myself.

In my first letter to Bill and Marilyn I predicted that, when I finished the home, I hoped to be a more conscious and evolved human being. And as I reread my old letters, this vague premise, stated more than fourteen years ago, took on new meaning.

As a coach I am aware that a person could best understand himself or herself by observing their behavior and thoughts as they interact with the larger environment around them, and within the relationships in which they are embedded. Therefore, it would follow that, if I intended to consciously touch my true

Nature, it would more easily happen by observing myself in relationship to a new environment, new relationships, and new challenges. So, review and reflection on the letters I wrote more than a decade ago offered a key to new understanding and appreciation of myself. And since we are all participants in the grand human experience, my discoveries and insights might also prove interesting and helpful to others.

I offer these letters and journal entries – extracting old insights in search of new coaching principles, tools and practices. The hope is that by looking deeply into my experiences, we will discover and share the *universal* processes and dynamics that lie behind all human growth and true evolution. I am not promising to show "the way," because I do not believe that anyone else can give us the map to our true self. With this thought let me now reveal what I plan to do.

The Format of the Book

I will share my letters and journal entries exactly as I wrote them many years ago. You will see the good, the bad and the silly. There was an impulse to change some of these letters. As you know, human beings are pretty adept at rewriting our personal history. I left the letters in their original form because I have come to accept and love myself, more now than at any prior time in my life. True love is seeing things exactly as they are and accepting them without judgment.

After I share each letter, I'll select individual phrases or passages that point to a deeper insight or principle that may be useful to coaches. These phrases and passages are written in bold italics within a post-chapter section called *Coaching Principles and Practices*.

You will note that I come back to some topics over and over again – like listening, silence, language, and especially emotions. I do this because it's the way we create mastery. Mastery is a product of deep, continually evolving distinctions -- in this case, distinctions within coaching. My distinctions will mingle with your own to create a deeper understanding. In this way, your coaching behavior will *naturally* and *automatically* change and improve. That is the magic of distinctions.

A summery of each chapter that includes insights and principles, along with tools and techniques, can be found in a special section at the end of the book. Unlike the toolbox in my garage, I hope to make it easy for you to find and use the right tools as you go about your own coaching practice. Let me illustrate how this process and format will work using the introduction you have just read.

Coaching Principles & Practices

"I used to think I was special."

Feeling "special" doesn't seem like a bad thing, but it limits us in several ways. I distinguish "special-ness" from the personal gifts we all possess. Indeed we are each unique, and have abilities and potential abilities, that make us distinctive and unique. However, feeling special is often a way for us to compensate for some self-perceived inadequacy. Feeling special also implies a judgment that we use to create a higher rank and status for ourselves. Our special-ness makes us different than others. You might ask, "Is that so bad?" Alas, it usually is.

The moment we begin to define others and ourselves by how we are different, the seeds of separation are planted. We have all seen this seed grow, if not in ourselves, then in other ways around the world. It works like this:

They are different.

We are better.

They are less.

They are animals.

They are a threat.

They must be stopped.

It's okay to kill them.

This compresses and exaggerates how the seed-of-separation grows, but I trust the point is made.

However, if we define others and ourselves in terms of what we have in common – how we are the same – individual and collective possibilities are almost limitless. We now have a way to use our innate gifts as they were intended – cooperatively, in service to all.

A lament I hear from some of my clients is that they are different than their colleagues, their boss, their generation, their family, most people . . . take your pick. Whenever I hear the seed-of-separation being planted, or in some cases growing on a robust vine, I shift the coaching conversation to focus on what my client may have in common with those around them. This theme plays out beautifully in Robert Heinlein's classic science fiction novel *Stranger in a Strange Land.* The main character, Valentine Michael Smith, has human ancestry but grew up on Mars. When he comes to earth for the first time, people are obsessed with what makes him different, but what they find is what they all have in common. The most important thing we have in common is our innate empathy that proves our interconnectedness, and related to that, our need to love.

"I will share my ten-year journey with you."

Human transformation is typically a long process. Many would say that takes a lifetime. While that can be true, the reality is that, like biological evolution, psychological, emotional and spiritual growth in human beings is not usually a slow, gradual climb. In our animal world, corporeal evolution often happens in spurts created or punctuated by cataclysmic events. For example, wings on birds did not likely develop from a slow, gradual evolution of front legs. After all, what do you call an animal that lost its four-legged ability to run and, instead scampers awkwardly on two hind legs waving wing-like appendages to and fro? I call it lunch.

Evolution only looks gradual when viewed over a period of millions of years. Our psycho-spiritual evolution is no different.

Our lives drift along with little significant change, then something, a big problem or unexpected opportunity, suddenly forces fundamental change – or at least invites it. In this regard, challenges and breakdowns are a coach's ally.

It is the mission of the coach to work with people who have accepted the invitation to grow. Through conversation, interactions, and holding that person in your consciousness, the individual's transformation accelerates. This process often takes longer than most coaching engagements – measured in years, not months. So, a coaching engagement is only *part* of a larger, ongoing process.

About fifteen years ago, I was beginning one of my evolutional spurts. To everyone else it looked like the proverbial mid-life crisis. I call this middle-age passage my "regretorama." I had it bad. A friend recommended a book – Executive in Passage by Donald Marrs. As I began reading, my body shook with resonation as Marrs started his tale:

"I felt trapped by my lifestyle. Trapped by my career. Trapped in the high-rise I lived in. Trapped in my skin."

I had definitely picked up the right book. At least I thought so until the author revealed, at the end of the first chapter, "this was the *beginning* of a seven year journey."

The words, "Oh shit!" definitely crossed my mind, if not my lips. I wasn't prepared for the long journey ahead. I wanted to move on. I wanted to move *around* my regrets. But if we try to sidestep emotional and personal barriers, we inevitably fall back into our old patterns of thinking and acting.

Related to the longevity of the transformation process, some of my clients will tell you that I often stay in touch with them long after our formal coaching engagement ends. This connection is necessary because these people are forever a part of my consciousness. I believe it is helpful for them because my presence fans the coals of the commitment that originally brought them to me. Those embers of commitment may have cooled a bit, but they are seldom snuffed out. As much as anything, I am a point of loving accountability in their life, and I like to remain so. Sometimes the most powerful coaching act is just showing up.

"These ingredients for transformation stew are familiar to most coaches – a commitment to change, compassion for self and others, time to reflect, and breakdowns."

Most of these transformational ingredients are well known. And they generally make sense. However, that may not be true of the last one – breakdowns. Breakdowns are a gap between what you want, need or expect, and what you perceive is happening.

One principle of my coaching practice has to do with the awareness that breakdowns are a key ingredient in human transformation. Often breakdowns come to us unbidden. Illness, death of a loved one, a new job, a new baby, divorce, loss of a job and the like, bring our lives momentarily to a standstill. Although we may not realize it, we are at a crossroads. We must choose a path forward in order to move on.

While it may not be obvious at the time, we always make a choice. We *choose* the past, or we *choose* a new, alternative future. Our inability to choose a new future, by default, ensures that our life will continue on as it has in the past. The past is tempting because it is familiar and safe. Though we may be dissatisfied, or even in pain, our old familiar existence can seem preferable to an unknown future.

Oftentimes people come to coaching in a breakdown. Peoples' immediate response to their situation is, "This should not be happening to me." In reality the opposite is true. Life happens. Life brings change. But when what happens doesn't meet our expectations or needs, we find ourselves upset and concerned by our own assessment, judgment and needs.

As a coach I help people to see that this breakdown presents a choice – and maybe an opportunity. I don't do this in a Pollyanna way, by asking them to find the "silver lining," but rather I suggest that they picture themselves standing at the intersection of several roads. I ask them to read the road signs and tell me where each path is going. Initially they can only see a small distance down each road. But, I suggest that each path goes a long way and represents a journey of *years*, not just months. I say, "Let's see where each of these roads might eventually take us, then we'll have a better idea about what steps you might wish to take today -- to get on with your journey."

What road a person takes is their choice. Their *ability* to wisely choose a new path depends on the other transformational ingredients – commitment, options, self-awareness, etc. My objective is to help the client see that they have *many* choices, and that failing to choose keeps them on their current road with little change. Suddenly the breakdown looks less like a problem and more like an opportunity.

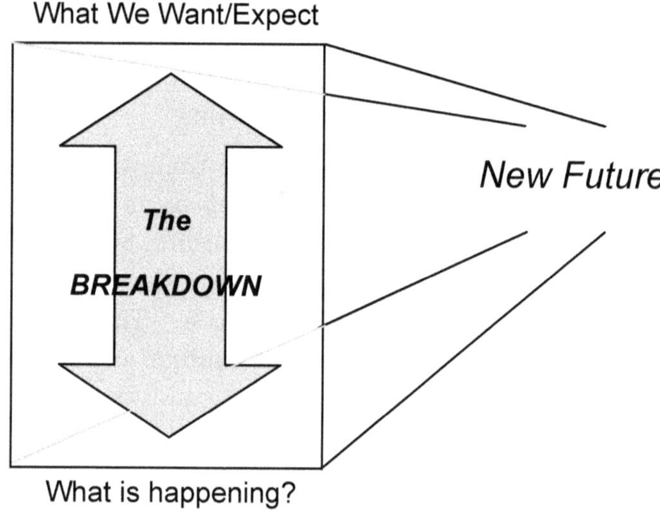

So, at first human beings see a breakdown as a *gap* between what is happening and what they want or expect to happen. A coach helps them see this breakdown as a doorway to an alternative future.

"The gap I perceived between my resources and my realized dream was large enough to create the breakdown I was seeking."

As I said, most breakdowns occur as a natural part of life. However, we can *intentionally* produce our own breakdowns when we consciously endeavor to change and grow. You may have attended a meditation retreat or workshop that does shadow-work[1] knowing you would encounter breakdowns.

[1] Carl Jung popularized the notion of "shadows" inside us. We have all been hurt, and we learned to hide parts of ourselves to prevent getting hurt again. These emotional barriers limit our ability to live and love. Shadow-work explores the hurt, fear, and anger inside us so we can beyond it to live more fully.

Nonetheless you chose these experiences because you understand that they might lead to improved awareness and greater personal growth. Interestingly enough, this same developmental dynamic is the "engine" that drives businesses and organizations.

When a leader or leadership team states a bold vision, a "stretch-goal," they are creating a breakdown. The vision or goal, by definition, is typically beyond what is happening, or likely to happen, of its own accord. So, in essence, leaders *intentionally* cause organizational breakdowns. I simply applied this same transformational process to myself.

Knowing I had the other ingredients – a commitment to change, compassion for self and others, and time to reflect – I provided the missing piece. I intentionally produced a breakdown by designing and building my own home, thereby challenging my capacities.

As I look back, the breakdown gap I perceived at the time seemed smaller than it turned out to be. As you will come to know, I quickly became the proverbial voice crying out in the wilderness – a madman talking to the trees.

"Bill and Marilyn are coaches, colleagues and dear friends (and angels)."

We all have special people in our lives. It's easy to think of them as angels. I have been blessed with more than a handful – a dozen or more angels who showed up at critical times to keep me pointed toward "my star." Bill and Marilyn are on that list, and I will tell you about others along the way. One of the first to come along was Felix.

I was thirteen years old. I met Felix in the last coffee house in the Old Town district in Chicago. He cast a spell and made a prediction about when I might "wake up" – and his prediction proved true.

The next one was Jessie, a causality of the '60's, who lost his sight using bad drugs and ended up opening a home for abandoned women and children. He taught me about the healing properties of loving. Not *being* loved, but loving.

Then came Buford. We drove through much of the Midwest making non-theatrical 16mm films for a living. He showed me the power of authenticity. He was a black man on the outside looking in, the place where I find myself now.

Around 1980 I entered the business world, I lost touch with angels for a long time. I guess I wasn't looking for them. Maybe I believed I didn't need them. However, they began to reappear when I leaped from the corporate carousel in 1990, went through a divorce, and began the long transition to my Colorado mountain home. Suddenly, angels reappeared. You will read about some of them in the pages ahead.

"In my first letter to Bill and Marilyn I predicted that, when I finished the home, I would hopefully be a different human being."

The word *human* comes from the old Latin "hemo" meaning *earthly being*. The biological term we commonly use to describe ourselves is the Latin "homo sapiens" meaning "wise humans." This book has to do with getting from "hemo" to "homo sapiens."

In that effort, I offer my experiences and insights with the hope that my perspective will provide some elevation – a place to stand and see your own pathway. This is why I wrote this book.

It is primarily through our own evolution that we grow in our ability to coach others. In the absence of ongoing personal growth, everything we might do is merely techniques, practices, and processes. In the end, it is who we are at our deepest level that determines our effectiveness as coaches.

"I am not promising to show "the way." Indeed, I believe no one can show us the pathway toward our true self."

Most of the great teachers have said that no one, other than oneself, can provide the answers to the big questions. But it is not without trying. Indeed, it seems EVERYONE and EVERYTHING is giving us the answers to these important heart and soul-centered questions from the moment we are born.

Our parents, teachers, churches, communities, governments, our culture, our society, are all programming us with answers to the big questions. Eventually we can no longer distinguish between their answers and our own. I suspect that most people grow up without ever having asked or answered existential questions such as:

Who am I?

What am I?

Why do I exist?

What is my purpose?

Felix, the angel of the Chicago coffeehouse, knew this. His words echoed those from thought leaders like Friedrich Nietzsche who, in Thus Spoke Zarathustra, said, "This is my way. What is yours? As for *the* way, it does not exist." It is well for coaches to remember this.

As a coach I seldom catch myself pointing directly to any specific solution or action. Occasionally I will point to a particular *pathway* where a solution, direction, or answer might be found. This often happens if I share my personal experiences with a client – usually outside of a formal coaching session.

In my role as a coach, some clients tend to endow me with greater intelligence or wisdom than I have. Therefore, I am always aware that when I relate my personal experiences, I might be *indirectly* pointing to "the way." And so, I have the same concern as write this book.

I will offer coaching concepts, practices and processes so that, first and foremost, they catalyze *your own* psycho-spiritual evolution; and second, that they become useful tools in your coaching practice.

We must walk that thin line between supporting our clients as they find *their* way, while we only point in a general direction. We are able to provide proper orientation to the degree that we have learned, in our own lives, what does *not work* – not necessarily what does. The clearer we can make this distinction, the more honest and effective we become as coaches. For example, a client may say that they are intending to quit an unfulfilling job on Monday morning. While you cannot know or suggest this choice is either good or bad, you could suggest that they give themselves a week to make this decision if, in your own experience, you had impulsively quite a job (as I have). It's not that quitting is necessarily a bad choice, but rather that you know that *impulsively* making that choice might likely lead to doubts, regrets and recrimination later on.

With this orientation to the format, let the journey begin . . .

FOLLOWING THIS EXAMPLE, CHAPTER SUMMARIES WILL BE FOUND IN A SPECIAL SECTION AT THE END OF THE BOOK.

Summary

Insights and Principles . . .

- Only through our own evolution do we grow in our ability to coach others; everything else is merely techniques, practices and processes.
- What makes us effective as coaches is who we are at our deepest level.
- A coaching engagement is only part of a larger, ongoing process that can stretch for years, not just months.
- The basic ingredients needed for personal growth and transformation are:

  1) A *commitment* to change,

  2) *Compassion* for self and others,

  3) Time for *reflection*, and

  4) *Big challenges* or *breakdowns*.
- Emotional and spiritual growth in human beings does not typically occur in a slow, gradual, linier climb. Human growth is characterized by spurts created and punctuated by challenging events, circumstances and opportunities. In this regard, challenges, problems and breakdowns can be a coach's ally.
- Breakdowns and challenges typically show up in life unbidden; but they can also be *intentionally* invited and created. Either way, coaches can play the role of a guide accompanying their client on a fascinating new journey.
- Psychological breakdowns often place a client at an unseen "crossroads" where they must choose the past or a new alternative future. It is up to the coach to help the client see these "crossroads," and make conscious, thoughtful choices.

- Whenever a person tries to work around, rather than through, life's challenges and breakdowns, they inevitably end up recreating old, well-engrained thinking and behavioral patterns.
- Coaches must walk the thin line between supporting clients as they find *their* way, while only pointing in a *general* direction. Though it may be helpful to identify what *does not* work, it is neither helpful, nor possible, to show another human being what works.
- Whenever anyone defines themselves, their enterprise, their team or organization in terms of how they are *different* from others, and who is *not* included, their behavior tends to become dysfunctional. Rather we should strive to build on what we share, have in common, and who *is* included.
- A key role of a coach is to act as a point of accountability for clients. Often the most powerful coaching act is to remain present in a person's life because it stirs and supports the deeper commitments upon which the original coaching relationship was built.

Models and Tools

SNAPSHOT OF COACHING

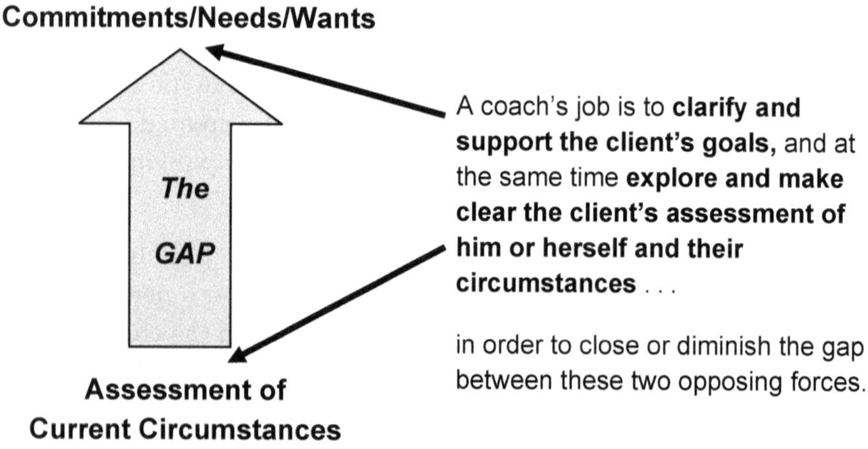

Commitments/Needs/Wants

The GAP

Assessment of Current Circumstances

A coach's job is to **clarify and support the client's goals,** and at the same time **explore and make clear the client's assessment of him or herself and their circumstances** . . .

in order to close or diminish the gap between these two opposing forces.

THE FIRST YEAR

I

"Living is precisely the inexorable necessity to make oneself determinate, to enter into an exclusive destiny, to accept it – that is, to resolve to be it."

José Ortega y Gasset

May 1, 1997

Dear Bill & Marilyn,

Greetings from Colorado!

My trek to Colorado is turning out to be one of the most challenging adventures in my life. Each day I am greeted with new obstacles. I would feel all right about bitching and moaning if we were talking on the phone, but delineating my trials and tribulations in writing seems demeaning somehow. With a slightly different perspective, it would be comical. Indeed, I am certain my escapades would put *Mr. Blanding's Dream House*[2] to shame.

Suffice it to say that in the last few weeks I've had my fence run down, the straw for my house unexpectedly dumped in the road (I am building a straw-bale home), the only bridge to my land restricted to cars only, and a host of other problems leading to a $8,000 budget overrun in the first week. It is frustrating, but somehow okay. It may even be a good sign. As Walt Whitman said, "It is provided in the essence of things that from any fruition of success, no matter what — shall come forth something to make a greater struggle necessary." I cannot usually quote Whitman, but his poems, along with Thoreau's essays, Rene Dubois' <u>A God Within</u>, and other treasured books are among the relatively few personal belongings I brought with me. As I pick them up I am reminded of a sentence in Quinn's <u>*Ishmael*</u> – about a telepathic Gorilla. One of the many great lines that haunt me was Ishmael's question, "Why is it you humans have to be told how to live?"

---

[2] Cary Grant and Myrna Loy – 1948. For younger generations recall *The Money Pit* with Tom Hanks and Shelly Long 1986.

I should be more upset at the setbacks than I am, and I'm surprised that I'm not. For a while I thought I was in shock or denial, but I don't really think so. Something is telling me everything will turn out okay.

I had hoped to be able to work full-time on building since my home has a unique and demanding design and will take most of my personal time. I can't recall if I mentioned it before, but I designed the home using principles of feng shui. And, while building on rock poses enormous building problems, it is great from a feng shui standpoint. Of course, the abundant wild life bodes well also. Elk, bear, wild turkey, rabbits and coyotes are plentiful. Hardly a day goes by when I don't enjoy the sight of wildlife nearby. I suppose that is what attracted and appealed to the Taos Indians and other native people who passed through this canyon centuries ago.

I have a dog now. She's a full-blood Australian shepherd. I call her Phantom. I have wanted a dog for a while, but thought I should hold off until my home was underway. My daughter Jennifer offered some coaching and advice, urging me to get a dog *now*. She was right. Phantom is a great companion and affords me an outlet for my need to care for others. She is also a good coach. Her insatiable curiosity and youthful vitality reminds me to enjoy the process and journey. Without that I might well see this effort as "work" - something I need to get through before the "good life" can begin. That's a mistake I have made in the past.

Working all day affords me little opportunity to be with other people, and I'm so tired at night that I seldom go out. I have a lot of conversations with Phantom as she helps satisfy my need for intimacy (although not totally). At any rate, I am bonding with Phantom in a special way. I am discovering her true nature and personality. The best words to describe Phantom are "sassy and sweet."

I will be working on my foundation (slab), plumbing and heating in the next few weeks. I hope to have that wrapped up in late May. Two 14" snowstorms put me behind schedule.

I took a small apartment for two months since the deal I had to buy a small travel trailer fell through. I bought some furniture at a second hand store and am living a monk-like existence. I have one chair, one bed, one lamp, one table, etc. I write in a diary every day, which helps me to blow off steam and extract the learning from the day.

Among other things, I have had to confront my fears and uncertainty head on. Like everyone else, I face my share of difficulties, fear and insecurity, but in the past I had others I could share with to lighten the burden. I am making friends, but it is difficult because I work all day and crash at night. I'm mostly by myself.

The silence that surrounds me acts like a mirror - reflecting circumstances as they are . . . reflecting me as I am. Little by little my ego, and the fabricated self-concept that protects it, is being torn down. By the time I finish this house I suspect the "essential" Kim Krisco will be all that remains.

I am anxious to hear about how you are doing. I don't believe you have time to write letters, but a note would be appreciated - or even a brief voice mail message. Please write if you can find the time, and let me know what's going on with you - what you're up to . . . where you are going . . . etcetera, etcetera. I don't have a phone, but you can reach me in the evenings at my landlady's phone. Her name is Sara.

Love and warm regards,

Coaching Principles & Practices

"Each day I am greeted with new obstacles."

Breakdowns often turn out to be larger than originally perceived. There are a lot of reasons for this, the primary one being that most circumstances are more complex and challenging than we can initially appreciate. Also, once we step into a breakdown it becomes more real, and its true nature becomes apparent. More importantly, when we experience a breakdown, there is a powerful emotional response generated in our bodies. This is true whether the breakdown has an external source or is intentionally generated. As coaches we have to be ready for the wave of fear, regret, and other emotions that come just before a person commits to taking the road to an alternative new future.

"Why is it you humans have to be told how to live?"

As I recall, when the character Ishmael uttered this line, it was with an insinuation that animals don't need to be told how to live. They are simply being who they are. So, why can't people live this way? I believe we strive to, but we have something animals do not have – and this gets in the way.

We are conscious. This consciousness or self-awareness does at least one significant thing. It gives us foresight – the ability to envision the future. This miraculous ability might be seen as a blessing *and* a "curse."

The "curse" is that consciousness and foresight allow us to know with certainty that we will die. The blessing is that it enables us to intentionally shape and change our future.

Animals have a future shaped by genetics and circumstance. My dog Phantom was not aware of tomorrow or next week. For Phantom next week seemed, and usually was, an extension of yesterday. There was no way for her to intervene in any significant way to change her future. On the other hand, human beings have foresight and can imagine a future that is not a logical extension of the past.

So, our consciousness creates an *ontological dilemma*. This means that our animal nature has us rooted in the past. In every moment of life, our biological and psychological characteristics and behaviors are an expression of past experiences that have become incorporated into our body-mind. At the same time, we struggle against these constraints of determinism by using our innate ability to choose. "Man becomes truly human only at the time of decision," wrote the German-born American theologian Paul Tillich. This dilemma is apparent on the worried faces of human beings when we make decisions. At both a conscious and unconscious level, we understand that our choices have significance, power, and consequences.

We know from experience and history that some choices may prove good for us, and others may be bad. However, we do not always have enough information, intellect or time to make good choices all of the time. So, we seek other sources of knowledge and wisdom outside ourselves. We seek knowledge and counsel from friends, religious books, philosophers, the media, celebrities, wee gee boards, etc. Coaching turns this paradigm around and reconnects us with our most important source of wisdom – our heart, our soul, and the Truth that seems to permeate the universe and everything in it.

We have access to great sources of inner wisdom. Each of us, at different times in our lives feels the fullness and connection with our own Truth. That connection is easily lost in today's busy world. It takes a discipline, and often a lot of time, to reacquaint and to reconnect with the Truth. Coaching can help us do this.

As much as anything, coaching is a consciousness raising discipline, in large part because coaching is firmly planted in the fertile ground of self-awareness. As you know, a key part of the coaching process is *reflection*, wherein awareness can emerge. It is easy to think of coaching as "a conversation," but verbal interaction is only part of the process we call coaching.

Coaching has four primary process components: 1) Preparation for the coaching conversation, 2) the coaching conversation, 3) the reflection - or review of new knowledge and perspectives that come through and after the conversation, and 4) integration of the new knowledge, perspective or awareness now manifesting. We may delve deeper into each of these parts of the coaching process later on; but for now we will simply hold this as the process we use to tap into the inner wisdom we all have. Without a doubt, this is the very process that enabled us to evolve from Homo erectus to Homo sapiens.

"The silence that surrounds me acts like a mirror -- reflecting circumstances as they are . . . reflecting me as I am."

My move to the mountains was motivated by many needs . . . the most important is the quiet atmosphere. People who visit often remark about the total silence that surrounds them here because it is so rare today. At first I was unnerved by the quiet of Longs Canyon. I struggled to figure out why the silence was so disturbing. I realized that silence acts like a mirror, and at first, I didn't like what I was seeing.

I saw a fool standing in the middle of the woods with a hammer, contemplating how many swings it would take to build a home.

I saw myself standing at life's tipping point, closer to death than birth, and tilting toward my grave under the weight of a thousand small regrets.

I saw a man standing in the dark, yearning for the sunshine of people's love and appreciation – a man whose identity has too often been contained in other peoples' assessment of him.

I could barely distinguish myself from the bundle of fears, doubts, regrets, anger and loneliness that was bubbling up in the quiet. I knew something else lay underneath. I knew I would have to dig through all the crap to find it. I didn't want to do it. I wasn't sure *how* to do it.

There is a Chinese proverb I love to quote in my work . . .

The three great mysteries are:

Air to a bird,
Water to a fish, and
Man to himself.

I've heard it said that man is creation's mirror. We are that part of ongoing creation that allows it to see itself. And, being part of creation, we need to see ourselves as well. And how can the observer see him or herself? A mirror of some kind is necessary.

Certainly Nature is a mirror. That is part of the mystery and power of the natural world. Silence is a mirror too. Ultimately, it allows us to peer deeply into our inner waters, past the flotsam of yesterday's regret and the jetsam of tomorrow's hope, to a still place where the truth lies. Coaching is a mirror, fostering the silent reflection before, during and after the conversation.

So much of the coaching process focuses on creating a viable future. This dauntless task is impossible unless we come to know ourselves as we are *now* – in the present. It is in our exploration of our gifts, our beliefs and our unique perspective on the world that we find our personal destiny – *our* future. The ability to wisely choose a path forward only happens when we are in touch with the values, beliefs and gifts that form the basis for our choices. *A coach's primary job is to facilitate inner exploration.*

Coaching conversations provide a catalyst, but it is within the coaching process, in reflection, that our clients are able to peer into their deep "inner waters." Essayist Michel de Montaigne noted, "There is no one, who, if he listens to himself, does not discover in himself a pattern all his own . . ." The operative word being "listens." To hear our innate wisdom requires silence.

Silence is, of course, a useful tool within the coaching conversation as well. Indeed, the use of silence may be one of the things that distinguishes a coaching conversation from day to day interactions – where silence is sometimes abhorred, and generally avoided. The use of silence facilitates self-awareness and taps the collective mind. It has that same impact during other stages of the coaching process as well.

Like most coaches, I recommend quiet contemplation in whatever form might seem appealing to my clients -- meditation, yoga, hiking alone, tai chi, journaling, etc. I am especially fond of journaling and strongly advocate for this practice. However, I am often working with people who are not willing or able to get quiet. To them I suggest another process that has proven to be useful. I refer to it as "audio journaling."

Audio journaling is simply a process where, with the use of a small cassette, micro-cassette, or digital recorder, a person records their thoughts and feelings in a stream of consciousness. My instructions are:

AUDIO JOURNALING

- Find a quiet place where you will not be disturbed for at least 20 to 30 minutes.
- Start with a question that focuses your initial comments, such as – What is the biggest barrier to my fulfillment? OR, What's the single change that would make the biggest difference in my life?
- Turn on the recorder and begin to answer that question.

- As you speak, let your conversation wander where it wants to. As thoughts and feelings bubble up, share them freely.
- You don't have to make sense or have a logical flow. Just keep speaking and sharing whatever comes to mind. One thought or phrase will inevitably lead to another.
- Go for at least 20 minutes or until you feel the energy dwindling, then stop the recorder.
- Put it away for at least 24 hours – a few days ideally.
- Then, get a pad of paper and pen if you want to make notes.
- Rewind the your tape recording and play it back.
- Listen to yourself. Remember and make note of what you hear. Listen, not just to the words, but what is *behind* the words.
- Don't get so caught up in note taking that you aren't listening. If you feel compelled to scratch down more than a couple words, stop the recording and write. Then, continue again when you are finished writing.
- When the recording is over, sit quietly for a while and consider what you may have learned about yourself.

It's important to experiment with this process yourself before you recommend it to others. People always report that they learn something new about themselves through what was said, as well as what was not said.

A common report is that they heard a lot of B.S. That's a *great* report. It tells me that the person is beginning to comb out and distinguish *their* beliefs, values, goals and plans from the tangle of beliefs, values and goals heaped upon them by their culture and society. Once an individual realizes that many of the values and beliefs guiding their actions are "inherited" so to speak, you as their coach can augment their exploration with a few questions:

- What were/are your parents values?
- Can you recall the first thing you did that pleased your mother? Your father?
- Who were your childhood heroes?

- What would you say your first big decision was? How did it turn out?
- Who would you hold up as a model for yourself?
- Can you tell me about a couple of experiences you had that were extremely gratifying?
- What would you number among your successes? Your failures?
- How would you like people to remember you?

The Spanish philosopher Jose Ortega y Gasset defines living as determining who we are and being it. Not a bad one-sentence definition. If that is true, then coaching is a vehicle for catalyzing, or expediting, this natural process.

The Old Town beatnik Felix referred to in the introduction, issued an invitation to me to explore and answer the big questions fifty years ago. So, half a century later I woke up, climbed into my Chevy pick-up, and drove to Trinidad Colorado.

The only thing worse than waiting so long to live my life would have been to believe that it was too late to do so. The weight of that resignation would have ended all my joy, if not my existence.

II

"If we cannot imagine ourselves as different from what we are and assume that second self, we cannot impose a discipline upon ourselves. Active virtue is therefore consciously dramatic, the wearing of a mask."

William Butler Yeats

JOURNAL ENTRY -- May 6, 1997

How did I get here? I have the whole story down pat when someone asks, but when *I* ask, that story seems to fade away. Was the story of my journey to Colorado created before, during or after I came here?

Why is a story necessary?

Maybe it's only for others. It seems I continue to tell my story in a town where I can count the people I know on one hand. Is it my ego? I want to "be somebody." I recall what Lily Tomlin said, "I always wanted to be somebody. Now I realize I should have been more specific."

Am I wearing a mask to cover up who I am, or am I in the process of creating a new me? I did that in years past, but I found that I often created a future that didn't include the real me. Am I doing this again? How would I know?

Too many questions. I better get to work. It's been said that idle hands are the devils playground. During this lonely transition, the devil will build a theme park if I am not careful.

Let it be resolved that I will work every day on my home – no matter aches and pains, no matter feelings, no matter weather . . . no excuses.

Coaching Principles & Practices

"How did I get here?"

Hindsight has woven its magic once again. It's ever so clear now, that my decision to put all my stuff in storage, leave the Dallas-Fort Worth metroplex, and undertake a huge building process in the wilderness was *emotionally* driven. How can I tell? Well, that decision doesn't seem logical and rational, and that's the clue.

I was an emotional mess in DFW. I had quit my corporate job years earlier, messed up and ended a marriage, and found myself barely able to scratch out a living as a writer and coach. I lived a meager existence. My primary sources of pleasure were walks in a park where I fed a murder of crows, and the dollar movie theater a few blocks away. Every weekend I saw each of the three movies that were showing -- no matter what was playing. I usually enjoyed the movies, but primarily I did it to be surrounded by happy people. I tend to be a loner, and back then I was a hermit.

The Dollar Movie House in Euless Texas was no other I had known. It was in a Hispanic neighborhood where going to the movies was a multi-generational outing. Entire families came – grandma Theresa, uncle Armando and two-month old baby Maria Elena. The theater sold popcorn, candy and such, but many families came with shopping bags full of food.

As the lights dimmed I could hear Tupperware containers popping. Suddenly the entire theater was filled with wonderful smells, the most noticeable being jalapeño peppers. People ate them like candy. The bag of popcorn in my lap looked pretty boring – like my life back then.

The desire to escape and start fresh was overwhelming. So overwhelming that I ignored the logic that would tell most people that they didn't have the money or skill needed to construct a large home in the mountains.

I often make decisions emotionally and then -- later -- create a "logical" explanation. In doing so I can fool myself into thinking I made a rational, well-thought-out decision. (This is the same process often used to write history books.) I endeavor to remain cognizant of this ontological process, but the light of awareness seems only to shine on me *after* a decision is made – not while I am making it, *unless* I seek coaching.

Like most coaches, I am careful to modify my approach when coaching someone who is in a highly emotional state. For example, I back off when a client displays anger, or if they show up as depressed. However, I do not end this rich interaction. I not only offer help and support, but facilitate exploration that will sort out and reveal the emotions they are experiencing. I do this knowing that, in subsequent coaching sessions, we will need this emotional information.

In addition, believing that many choices people make are driven more by emotion than reason, I also gather emotional information *during* coaching conversations. Emotion mostly shows up in our bodies. Some people are better than others at concealing their emotions, but few can hide them completely.

Knowledge of nuero-linguistic programming (NLP) and other psychological tools can help, but it doesn't take special training to be able to tune into another person's emotional state. We all do it in our everyday interactions – primarily via non-verbal communication. Coaches need to be especially good at this.

Decoding emotional information can be as easy as asking, "How does that make you feel." Sometimes, I simply reflect the somatic information I am receiving. For example, "You shook your head when you said that. What does that mean?"

No doubt these approaches are familiar to you. I am sharing them in support of the assertion that, while coaching is a logical, intellectual, methodical process, it must take into account the deeper emotional body of a person, because that is where much of "the truth" for that individual lies.

As coaches we help people find new opportunities for action. From there they can make committed choices that will ultimately lead them toward accomplishment, fulfillment and peace. Since many past and present choices are driven by emotions, emotions must surface so they can be explored *before* new choices are made, or less ideally afterwards. Either way, it is by revealing these emotions, exposing them to the light of awareness, that they take their rightful place in the decision-making process.

"Why is a story necessary?"

Stories are at the heart of the human experience. Our unique ability among all creatures to consciously shape our future, depends on our ability to create, tell, hear, and – yes – live our stories.

We share our stories, not just with words, but by the way we dress, the surroundings we choose for ourselves, and through the work that we engage.

We have little control over the world around us that tries to tell us, not just who we need to be, but who we are. We live in a constant interplay between the "world's story" that we live within, and the one that we are currently creating for ourselves. I would assert that the measure of a human being is their ability to put the world's deterministic story about us into the *background*, and then step forward to create and tell our own story. The ability and decision to become the primary author of our story is the finest criterion for human beings. This is the work of a coach.

Coaches help others create a better tomorrow. However, I know through personal experience, that it is possible to create a future that is not only unfulfilling, but also sad and lonely. How does this happen?

It happens when we let the world around us – our society and culture -- write most of our story. "Living your parents' life," my beatnik angel Felix would say. This is determinism. This is the way animals live. Even when it comes to who we are and what we do, those chapters are, at least initially, written for us. We tend to grow up playing a scripted part -- adding a few "adlibs" along the way. However, the moment we take "pen in hand," the possibility of becoming more authentic exists. It is often this choice that brings clients to us.

Coaching clients come seeking to rewrite their story. Our job as coaches, then, is to help clients distinguish between the larger story that has been written for them and the one that they are now rewriting for themselves.

"Am I wearing a mask to cover up who I am, or am I creating a new me?"

I was onto something when I scribbled this in my journal. I can see now that it was as much an answer as a question.

I have always been fascinated by masks. One of the five college majors I explored was theater. In one acting class I wrote a paper entitled Personal Facade: The Use of Masks in Theater. Masks have been used in theater for thousands of years and are still used today. I mention this theme paper because, in my research, I ran across a story that stuck with me.

Someone wrote an article about a revival of *The Frogs* by Euripides in a London magazine. The author told of an interview with one of the actors who played an angry, snarling Greek god. The actor was wearing his mask at the start of the interview. With this bit of theatrical flair, he approached the interviewer in character. However, the interviewer was distracted by the mask and wanted to interview the *actor,* not the character Aeacus. So, the interviewer snatched the mask from the unsuspecting actor. As he did so, he noticed that the actor's face was contorted in a way that *exactly* matched the expression on the mask. The interviewer wondered why, and asked the actor why his face matched the mask's expression when he didn't really need to do that. The actor responded something to the effect, "I believe it helps me get into the part." Indeed it does.

The point here is that the human transformation process often includes the creation of a *persona*. (Persona, by the way, is from the Etruscan "phersu" meaning *mask*.) As we choose who we want to become, how we want to live, what values we wish to express in our life, we *initially* try on the attributes and actions of the "character" into whom we want to transform. It is not so much an attempt to deceive or hide, but an intermediary step to get from who we are to who we want to be. My former neighbor in New Mexico is an example.

Greg moved from Arizona where he retired from truck driving. He and his wife moved to New Mexico, bought a ranchette and a couple horses. But that was only part of his new persona. Most every day he wears clean jeans, high over-the-calf-boots, a bandana over a western style shirt and a Stetson with character. He is definitely one of the good guys. On the way to becoming a cowboy, it helps to dress the part. By now I suspect he has registered his own brand.

My "wish to be cowboy" ended a long time ago, but Greg's did not. In getting to know him, it is clear that his cowboy persona is more than clothes-deep. Greg is committed not just to the *ways* of the cowboy, but to the values and beliefs – hard working, close to the land, plain speaking, etc. Taking on this wild-west persona was part of the transformation from an urban city detective to an uncomplicated man of the range.

Taking on a persona can be a good thing if it helps us to explore what we are seeking. So, while trying on a new guise can sometimes be used to cover-up or deceive, it can also facilitate personal transformation. Certainly it did that for me.

I wanted to live what I then described as an "authentic life." In part, that translated into living in Nature. In Nature I am constantly reminded of what is real. When I see a bear lumbering around the property I am pretty sure that that animal is not pretending to be a coyote or elk. It only knows how to be a bear.

I seek a peaceful, more contemplative life. And in pursuing this end, I am learning about the power of place. In my coaching practice I carefully choose where coaching conversations are held. I not only remove the client from their office, but often arrange to meet them in a park, or another place that supports protected introspection.

I also studied feng shui and environmental psychology to better understand how our surroundings impact us. For example, while modifying an existing dwelling is helpful, *creating* one allowed me to design the optimal environment for coaching and writing. And so I built a unique straw-bale structure where the heart of the home is a garden.

I could go on and on about the persona I created for myself, the pragmatic pickup truck, the "working" Australian shepherd, etc. All of this helps me live a more authentic life – one closer to who I intend to become.

But is there a difference between creating a persona to hide or deceive and using one to facilitate growth and evolution? Of course there is. But the only one who knows for certain is the individual in question. It has to do with the intention behind the persona and how ego-bound we are to it. I have a great example.

Just after 9/11 my practice, like many businesses, tanked. I struggled in vain to generate income for five months. I worked at it every day – cold calls, book giveaways, etc. Finally I asked myself, what else can I do to make a living in Trinidad? The answers came easily – building.

I strapped on my tool belt and made appointments to meet with the three primary building contractors in town. The first two turned me down flat. A 57-year old carpenter wasn't in high demand. My last hope was Joe. Joe knew me, but not as a carpenter, so I modified my pitch. "Here's the deal Joe. Put me on the job for two weeks. If I don't cut it, when you give me my first paycheck, simply tell me you don't need me anymore – no explanations needed. I just want a chance."

Joe gave me a chance and I worked for him for almost a year before I partnered up with another fellow I met on the job. The two of us continued building and remodeling for another 14 months. For over two years I did construction.

Did my persona change when I was a carpenter? You bet. I wore jeans, a canvas hat, tool-belt, and drove a pick-up. I took regular breaks and had lunch with the guys, and had the occasional beer with them after work. A change in role required a change in persona. Or more accurately, the persona facilitated my changing role. It was authentic because my intention was to be a carpenter -- not a writer *doing* carpentry.

Working with people committed to change and growth, we will notice them taking on a new persona, and we should cautiously support this process. One of the most useful things we can do is to help a client explore the *true intention* that lies behind the "mask" they are shaping.

An interesting footnote to my carpenter story came in mid 2003. I received an unexpected phone call from a large national non-profit. I had done a little coaching for people in that organization, but not much more. I took the call on my cell phone from a scaffold twelve feet above the ground. I was installing siding on a house. After introducing himself, the caller asked if there was any way I was free to facilitate an important team meeting in Puerto Rico the following week.

"Let me check my calendar." (*Count to ten*). "What do you know, I am free. What exactly are you looking for?"

I took off my canvas hat and my tool-belt.

III

"In language we build our own identities, our relationships with others, the countries we live in, the companies we have, and the values we hold dear. With language we generate life. Without language we are mostly chimpanzees."

Fernando Flores

May 11, 1997

Dear Bill & Marilyn,

Greetings from Colorado!

Got your letter a day before my birthday. Letters from friends are the best gift. I baked cupcakes as a way to celebrate. I forgot to use the high altitude recipe, which calls for me to add flour to the mix and raise the oven temperature. They rose more than usual and overflowed the cups. They are edible, though a little fragile. Live and learn . . . which brings me to your query as to why I chose *this time* to build a home in the mountains.

It's a question I continually ask myself these days, particularly as I seem to face adversity at every turn. As with most big decisions, there are several things driving my action. On the surface, my divorce freed me up to move. Then there is the part of me that simply wants to hide, heal . . . or maybe just run away. There are many forces at work.

Many of my friends took "early-out" packages when their company "downsized." Now they spend their days tinkering a workshop, touring in a Winnebago, or playing with grandchildren. Somehow I seemed to be surrounded by people that appeared to be pulling back from life. On the other hand, maybe they are finally living life. Either way it may be the only escape from the corporate carousel that seems to be spinning out of control. You're either on the carousel or off of it. I seem to be seeking a middle ground.

I may be in some kind of denial, but I feel as though there is still much for me to do. I'm winding-up, not down. Of course, to accomplish all I intend, I will need to keep my mind, body and spirit in tip-top condition — and I don't mean by power walks and herbs. Most of my friends say that one man, especially a 51-year old man, can't build a house and center with his own hands. I can't see why not. What I may have lost in energy, I can make up for in ingenuity. I wonder though . . . maybe my purpose in life is to act as a warning to other aging men.

Late at night, when I mutter silent prayers to the trees, I don't ask for miracles. I give thanks for what I learned during the day and ask for the strength to get through the next one. But I wonder if the trees are listening.

Tomorrow, I'm not building a house, but rather cutting 300 sticks of rebar. And the next day, I'm not building a house, but grading and leveling my floor. We can do the "impossible" if we do the possible one-day at a time.

All this is a philosophical cliché, but it is how breakthroughs are created. If I thought about building a coaching center and all it entailed, it's unlikely I would ever try to do it. I would compromise - buy the land now and build later, or rent a building. Most people take what already exists and improve it. Yet within each of us there is spirit that gives us god-like powers. We have the ability to create something from nothing. We can speak things into existence by simply saying, "I will . . ." And so, I say, "I *will* build this house and center."

There is a Paul Simon song that poetically makes the point I'm struggling to share. I believe the song is called *Slip-sliding Away*. Part of the lyric quotes a woman who says, "A good day ain't got no rain, a bad day's when I lie in bed and think of things that might have been." I won't let my future "slip-slide" away.

Love and warm regards,

Coaching Principles & Practices

"It may be the only escape from the corporate carousel that seems to be spinning out of control."

When I connect in with old friends and colleagues the most frequent remark I hear is, "I wish I could do what you're doing." They don't necessarily wish to build a home and coaching center in the mountains, but they are tired of playing the games that comprise so much of the typical work life. They are tired of starting every day girding themselves emotionally for the stressful day ahead. They want to escape the corporate sirens constantly singing in their ears:

"To get ahead you must:

. . . put your entire heart and soul into the business.

. . . stretch yourself thin.

. . . stress yourself out.

. . . work longer hours than are sensible.

. . . take on more responsibility.

. . . sacrifice time with your family.

And you will be rewarded with executive approval and more money."

By working hard nine hours a day you earn the right to work ten.

When I suggest to my friends that they CAN do what I am doing, they often scoff and describe the "burdens" they are carrying that they cannot set down. And like the Greek hero Atlas they grasp more firmly to that pillar that seems to be holding up their heavens. Then come all the reasons why their work is so vital and important. As they list their reasons, I recall that Bertrand Russell once remarked, "One of the symptoms of an approaching nervous breakdown is the belief that one's work is terribly important."

A recent study by the International Labour Organization revealed that America is the only country in the world where working hours are increasing. The average American works about 2,000 hours per year. This is the *highest* in any industrialized nation. European countries work 16% fewer hours per year and, on average, have a GNP growth rate only about two-tenths of a percent less than the United States. These two-tenths of a percent must be very precious because we pay for it with the shortest vacations and the highest rate of depression in the modern world. According to a recent survey by Expedia.com, Americans have the fewest number of vacation days in the world – 13 days on average. Even when on vacation, 42% of Americans say they call into work regularly. In making a living, American's have forgotten how to live.

A crisis point comes when a person realizes that all their "success," "progress" and "achievement" has not seemed to increase joy, fulfillment, happiness or delight in life. Understanding this dynamic is critical to coaching because many of our clients feel trapped on the "corporate carousel." Being good coaches we often suggest they explore alternatives and ideas for a different kind of life. But how do you do this without falling into a "wishing conversation" about "what I'd *really* like to do?"

I play a game with some client-leaders. It's a classic therapeutic process called *The Magic Shop.*

A deeply relaxed state is created in the Magic Shop by moving closer to my client, lowering my voice, and speaking slowly to signal that we are changing the focus of attention. I tell them a story about a Magic Shop where people can go to get anything they want. The storeowner, the Magician, doesn't want or accept money. He likes to barter. The Magician is shrewd, but wants the trade to be fair for everyone. I then ask my client if she or he would like to visit the Magic Shop.

If they decide to continue, I ask them what they are shopping for – an attribute, a feeling, a goal, etc. Usually it relates to the issue(s) they have brought to coaching.

Once they can clearly say what they want, I ask them what they are willing to trade. At a deep level, every person has some idea regarding what he or she will have to give up in order to gain what he or she wants. However, it may take some time for the client to get in touch with this, and then to articulate clearly what it is. I remind them that the Magician will insist on a fair trade. What they trade must have value.

There is sometimes a tendency to help clients find a way to avoid giving up *anything*. For example, if they want a new career path, they might say, "I will give up financial security." While that may not be necessary, I do not intervene. The primary goal of the Magic Shop exercise is to have the client realize and accept the notion that they must be willing to give up something to get what they want.

A visit to the Magic Shop can be a powerful experience for most people. It goes far beyond a conversation about "what I'd really like to do." The process of shifting the focus of attention encourages people to look deep inside themselves to find what they *really* want . . . and what they fear.

The fact that they have to give up something of value tests how badly they want a change. It puts them firmly in touch with the reality that fundamental change requires discipline and sacrifice. The Magic Shop exercise leads to greater clarity, and more importantly, it puts clients in touch with their commitment, or the lack of it. Commitment begins to be generated the moment we let ourselves know what we really desire. Since commitment is what fuels the coaching process, this is no small accomplishment.

"We can speak things into existence by simply saying, "I will . . ."

My practice is built on the shoulders of many people, Fernando Flores, John Searle, Julio Olalla, John & Laurie Ford, Alan Scherr, John L. Austin and others. Advancing the work of these and other pioneers, I continue to explore the awesome power of language and how to use it more constructively, wisely and effectively. Today I have deep appreciation for the significance and power of language.

I believe that language is not so much what separates us from animals, but what takes us closer to God. As Flores points out, we use language to create our reality. But my shouting to the trees, "I will build a house in the mountains," was not enough. By itself alone, even the most powerful declaration doesn't manifest anything. Mind you, words are an indicator of what I am thinking and they shape my thoughts. That is what affirmations are all about. But when it comes to speaking and creating, involving other human beings, seven elemental that things must be present if language is going to give birth to co-creation.

1) A clear *intention* and strong commitment within the speaker.
2) The ability to say what is meant.
3) A receiver (listener) who knows that the speaker is trying to communicate.
4) Listening (message reception) by the receiver.
5) A listener that knows and understands the *intention* behind the communication.
6) A listener who understands the message itself.
7) A shift in perspective and intention within the listener that leaves them poised to respond or act.

The need for all of these prerequisites is what makes human communication so challenging. Let's take each of these in turn and see how they relate to coaching.

A clear intention and strong commitment within the speaker.

Words themselves carry the meaning, but not power. The dictionary is full of words, yet I wouldn't consider the dictionary a powerful book. The power lies in the human intention and commitment behind the words, and the context in which the words are used. I have experienced people whose intention and commitment are so strong that they only have to show-up. They don't have to speak. And, when they do speak, their intention and commitment is focused in a way that changes you. For example, I have experienced this phenomenon with a Buddhist monk in Irving Texas. He is one of the "angels" I referred to in the introduction.

More than fifteen years ago, I read an article in an Irving Texas newspaper about the coming Vietnamese New Years celebration. It is celebrated in early February, and this particular year Tet was celebrated February 12. Curious to learn, I decided to attend the celebration and went to the Lien Hoa Temple in the early evening.

I was surprised to find that no one was around. I was going to leave, figuring I had the date or location wrong, but decided to inquire at the monk's residence next to the temple. The monk answered my knock with silence. "I wanted to join in the New Year's celebration," I said, "but I must have the wrong day." The monk smiled and opened wide the door.

I entered his small chamber and sat down. He had a smile and casual manner that made me feel like an old friend coming for a chat. He served what he said was a special tea, and asked about me, who I am, what I do, what brought me there, etc. He said he was a writer too. I later found out that he spoke several languages and had written books in many of them.

I recall feeling very comfortable. After a bit, he explained that Tet, like our New Year's, was celebrated the evening *before* New Year's Day. I was a day late. I should have been embarrassed, but I laughed at my mistake and he chuckled too. He noticed that I had brought some oranges. I understood that people brought fruit to be blessed during the celebration. He asked if I wanted to take my fruit to the temple.

We entered the beautiful temple and he told me to place my oranges at the Buddha's feet, and take some fruit that had already been blessed from the altar. He then taught me a walking meditation and we meditated around the Buddha for some time.

Without a word, he put his hand on my shoulder and walked me back to his small residence. Still without speaking he crossed the room, picked up a small, carved wooden box, and brought it to me. He opened the lid and took out what appeared to be a large, fuzzy, dried almond. He held it up and motioned to his mouth to show me I should eat this. As I opened my mouth, he said a few words in Vietnamese as I chewed and swallowed the spongy, almost tasteless "almond." He looked a long time into my eyes and I returned his soft gaze. I felt my chest get warm and tears began to gather in my eyes.

He sat back in his chair and sipped his tea in silence. I knew it was time to go, and I simply said, "Thank you." As we rose to go to the door, he asked if I wanted to know what I ate and what he said to me. I nodded my head in the affirmative.

"You ate the heart of the lotus," he told me, "What I said to you was, 'I give to you the lotus, because I see in you the Buddha."

That visit changed me. I had experienced love . . . pure and simple. The word love was never used once in our conversation. His intention and commitment to love was in his *being*. And that's what I experienced. I didn't understand his words, but the message got in, and went so deep that I carry it with me today.

So, what's the difference between saying something and meaning it, and saying something and not meaning it? Intention -- intention is key because we are not always able to find the exact words we need.

The ability to say what is meant

Even when we are clear about our intention, we must have the vocabulary, the speaking skill, and the proper context, in order for our words to produce action and manifest a result. There are many times, even with a clear intention, that I am not able to say what I mean.

Like many adolescents, I was awkward in most things I did, but especially when it came to addressing the opposite sex. At thirteen the love of my life was Mary Ann. My intention was clear and strong. I wanted her to be my girlfriend. But in every encounter I was never able to find the words to tell her what I felt. Mary Ann . . . if you're out there . . . Will you be my girlfriend?

A receiver (listener) who knows the speaker is trying to communicate.

As human beings we often have the ability to transform our intention into a result by simply taking action ourselves. If I want to build a concrete floor, I make and set the forms, place the rebar, pour the concrete and finish it. Many things in life are that way – except communication. Communication is one of the only things we cannot do by ourselves.

In order for communication to occur, we need another party to know what we are trying to tell him or her. Have you ever said something in a casual manner so that it was heard as idle chatter and, as a consequence, it never registered with the person with whom you are speaking?

In order to ensure that our messages are received, we have developed subtle ways of getting someone's attention so that they that they know we are trying to communicate. We make eye contact. We touch a person as we speak. Or we intentionally insert silence into the conversation to focus attention on what we are about to say. I often use these and other techniques to *change the focus of attention* when I deliver feedback and observations to a coaching client. As I mentioned with the Magic Shop exercise, I draw in closer, lower my voice, and speak slowly. This whole notion of shifting the focus of attention is key in the coaching process. I have created a ladder of distinctions for attention that is useful in coaching:

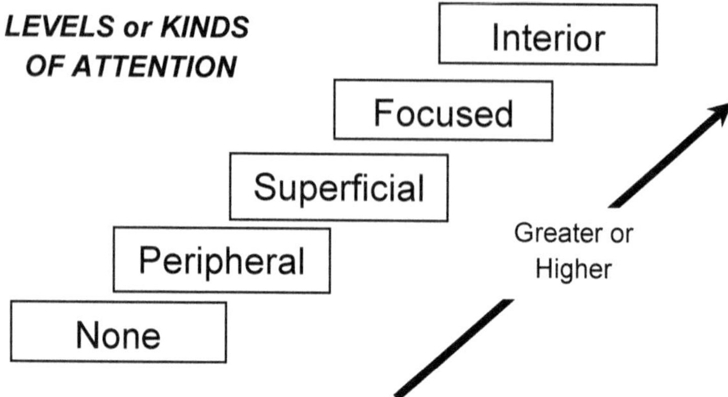

Most of these levels are self-explanatory. Most day-to-day conversation is superficial at best. Most people are paying more attention to the running dialogue in their heads than to what's going on within their interactions.

Focused attention is when we are engaged emotionally and intellectually – fully sentient. The voice of judgment in our heads is fading into the background and we are fully present to the conversation. An indication that you are in a state of focused attention is that you lose track of time. Ideally most coaching occurs at this level. Even then, it is unlikely that any individual will remain in a state of focused attention for an entire coaching session. For that reason, coaches must be sensitive to their own attention level, and that of their client, and continually shift the focus of attention higher on the ladder.

There are times when you will want to get and keep someone in a focused state. Then there are times when you want to bring them into **interior attention**.

Interior attention often shows up during meditation, yoga, and prayer. Although I know of no definitive research to support my assertion, I would imagine that our brainwaves, when we are in "interior attention," are in a theta pattern. When in this state we are completely present to what's going on *inside* us. We are more susceptible to suggestion in this state and, I believe, able to take thoughts and ideas directly into our subconscious.

There are moments in a coaching conversation when you want to create interior attention. For example, when you suddenly stumble upon a critical insight and you want it to register deeply with the person you're coaching.

On one occasion I was working with an individual -- call him Jim -- who left an organization under a flood of mostly erroneous accusations. He found new work and was doing well, until he was asked to come back to the organization he had left years earlier. He sought coaching to help him gain clarity and decide if he should take the new job at the old place. At one point in our conversation Jim said he had been vindicated, but he said it with an unusual twist. "I guess they learned they were wrong about me. I guess that should be enough for me." I held my hand out to create a pause to signal for interior attention.

When I put my hand down, Jim continued, "I'm not taking the job." In that moment Jim realized something important. I wasn't sure what. Did he realize that this betrayal ran so deep that he wasn't content to be exonerated? Was turning down the job a way he could get revenge? Or did he feel that he had not really been exonerated? I signaled again for greater interior attention.

I moved in closer to Jim and put my hand on his. I slowly repeated his words, *purposely* paraphrasing him incorrectly. I said, "Jim, did I hear you correctly? Did you say . . . 'I guess they learned they were wrong about me. I guess that should be enough for me, but it isn't." I asked if I got it right. In this important moment I was being a bit of a trickster.

Jim slowly came out of a trance-like state and said, "I'm trying to get even with them for what they did to me." In that moment Jim found his answer.

Listening (message reception) by the receiver.

In past books and articles I have written about listening, but I have barely scratched the surface. I focused on the little "pundit" in our heads who does a running commentary on everything we think, see, feel and hear. As you know, a pundit is a critic of sorts, sometimes wise, and sometimes not – but always chattering away. Managing this omnipresent critic is not easy and not always necessary. The key is to be aware of our inner pundit and take what she or he says with a dash of skepticism – without totally disregarding all that's said. There may be insight and wisdom to be gained.

It is true that the little pundit usually comes from the past. This is not surprising since the largest percentage of our thoughts and words emanate from the past. Sometimes our little censor is in the future – imagining, creating, and anticipating. Sometimes the pundit is in the present moment gathering minute sensory data – giving voice to intuition.

It is difficult if not impossible to quiet the little pundit, but we can be aware of him. Practice some inner aikido, encouraging the pundit to move aside. It's the only way to manage this imp who has outposts in your head. Your hearing works at the speed of sound – about 1,100 *feet* per second. Our brains work at near the speed of light – 186,000 *miles* per second. Thus, our brain is working almost nine million times faster than our ears and this discrepancy shows up in our listening process.

Even when our little pundit is operating from the past, it may be helping us validate and integrate information. When it is focused on the future, it is creating and planning. And when it is in the present, it is in touch with our body-mind and emotions. These are good things, so don't throw the baby out with the bath water. Even if you could stop the little pundit, why would you? Instead you want to manage the imp because not *all* of his information is valid. And invalid information can limit possibilities, relationships and action. So, when you catch yourself discounting, dismissing and/or resisting, take heed. Your pundit is getting nervous because your world wants to bust out of its box.

At any point in time, our world, our reality, is a tidy little package tied up with a neat tag that reads, "The Way It Is." When we encounter something, someone, some idea or thought that cannot be validated within our little package, we are faced with a choice. Either we ignore this new bit of information . . . or we unwrap the package, find a bigger box – one that will hold the new idea, thought or belief -- and then wrap it up again and put our now tattered tag back on.

We will explore listening again in future chapters, but for now, be cognizant of the little pundit in your head. When he is shutting down the conversation by dismissing, discounting, resisting and judging something as 'wrong," he's giving you an opportunity to explore the boundaries of your current reality.

One of my biggest challenges is managing *my* listening. Indeed, my focused listening is one of the biggest gifts I have to give. Listening is a manifestation of love that energizes coaching conversations.

A listener that knows and understands the intention behind the communication.

The first thing that gets communicated to a listener is your *intention*. At the beginning of the conversation the listener gathers verbal and non-verbal information about your intention that will provide the context for your message. Obviously, you want to make sure the listener receives a clear, positive intention. The easiest way is to simply declare your intention. As you do this be sure that your stated intention is in total alignment with your *true* intention. For example, recently I heard a peewee football coach here in Trinidad stating his intentions to his team before their game. After reviewing all of the mistakes the team made during the previous game, the coach said, "I'm not doing this for me. I don't care if we win or lose." Really, you had to be there. But suffice it to say that his true intention came through loud and clear . . . he wanted to win that game.

A listener who understands the message itself.

As we can see, understanding the spoken word is only one of the conditions that must be present in order for communication involving others to happen. Nowhere is this clearer than when I am in a foreign country where I do not speak the language.

I do not speak any language other than English. I nibble at the edges of Spanish when I visit Mexico, and I am continually amazed that I can communicate fairly well. In fact, I am able to conduct some rather complex transactions. This is because the other six necessary elements of communication are firmly in place – not to mention the patience and generosity of the majority of Mexican people with whom I interact.

An overt or covert reaction within the listener that generates a change, leaving the speaker or listener poised to respond or act.

Two decades ago I discovered John Searle, and what he called *speech acts* – language that generates a response. Searle noted, for example, that *requests* were among the forms of speaking that could create action. Actually, there are many action-generating speech acts.

John L. Austin, in his seminal work, *How to Do Things with Words* (1962), created some powerful distinctions for speaking. Austin distinguished between what we say, and what we accomplish by saying it. He labeled these two kinds of speech acts *locution* and *perlocution* respectively. Dipping into his body of work, he pointed out that there are over 1,000 illocutionary acts – acts that can produce action. Requests are among them, but so are – order, censure, pledge, approve, object, demand, etc.

While these illocutionary acts are useful to coaches, I have come to find that what Austin calls perlocutionary acts are even more interesting. These are the spoken words that not only impact a listener's behavior, but their thoughts, beliefs, feelings, viewpoints, manner, mind set, position, etc.

An illocutionary act is actually a *prelude* to action. For example, making a request is not, in itself, an action. Pronouncing a sentence is not carrying out the sentence – nothing has actually happened.

A perlocutionary act is *doing* something by saying something. It has to do with manifesting your intention within your speaking and being – sometimes using illocutionary acts. For example, a coach typically asks many questions – illocutionary acts. They elicit a response or action – an answer. This is a perlocutionary process – one that changes a person in the moment that words are uttered. For example, when a client makes a matter-of-fact assertion that you suspect is flawed, you might offer a perlocutionary response. One of the most common is, "Is that the truth?" I've seen that question transform a person in that moment.

IV

"The only service a friend can really render is to keep up your courage by holding up to you a mirror in which you can see a noble image of yourself."

George Bernard Shaw

May 12, 1997

Dearest Jennifer,

Thanks for the great birthday package and the lovely gifts, my daughter. I savored them, opening them a little at a time throughout the day to prolong the joy. It was a poor substitute for having you with me, but your love and spirit was certainly here. I particularly loved the tapes you made. I suppose you knew that I had but a few tapes to play, so they will brighten up my place and will undoubtedly get worn out. I know it took a lot of time to record and label them — time which is precious to you. So thanks for your time also.

Phantom loves all of her gifts, especially the green squeaky frog. Of course, the treats are appreciated too. I had to give her a bath today - long over due. She was dusty and caked with mud in places. This land and way of life suits her. She loves to run in the woods and play in the dirt with sticks, pinecones and elk and deer bones that she drags home to lie at my feet.

I am resting today because I can't seem to shake this cold and sore throat I've had for almost two weeks now. The physical work is more difficult than I had anticipated. I'm fine during the day while I work, but I ache in the evenings and my right elbow throbs during the night.

I took most of the last weekend off, something I rarely do. What prompted it was a library book sale. I needed to replenish my library. I go through about two books a week these days. As I rummaged through the books I ran across Norman Vincent Peale's book The Power of Positive Thinking. My first thought was, “What good will that old book do?” Fortunately I’m more aware of my thoughts these days. I bought the book.

I poured about two-thirds of the stem walls Friday. As with many tasks thus far, there where complications. The first of four cement trucks to cross the bridge broke the planking. It was lucky to make it across, but the other trucks had to take the long way around — adding twelve miles to the drive and my delivery costs. But that wasn't the worst part. The long way around goes through a private association road and because of the difficulties with the bridge, they closed and locked a gate that is normally open to everyone. The drivers refused to take responsibility for crashing the gate, so I rushed to them with a gas-powered demolition saw and cut the chain. I plan to follow up and make amends. No doubt there will be complaints, but I had little choice. It was that or eat $3,000 worth of concrete and delay the pour longer. As the Japanese proverb goes – “fall down seven times, stand up eight.”

As I returned with the concrete trucks, the crew gathered around. The foremen Jerry said there were bets that I might be in the county jail by now. There was a round of “way-to-goes” from the gang. As he was walking away, Dan slapped me on the back and said, “You may just have what it takes, city-boy.”

This week I'll finish grading the sight and installing the plumbing and heating. I expect it will take almost three weeks until I can pour the rest of the slab. I imagine all this is rather boring for you, but it's my life these days. At this point I can’t even imagine how I will do it, but I am certain I will finish this project.

After the pour on Friday the concrete crew asked if I wanted to join them for a night out with "the guys." I was tired and sore but honored by their invitation, so I accepted their offer.

They were all great, tough on the outside but with hearts of gold. We drank beer, ate pizza and played pool. My pool playing was a joke, but I made no pretense that I could play, so it was okay. As the night went on some of them shared their stories with me. Most of them have lived a tough life and yet still hold on to their values and hope for a better tomorrow. Farley is the father of the boy who, just six months ago, was killed in a military accident during basic training. Jerry recently lost his home and most everything he owned fighting charges because is fifteen year old son, who didn't have a driver's license, got in a bad accident that injured several people. He and his wife came home one evening to find police cars in their driveway. They eventually found their way through the legal tangle, and were eventually acquitted, but the lawyer's fees and other expenses caused them to miss four house payments and the bank is foreclosing.

All of this brings me back to my early days in the steel mills. There remains a special place in my heart for working-class people. The values I hold are working-class values. Maybe that is part of the attraction of Trinidad for me. These are people who are mostly about making a living day to day. Money and status seems to soften the bumps along the road of life, but it can also isolate you from the bittersweet human experience. Working people seem to feel more, do more, and have more intense relationships. Of course, this means they feel more pain too -- that seems to be the trade-off.

Jen, I want to leave you something more than pictures, memories and money. All of those things seem to vanish in time. I don't think this is a place you could live, but I think you just might enjoy spending time here. I am not asking for anything other than a visit. And when you come, listen to the wind in the pines. You'll hear me saying "I love you."

Much love and many warm regards,

Coaching Principles & Practices

"Dan said, "You may just may have what it takes, city-boy."

We come to know people not so much through their work or words, but through their being – some call it their heart. The people who came into my life when I took on building our home and center became a family. We came together because of what we *do*, but we remain together because of who we are to one another. Above any imperfections I see the courage and nobility in the men I work with, and they seem to see something in me.

Jerry's slap on the back and invitation to pizza and pool meant more to me than the plaques and certificates I received over the years from the companies for whom I have worked. Jerry, Farley, Eddie, Spider and the others were able to see me, and their friendship reflects back to me a "golden" part of myself. To a large degree, coaches do this – maybe it's the most important thing coaches do.

Coaching as a mirror is almost a cliché. And like most clichés it's true. But that is only *one* role a coach plays. Some of the many roles a coach can play include:

Action generator – the client leaves every interaction committed to action. Remember, "getting ready" to act, even seeking more coaching before taking action, can be a stalling tactic.

Agent – sending the client-leader on a journey (e.g. The Magic Shop) to foster experiential learning.

Appreciator – communicating positive regard and acknowledging whom the client is being and becoming.

Change manager – supporting the creation of a compelling vision by reducing the perceived cost of change, reflecting their dissatisfaction with their current circumstances, and encouraging their first step.

Clarifier – reducing confusion and chaos by separating real from imagined aspects of a situation – fact from opinion or fear.

Commitment generator – understanding that commitment can and must be generated, maintained and enlarged in order for actions to manifest powerfully.

Confronter – pointing out when the client is out of integrity, playing games, or may be lying to him or herself and/or others, etc.

Context Creator – creating a place and space to safely explore and try on a new persona, or explore new ideas and directions.

Distinction creator/explorer – using language to make the invisible visible. If we can "see it," we can acknowledge, manage and use it to grow our awareness and mastery.

Edge finder – pointing out when the client hits the edge of their "box" or paradigm, and supporting exploration outside of it.

Explorer of limiting behavior and thinking patterns – these are our defenses against randomness and chaos that seem to facilitate our survival by creating the illusion of safety.

Giver of feedback / mirror – there is no growth, improvement or evolution without feedback.

Grower of awareness – increasing sensitivity to our inner selves, to those around us, and the world. Being more aware of what's going on in our bodies is a starting point.

Guide – encouraging exploration of new pathways, or sometimes modeling the "explorer spirit."

Perspective shifter – changing the point-of-view. A perspective is neither right nor wrong, but rather useful or not useful.

Point of accountability – a witness to promises and commitments made.

Seed planter – sharing useful notions, reactions, observations, etc. with the understanding that nothing escapes the subconscious. The subconscious will eventually create a new thought.

Shifter of time – moving out of the past to explore the future, and especially focusing on the present.

Trickster – provoking, prodding – e.g. intentionally incorrectly paraphrasing.

Within these various roles, a coach utilizes a wide variety of *tools*:

Awareness – This is different than "attention." Attention, of course, is necessary. It is a focused presence. But *awareness* is more defused and expansive. It is possible to be paying attention to a person and, at the same time, be aware of others around you, or the energy shift in the room, and most importantly YOURSELF. As Anthony DeMello said, "Attention is a spotlight, and awareness is a flood light."

In a coaching conversation it is as important to be aware of what is going on inside you, as it is to be paying attention to your client. What judgments or assessments are you making? What is coming up for you at an emotional level? If you don't do this, your issues and programming will get tangled up with those of your client. The boogeyman of coaching is the coach's own projection.

Compassion – Feeling compassion is critical because it tells you and your client, that you are aware of your connection, and are listening at a deep level. That said, there is a difference between feeling compassion and expressing it. You do not need to give voice to your compassion. If you feel it, it will be present for all to experience.

Dialogue/Inquiry – This is one of the most useful forms of conversation in coaching, and in all interactions. Without going too deeply into dialogue and inquiry, a coaching conversation is primarily an *exploration*. The purpose is greater clarity and understanding, not necessarily making a decision or acting on a solution.

Distinguishing – A distinction is a deep understanding of something such that, when present, it *automatically* and fundamentally changes perception, beliefs, values and/or behavior forever. The process of distinguishing involves subtle uses of language – using language in a new ways, to create a meaning that heretofore did not exist. This process sometimes goes beyond language. Indeed, some of the most powerful distinctions are created in action and held within our body-mind. For example, in distinguishing "leadership" for a client, I put his hands in mine. At first I simply held them firmly. Then I gradually pulled them toward me. The client instinctively pulled back, creating resistance. Then I relaxed, and so did he. Then I let go of his hands, and turned my palms up in front of him. After a moment I asked, "What did you just experience that might have something to do with leadership?" His answer reflected a deeper understanding of the nature of leadership versus management. This understanding was not only in his head, but understood in his body-mind.

Intuition – This term comes from the Latin – intueri – meaning "to see within." It was first used in text in the 15th century to mean a "prior or existing truth." In the 17th century it came to mean what is does today – immediate apprehension of the senses, or coming into direct knowledge without reasoning or inference. Suffice it to say, if a coach is fully aware, intuition will be available for use. And it should be used as much as possible.

Joy/Optimism – This is another great gift coaches can give their clients. Clients come with issues and problems. They come to *you*. You represent hope and possibility. Be just that. And when you are not hopeful or joyful, be aware that you are not.

Listening – A meta-tool tool for coaches. A coach must continually endeavor to build deeper distinctions for this amazing cognitive and empathic connection.

Silence – Silence is underutilized – in life and especially in coaching. Silence creates the space wherein we can access awareness, intuition, our feelings, etc. Use it!

Will/Intention – This might be a new area to explore. The fact that "will" and "intention" are on my list of tools implies a belief that we have the power to influence and change the world around us in unseen ways. Intention is, at its core, a focusing of energy. It brings our life-force energies to a nexus. From there our will amplifies this energy much like a magnifying glass does with the sun.

Our will is a mind-body force, an assertion of our being. More importantly, the expression of our will is the precursor to action and change. As a coach, I want to leave my clients changed in some fashion and poised to act.

Just as intention and will are critical to a client, they are equally important to a coach. Before every coaching session I get in touch with my intention for my client. After the coaching session I align my own will with theirs as they leave. In this manner, my coaching is congruent.

The application of all these powerful tools sometimes gives me the feeling that I am powerful. So, I pointedly remember that I am no better than any other being. I have sought out tools and processes that are not immediately available to others. My auto mechanic is not a better or smarter person, he simply has some tools and knowledge with regard to automobiles that I do not have. He repairs cars. I coach. It's my job . . . and maybe more.

V

"Our doubts are traitors,
and make us lose the good
we oft might win
by fearing to attempt."
William Shakespeare

May 13, 1997

Dearest Bill & Marilyn,

Retrieved your voice messages a day after my birthday. Your words are "coin of the realm" (to quote someone I love).

Thank you for your coaching, words of encouragement and the muse-like magic. I also appreciate your offering up Tad (*Bill's son*) into indentured service. If the notion appeals to him in any way I would be happy to pay his way here and share my trailer and gruel with him. I will hold that possibility and await further signs.

I baked cupcakes to celebrate. However, I didn't use the high altitude recipe. They rose . . . and rose . . . and rose. My cupcake runneth over. Live and learn -- which brings me to what I am learning as I undertake the building of a home in the mountains.

Consciously or unconsciously we all choose how we will live our life. Will it be a déjà vu experience or jamais vu (excuse my French – "never seen")? There is a bit of underlying tension that's always in the background. But I can hear the words of my Tai Chi master Mr. Ho as my body strains in the form, "Relax, relax. Relax when your muscles are tense." I am long on tension and short on Mr. Ho.

This week I'll backfill, grade the site, and begin on the plumbing and heating. I expect it will be a while before I can pour the slab. It's amazing how what I describe in two sentences may take two weeks to complete.

I have been suffering from the classic two-in-the-morning-wake-ups. When I get tired my spirit flags. The gremlins tell me I'm not good enough and I won't make it. They challenge my commitment and urge me to go back. I have written a new affirmation that I hope will be part of my bedtime ritual.

"I have everything I need in this moment to be joyful and fulfilled. My intention is my strongest asset. When it is clear and present, it is irresistible."

It's not elegant, but it's appropriate. I use it to do battle with the gremlins. Maybe it's a smoke screen. Eventually I'm going to have to go toe-to-toe with those whispering imps that dance in the wee hours.

It has become my superstitious practice, when my fears surround me, to lean out of my trailer window and ask for help from the nearby trees. I wonder now if they are listening.

My doubts -- born of yesterday, haunt today, and hold back tomorrow.

Help, I'm being held prisoner by my doubts.

Love and warm regards,

Coaching Principles & Practices

"Eventually I'm going to have to go toe—to-toe with the whispering imps that dance in the wee hours."

Most of the principles in my last book are valid and useful as far as they go. Like a mythological Greek hero, I was on a quest then. I might have identified with Jason seeking the Golden Fleecc – in this case, the "fleece" was a future of my own making. I conveniently forgot that most heroes have to fight and kill a beast before they triumphantly return home.

It is possible to create a future that breaks the pattern of the past. This begins with getting in touch with what we truly desire, which fans the embers of commitment. The "bellows" that ignite those embers, and manifests our intention, is language. We declare our intended future to ourselves and to the world, thus growing our commitment and making it real. However, before our future can manifest, we usually need to do battle with "the beast."

The many imaginative monsters of Greek mythology – the Chimaera, Hydra, Minotaur – remind me of my past in that they arc formidable, clever, and hard to vanquish. But slaying them is the only way to escape and live.

I thought I could do some inner work and move on. My coaches, and most of the great thinkers I read, tell me that *deep*, sometimes painful, work on myself is a prerequisite to reinventing my life. But I never really understood what they meant until I came face-to-face with my old self in a small camper trailer in Colorado.

Before moving to Trinidad I went through a systematic, methodical process in which I identified aspects, experiences and relationships that were unfinished and, where possible, took action to bring closure. This is important work since so much of our thinking seems to be focused on what is unfinished – a sad waste.

Some time ago, I sought traditional counseling to help me take on my mid-life regretoroma. Psychologists tell us that we are usually doing our best, even when we think we are not. It's only hindsight that deludes us into thinking we could have done better, or done more. But the truth is we simply didn't have awareness in that past moment. Somehow, though, that thought isn't very comforting.

In an attempt to escape my past, I removed myself from my old lifestyle and acquaintances that seemed to be holding me back. I eliminated distractions. No radio, no TV, no phone, no nonsense. I paid my dues and was ready to move on! Or so I thought.

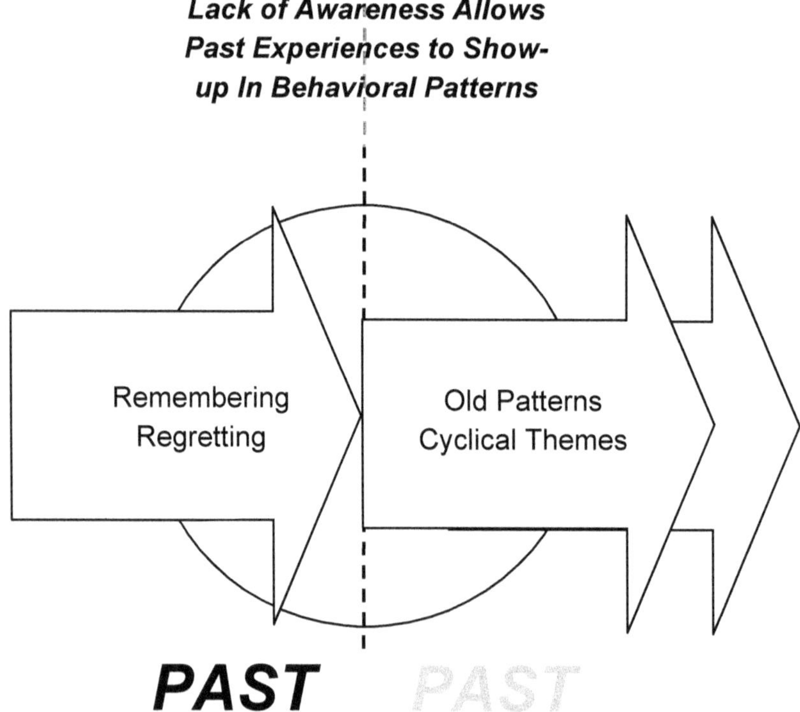

Many of my old patterns of thinking were still firmly in place. The most dangerous one being feelings of inadequacy. It shows up in my tendency to exaggerate. I knew there was a judgment within that tendency with which I would have to deal. If I could move beyond my own judgments of myself, I could take the next important step into wholeness – self-forgiveness.

I thought I did that work, but it was something that I completed in my head – not in my heart. I needed a different, less therapeutic way, to find self-forgiveness. I found it the most universal way. I found it by getting in touch with the God within me. I found it in loving – myself first, then others.

I had a love for others – most others; but there always seemed to be one or two people out there who were difficult to love. I chalked it up to their "*human imperfection*," and that gave me the clue I needed.

My cultural and upbringing had taught me to judge myself as "imperfect," and I had a past filled with errors and mistakes to validate my judgment. But this assessment was not the truth. In each moment my underlying desire and commitment to be a better human being makes me, not only okay, but completely worthy of love – especially my own. I am only okay in that moment, but that's the only moment that counts. We no not live in the past or the future. The only moment that counts is this one, and my intentions make me "perfectly loveable" in this moment. This is critically important for coaches to remember. And so our clients, by seeking coaching, are all "perfect in the moment."

If you can get past these words, to the truth of them in your life, you will love yourself and all others as well. This is critical work for a coach, since the coaching skills and techniques you offer are more potent when couched in unconditional regard.

As coaches we must come to this awareness in order to be masterful. Coaching is helping others break old patterns, and cyclical themes, to create a new future born of choice rather than conditioning. In order for this to happen, the client must do battle with their "beastly past" and "beastly self" and come away forgiving and loving themselves.

Forgiveness is what releases us from the past. We are not our past, but we tend to live as though we are. We are fooling ourselves when we proclaim a new future if we do not do the inner work that brings us to forgiveness, completion and self-love. Once we have done this work, the choices we make in the moment can and will create a fundamentally new tomorrow.

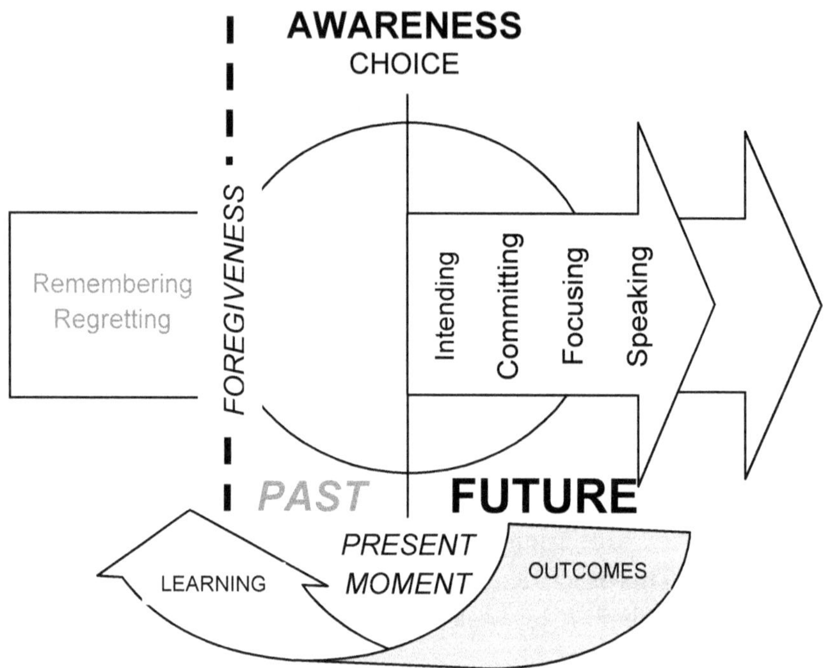

Our choices and our declarations grow from intention into being. Commitment driven speaking and actions usually attract most of the people and resources necessary to manifest our intention. We go on to create a result, and that outcome *always* provides learning. There is really no need for regret and recrimination unless you would regret learning and growing.

We can, and do, bring things into existence, and speaking plays a role. But, what comes *before* the speaking, and stands *behind* the speaking, ultimately determines what we create. For example, I worked with a client who wanted to escape from his current way of life. His actions were driven from the past. He was angry about his situation and had come to put most of the blame on himself and his past choices. I knew that this dynamic would not be a fertile context from which to create new opportunities. I felt that we had to deal with his past choices and decisions in a manner that allowed him to let go and forgive himself before he focused on the future. While he was initially reluctant to do this work, he eventually saw and felt the necessity of it. Once compassion and forgiveness were in place, we were able to focus on the future. More importantly, his conversations and actions were now driven from a pure, clear intention uncontaminated by regrets and recriminations.

As you may recall, one of the roles a coach plays is that of *agent* – sending the client-leader on a journey. A coach not only offers a ticket to the future, but also to the past.

"Help, I'm being held prisoner by my doubts."

Any inquiry into coaching would be remiss if the subject of *doubt* were not explored. Doubt is a "gremlin" that coaches encounter on a regular basis. For as any client considers new possibilities, a coach can be sure that doubt is waiting in the shadows. It slithers out of the darkness when a new commitment is made. I often see a fleeting frozen look on the faces of my clients immediately after they make a declaration. Hesitation -- a momentary stop in action. Doubt is dangerous because it often masquerades as reason and sensibility.

I not only look for doubt in coaching conversations, I *expect* it. Doubt is triggered by incoherence and/or contradiction with our experience, and what we have come to believe. Doubt lives in the past. So it stands to reason that, the moment we *break* with the past and begin to go in a new direction, we experience doubt.

Oftentimes a client cannot identify what they are feeling as doubt. They may simply feel discomfort, unease, or anxiety. There are a wide variety of emotions associated with doubt, most of them negative. On the more intense side of the spectrum, doubt can show up as paralyzing fear. However, it would be a mistake to think that a less emotional manifestation of doubt is of a lesser concern for a client, or for the coach. The slightest doubt decreases our emotional and spiritual stamina. Over time it brings sickness of the soul. As a wise yogi once put it, "Doubt is the tomb of the heart."

So, what is to be done?

As people set out to create a new future it is relatively easy to help them identify and overcome barriers and challenges that lay ahead of them. It's more difficult to fight a phantom nurtured by old wounds and faulty programming. It's like killing snakes.

I find a snake to be an apt metaphor for doubt. It travels low, unseen in the grass. It hides under rocks. And when you encounter one, you are frozen in your tracks. However, living where I do, this metaphor has special meaning.

You don't live in the southwest without encountering snakes. Most of them are not only harmless, but also beneficial – the bull snake, the hognose, the garter, etc. But we also have rattlesnakes – the western diamondback and the prairie rattler. The rattlers are good too -- but dangerous. My dog Phantom was bitten and barely survived. When we encounter rattlers on the land, we simple give them right of way. However, when I find them in our inner garden, or lurking under the deck, I sometimes kill them to protect my family, guests and pets.

The process of killing a rattler is not unlike dealing with doubts. First you have to see and acknowledge the snake. Next you need to find the proper instrument, institute a plan, and then take decisive action.

I stepped out on our deck one summer afternoon and heard it – that unmistakable rattle. I peered over our low deck and there he was – a five-foot diamondback warming in the sun just beyond the shadows. I was about seven feet away. I recall saying in a whisper, "Stay right there."

I quietly stepped away to get a long handled shovel. Then I crept up just behind the snake. I knew that diamondbacks cannot strike more than about one-half the length of their body, so I stayed outside of what I judged to be a safe distance.

I knew I must strike quickly. I had one shot. I raised the shovel, and pausing to take a deep breath, thrust the shovel down behind the head of the rattler. For a moment I thought I hadn't come down hard enough because the snake began thrashing widely. I wanted to run. But then the headless body suddenly zigzagged off into the brush. The head remained -- the jaws opening and closing over and over. After two minutes it stopped. I buried the head in the trees to keep the dogs and other animals from finding it and the poison.

And so it is with doubts:

1) **See and acknowledge them** -- give voice to them, describe them – don't let them hide in the shadows.
2) **Find the proper tool**. In the case of doubt, the only tool is *truth* -- truth about who you are *now*, and about what there actually is to fear. Doubt is most dangerous when you keep it closeted inside of you.
3) Then **act decisively** – calmly, quietly, but going straight at it without hesitation. While much of it will wiggle off, the "head" – some old deep-seated insecurity -- may often linger on for a long time. However, in the light of the sword of truth, it has lost its power.

I often experienced doubt as I lay in my narrow trailer bed, staring into the vast, dark night sky. I could see doubt slithering toward me into the moonlight. A snaky voice in my head whispered, "You're in over your head my friend. You're short of money. Your body aches. You're tired and alone. It's too late for this sort of thing."

I would take a deep breath and shout out loud, "I can earn money, and my body is in the best shape it's been in a many years . . . I will be rested in the morning." And then I began my evening ritual – one that I never talked about.

I would slide the trailer window above my bed open to feel the chilly air rush across my face. I took a deep breath, and at the very top of my lungs, I yelled, "Please help me. I need help! Let me complete this journey."

I did this most every night, for months. It may have been initially motivated by desperation, but at another level I knew that when a human being acts out of a deep commitment, the universe cannot resist lending a helping hand. As I cried out into the darkness I imagined the vibrations from my voice striking the giant ponderosa pines around me and taking my message deep into the earth through their roots. Indeed, when the realization that I may have bitten off more than I could chew – when the full impact of the breakdown I had created was fully realized -- I became a new-age Druid of sorts. Sometimes I walked deep into the nearby woods and, standing amid colossal pines, rapped my arms around an enormous tree trunk and prayed. Three or four minutes later, when I finally released the tree from my grasp, I walked back with my own deep commitment intact. I felt that the help I needed was on the way.

I am grateful to have experienced that power of intention, commitment and, yes, the power of vocal vibration in my life. It was on a small scale, but I was practicing a belief that our life intertwines with *everything else*.

I do not usually share my beliefs with clients unless they first share a similar experience. However, I know that they do not need to believe in this universal dynamic in order for it to work. They only have to identify and declare their commitments, and then take action to manifest them. At that moment I know help is on the way.

VI

"Our greatest pretenses are built up not to hide the evil and the ugly in us, but our emptiness. The hardest thing to hide is something that it not there."

Eric Hoffer

May 21,1997

Dearest Bill & Marilyn,

Greetings from the foothills of the Sangre de Cristo Mountains!

I am writing less and reading more. Indeed, I've begun reading fiction - something I seldom do. I suppose life is getting too real for me. I'm finally growing up. It seems a shame to leave my boyhood behind when, in another couple decades, senility may bring it back.

My reading selections are limited. The only stores that carry books are Wal-Mart, Safeway and Marty Drugs. I haven't taken to romance novels yet, but I enjoy science fiction and ancient adventure stories. There is adventure here to be sure, but it's coupled with hard work. Armchair adventure is more relaxing.

I will undoubtedly write about Trinidad someday because it's crammed with oddities and anachronisms that would tempt any writer. Aside from the people, Trinidad's most outstanding feature is its dog population. Most people in town have a dog or two . . . or three. Some roam free, but most are chained up outside of their house. I walk Phantom on a leash (or rather she walks me) when I am in town. I have yet to encounter another person with their dog on a leash. No doubt I'm a strange sight.

Chows seem to be the dog of preference - pretty but generally temperamental animals - particularly when on a chain. *Chows On Chains* would be a great title for an article. Of course, not everyone has a dog. Some have cats, others rabbits and one family up the street has a lamb in their front yard. It's as noisy as a dog, but somehow a bah-ah-ah is softer on the ears than R-R-Ruff Ruff.

Phantom loves all the animals - including cats. She is so curious and kind spirited that most cats aren't afraid of her. I am aware that I am growing a powerful attachment to her. I never fully realized how much a part of my life she is until I left her back in my temporary apartment one day. I did so because it was raining and she gets covered in mud, necessitating a big cleanup at the end of the day. The last time she got muddy I pulled into a self-service car wash and thought, for a moment, about popping a few extra quarters to hose her down. I felt it would traumatize both of us, so I didn't do it.

So, I worked an entire day without having Phantom around. To my surprise, I felt lonely. She isn't much company on the job site - usually running in the woods and dragging back old bones. But I know that she is there and would come if I called. It would seem that loneliness has little to do with being by oneself, and more to do with not having companionship *available*. This is a growing awareness in my new life.

Ashley Montague once asserted that women were responsible for civilization -- provocative but probably true. As evidence I offer last evening. I was waiting on two guys from the concrete crew to come by to shoot some grades for me. I waited all day, keeping busy of course.

As I was leaving, Frankie Sanchez and Jerry Montoya finally pulled in - beers in hand. They had just called it a day on another sight. As a gesture of appeasement for their tardiness they handed me a cold Bud.

After we shot the grades and were wrapping up the gear, it began to rain. Jerry cracked out another beer for everyone and, because it's not polite to drink and run, we chatted. The conversation began with advice for me about how to handle different imminent problems, but quickly drifted to talk of raising families and reaffirmation about what was *really* important and painful in life. All the while the rain came down.

In part, we did not even know it was raining because the conversation was so authentic and deep. It was either that, or we were too inebriated. It was not so much what was *said*, but the quality and depth of the listening. The hard work of the day, coupled with a little alcohol, had allowed the masks and facades to melt away.

We all wore hooded sweatshirts — warm, except when wet. It didn't take long for all of us to get soaked. This in itself is not strange, but the fact that none of us mentioned or seemed to recognize our soggy state was a bit bazaar — not at the time though. It's only in looking back that I find the incident so strange and delightful. We talked for nearly a half hour in the rain.

We finally parted ways after running out of beer. I extended my hand in goodbye. Both Frankie and Jerry took off their work gloves to shake it. I remember saying, "Oh, don't take your..." But this small gesture of respect was called for and most appreciated.

I was freezing when I got into my truck. When the sun goes down in the mountains the temperature can drop ten degrees in ten minutes. It was about 50 degrees then. So, I cranked up the heat, popped in a Paul Simon CD and sang *Kodachrome* all the way to my apartment.

I would assert that this kind of event might be uniquely masculine. There is only one woman I can think of who might stand out in the rain drinking beer . . . and she's dead. Do you remember Sophie Tucker - the last of the red-hot mamas?

No doubt, if left to their own devices, the male of the species would kill itself off in about two generations.

Speaking of Sophie . . . few people know Miss Tucker, so I was surprised to find that my landlady and new friend Sara did. She told an off-color joke in a small gathering and I recognized it as a Tucker joke. I later confirmed that she was a Sophie Tucker fan -- something that only another fan would admit.

I'm only familiar with Ms. Tucker because of the lure of the forbidden. When I was very young, my extended family gathered for holidays and family celebrations. Many times the evening ended with the playing of Sophie Tucker records. Of course, this was only after all the children were put to bed.

Hidden on the highest shelf of the front hall closet (so children might not accidentally stumble upon them) the tattered 78-rpm albums were dusted off and ceremoniously carried to the blond RCA Victor phonograph.

With ears against our bedroom door my brother Greg and I listened . . . and learned. To this day I know many Sophie Tucker's routines by heart. Sophie was always talking about her boyfriend Ernie. She had a series of three or four-line bits she fired out.

They began, "I was in bed with my boyfriend Ernie. He said, "Soph . . ." I'll tell you the rest when we are together again.

Love and warm regards,

Coaching Principles & Practices

"Loneliness has little to do with being by oneself, and more to do with not having companionship available."

It took me some time, both as a coach and human being, to understand that when exploring any issue, it is important to explore *all sides* – that is, explore it *thoroughly*. There is a tendency to believe that if we do *some* exploration of an issue, and generate action to address it, the issue will be resolved. The idea being that *action* is the key factor. Obviously, this can be a mistake.

Take the presence of the loneliness that emerged when my dog Phantom was not around. If I were operating at a superficial level, I might assume that a sensible action would be to bring Phantom with me the next time I go to work, and that this would resolve "the loneliness issue." However, I eventually became aware that there was another side to loneliness, *the root cause*. It was an inability to *accept* love that was available. By exploring loneliness more completely, not only as the absence of affection, but also as not accepting affection, I laid the foundation for truly effective action. Initially my exploration put me face to face with a classic dilemma – simultaneously feeling the desire for attachment, and the fear of becoming attached.

As the Buddha said, "Everything dear to us causes us pain." To choose a relational life is to choose pain. My solo adventure into the mountains of Colorado was an attempt to detach. The unraveling of my marriage had hurt me, and I sought escape in order to heal. But almost as soon as I detached, I was feeling the absence of love – and wondering if and how I would again bring love into my life. This initially showed up as simply feeling lonely. If I had just focused on *action* I may have adopted another dog, or hung out with friends. However, by exploring all sides of loneliness, a different, more effective approach was revealed.

Initially my lack of perspective motivated me to take on a building project solo, and care for a dog. I was in action – but not in action in any way that would get to the heart of my issue. If I had had a coach, he or she might have helped me explore another side of the "loneliness issue" sooner. As you can see, I am eventually coming to grips with it, but it took me a while to get there.

Today, when a client brings an issue to me, one of the first things I ask myself is, "What is *another* side of this issue?"

A client leader, I will call him Gary, recently brought up the challenges of collaboration across organizational boundaries as an issue. His perspective on the issue focused on how to increase teamwork between various regions in an organization that was spread out across the country. Gary had already been putting team members in temporary assignments in other regions. They were also taking time in quarterly team meetings to work on projects together. But after a while, he realized that team collaboration stopped when we discontinued facilitation. He didn't know what to do next, and he sought coaching.

By asking, "What's at the heart of collaboration?" we were able to conduct a deep inquiry that led to discovering the real *barriers* to collaboration within Gary's team. The biggest barriers were lack of trust, and a culturally imbedded inability to deal with conflict. Neither of these were being addressed in the actions taken to date. This led to a breakthrough for Gary and his team. I would add that, in order for him to accept and take action on these two issues, he first had to come to grips with these issues within himself.

I recall, when trust first surfaced as a barrier to collaboration he said, "I would hate to think that *trust* was an issue." His response revealed his dilemma: He didn't want to identify trust as the real issue, and at the same time he suspected it probably was. This realization made him sad. Our coaching conversations allowed Gary to see that he was not the sole cause for the lack of trust, but that he was nonetheless responsible for addressing it. Lack of collaboration was a stubborn issue because Gary and his team did not want to deal with the root causes. They were not in touch with the truth, and thus their actions were ineffective.

It is up to the coach to help the client get to the *truth*. This is not easy because issues are often presented in a way that takes the coach down the wrong path. As a consequence, we address the symptoms and not the cause.

An example of this unconscious obfuscation process that clients sometimes employ surfaced in work I was doing with a pastor on an extended leave of absence. His request for coaching showed up as the need to determine what career opportunities, outside of the church, he might wish to pursue. He told me he had been job interviewing for six months, and even had a couple offers. He said he turned down these offers because he wasn't sure it was the right direction for him.

Because a good coach initially goes through "the door that is open," we began a traditional career-path exploration. Once I established a sufficient quality of relationship, I brought another perspective to the conversation. I asked, "What about the church? Have you considered going back to the church?" I could tell from his emotional reaction, he didn't want to go down that path. On the other hand, I felt it would be useful. It wasn't so much that the church was a viable option, but exploring this question would give him greater clarity about what he needed in his life's work. In addition, he needed to deal with many past issues in order to let go of the church and move on to the next phase of his life. Again, he needed to look at all sides of the issue – not just what his next job should be, but also the *barriers* preventing him from moving on. At some level he knew this, but he didn't want to deal with it because the process was painful. So, he presented the issue in a way that might lead us *away* from this painful exploration. You see, it is not just the coach who occasionally takes on the role of trickster, but the client as well.

"It was not so much what was said, but the quality and depth of the listening."

In this age of digital technology, it is easy to conceive of all communication -- even linguistic communication -- as simply transferring of information from one point to another. In the case of speaking, words are used to move information from point A to point B. All this seems true until a deeper level of listening comes into play.

I am uncertain as to what combination of circumstances created the deep listening that was occurring when Jerry, Frankie and I were talking in the rain, but something triggered a quality of listening that transcends the everyday variety. I doubt it was the quality of the speaking, or even the beer, that made the difference. Indeed, much of the meaning was contained in what was *not* said. For example, because Phantom was not present, Jerry asked where she was. While explaining that I had left her home, Jerry was able to hear the loneliness I had been feeling. He talked about his dog and this sparked a conversation about the role that dogs play in our lives. That brought us to talk about relationships in ways that only men can. There were a lot of two and four word sentences.

"Yah . . . dogs."

"What makes'm special?"

"Love,"

"Yeh . . . love."

Sometimes we can say exactly what we mean. Other times we communicate more than words and sentences can – without using speech acts at all. We might even lack the vocabulary or context, skill or internal awareness, to share what is inside, but we can still communicate – if there is deep listening. This is because communication resides in our being. This assertion has led to the creation of a listening model that I use in my coaching practice.

The listening model begins with the realization that the individual communicates both by speaking *and* through being. Who a person is being is both conscious and unconscious. The conscious part has to do with the intention and commitment motivating their speaking. The unconscious part is the unique expression of empathy and that connects human beings. How much of both speaking and being is *received* depends upon the quality or depth of listening.

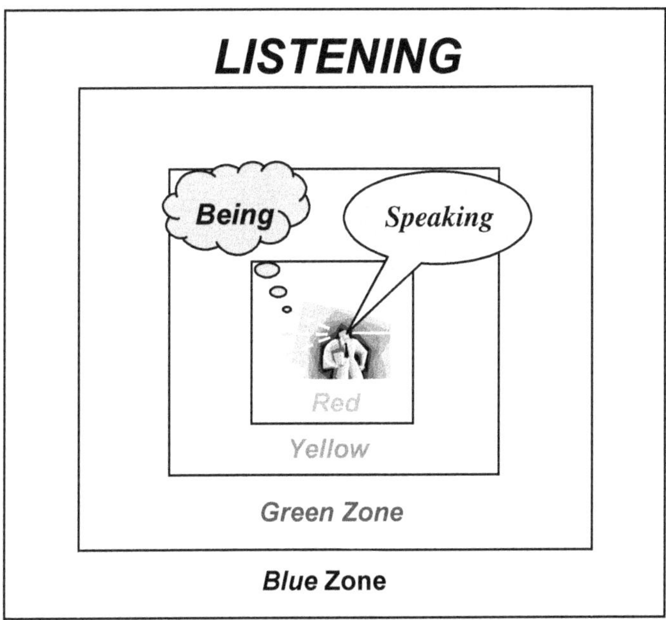

Again, this listening model begins with the realization that the individual communicates both by speaking *and* through being.

In the RED ZONE, words and sentences aren't even communicated. Our preconceived ideas about this person, this "type" of person, and this *kind* of conversation, are all that is present. The only thing that gets through is the data that supports our preconceived ideas. No aspects of *being* get through.

When we are listening in the YELLOW ZONE we are able to hear and understand the basic message. Sometimes we find the "gold" in what is being spoken and build on it. Being is felt, but it is not fully present for us in our consciousness.

When we practice GREEN ZONE listening the communication process begins to shift from a one-way transaction to a two-way process. Our listening begins to impact the speaker and draws out the genius in them. Intentions and commitments are clear and present. Often times we are reflecting them back in mutual appreciation.

BLUE ZONE listening shows up as an elimination of boundaries – between ideas, between egos, and between individuals. It is as if a third entity is created. Listening automatically becomes reciprocal. When we are in the blue zone, it is a flow experience. We tend to lose track of time and our surroundings. Words and sentences fade into the background. What is communicated is mostly *being*. We become agents in one another's awareness and growth.

My conversation with Jerry and Frankie was bordering on green-blue listening. It was memorable because it was unexpected. I did not bring an intention to create green or blue zone listening. But in my coaching practice I try to do just that.

Just as a client prepares for a coaching conversation, so a coach must also. While I spend a little time reviewing notes from the previous session, I spend some of my preparation creating an intention to listen at a deeper level. As you might suspect, I begin this process by getting quiet. This lets miscellaneous thoughts surface so that I can acknowledge and discard them. It also allows me to envision the person I am coaching in a way that enables me to "see" and appreciate who they are *being*. Typically, when this happens, I feel deep compassion that I can only describe as "sweet quiet." When I feel this, I know I am ready to listen.

Over the years, I have had the honor to coach other coaches. In most cases these coaches come out of a specific methodology. They have come to distinguish coaching through a well-defined series of processes and techniques. Such was the case with a wonderful coach who worked with a multinational computer company.

Cheryl was a masterful coach who came to coaching via a well-known school. We had had several coaching conversations before she stated that my approach was very different than hers. She was finding it difficult to stay in the conversation because part of her was always trying to figure out the processes and techniques I was using. This was becoming increasingly problematic for her. She said, “I can’t figure out what processes you are employing. Our conversations seem like normal everyday conversations – but I know they are different.”

We decided it would be best if I took off my coaching hat for a moment and, as a colleague, shared my approach to coaching. Things immediately began to get clear for Cheryl once I declared that I believe the power of coaching lies in listening. “That’s it, she said. “I know our conversations are providing new insights and perspectives, and most of these insights are coming from me, but I’m not sure how this happens.”

I went on to explain how deep listening (green and blue zone listening) allows for the truth to emerge. This principle emerges out of what most experienced coaches and therapists have come to know – that the Truth and the path forward is available to the each person, but not immediately known. Our job is to create a context and conversation that lets the Truth and the Way emerge. Focusing on how I listen, and not just what to say, allows this to happen.

VII

"If you treat an individual . . . as if he were what he ought to be and could be, he will become what he ought to be and could be."

Johann Wolfgang von Goethe

June 2, 1997

Dear Bill and Marilyn,

Greetings from Colorado! Sorry to be so long in writing. Work, fatigue and lack of electricity for a time delayed the telling of my adventures. And so the chronicle continues . . .

The title of a book or article flashed in my mind today - *Fifty and Alone*. Yes, I'm feeling sorry for myself. I think it's because I am bone-weary.

This feeling has cut down fantasies I've been weaving, and daily tasks used for distracting myself are no longer working. The entrepreneur in me saw a huge untapped niche market of lonely people. But the mercenary possibilities weren't enough to dull my own loneliness. As I reflect on my current state of mind, I realize this feeling came shortly after a visit from friends. Their departure triggered loneliness. Love was here, and then it was "taken away." But taken by who or what?

A psychologist might say "by you." A physicist might say, "by time . . . the illusion of linear time." A philosopher might say, "by your intellectual scrutiny." The jester would say, "How can you lose something that is always there?"

Knowing that mind and heart speak different languages I abandoned my inquiry and sought consultation and solace in the popular human pastime -- I tried to think of someone worse of than me. Fred quickly came to mind.

Fred runs a small antique and second-hand shop just outside of town. Among his treasures are used paperback books. I met him in search of new reading material. I was intrigued by his unique way of displaying books – fifty to one hundred books poured into large cardboard boxes. But his creative marketing approach didn't stop there. He decorated his store with old record album covers hanging from the ceiling by string. And then there's the unique name he choose for the store – *Fred's Second-Hand* -- stenciled on the front door next to a sign describing store hours with a single question mark. How could anyone resist a look?

My first foray into Fred's store turned into a two-hour conversation. I found Fred to have knowledge, awareness and wisdom that belied his circumstances and surroundings. We talked about everything from Bella Lagossi to bell curves. I surmised that he was a provocateur -- making statements intended to compel a response and keep a person engaged. He seemed to use this approach as a way to reach out and connect -- not willing or able to use more direct methods. Such a manner is sometimes misinterpreted by others who describe Fred as "odd" or "different."

Within a couple hours, I knew about his reclusive back country childhood, his attempts to create a new life for himself in Chicago and Fort Lauderdale, and his fateful decision to return to care for his aging parents. This move brought him back to the place of his birth -- where he has slept every night since 1982.

Both parents are dead now and he is struggling with a self-made dilemma. As Fred describes it -- "There is not enough time to make a life, yet there is too much life remaining to waste." I told him I do a little coaching and offered to spend some time to help him sort out his options. I've since returned several times for long chats with him. My focus is helping him surface new awareness around his circumstances and future. He keeps asking, "When are we going to begin the coaching?" I simply say, "Soon... soon."

Love,

Coaching Principles & Practices

"There is not enough time to make a life, yet there is too much life remaining to waste."

Like most of us, Fred was caught up in a web of his own making – spun, in part, from his own words. He was unaware of just how powerful his utterances were.

I often do an exercise with small groups of people on retreat at our home/center, or at leadership workshops. I write out a few sentences on some index cards and ask that we read the card aloud in unison. The index card might read:

My problems are impossible to solve.

I'm much too old and tired to be taking on this work now.

These problems may get worse, but there is nothing I can do about it.

There is nowhere to turn.

Even God doesn't care.

As you might expect, the recitation is often followed by a long silence. I ask the group what their mood is -- what they are feeling. I go on to ask what they are inclined to do? "Nothing" or sometimes "Not much" is the usual answer. They often appear numb. We then go on to discuss what they just experienced -- the power of language. This conversation sets the stage for more conscious conversation for the rest of the retreat.

Since coaching is a language-based process, it is important for both a coach and client to appreciate the power of language. Speaking is an act of creation. Language bridges thought and action to foster creation.

It has been said that the ancestor of every action is a thought. Conversation transforms thought into action, and ultimately results. But more is created than we might immediately perceive.

What coaching creates goes beyond future plans. An effective coaching conversation transforms mood, feelings, commitments, perceptions, understanding and even values and beliefs. These inner changes are not always within a client's immediate awareness, but they are always happening at some level. My clients often report that a particular coaching conversation did not yield any new opportunities for action, but they feel more hopeful, or positive, or calm. This shift in feeling and attitude may well as important as any new ideas or options that might surface.

One simple example of utilizing the power of language in coaching has to do with weaving affirmations into the coaching conversation. "You're doing great!" "You're on your way." "It feels like you may be closer to a breakthrough." "You are coming into your mastery."

In the end, coaching, like all communication, relays information; but not all information is equal. Some information is more valuable than other information. Often the difference is in the *context* and not the content.

Information is that part of communication that resolves uncertainty. And so, information has the highest value when the ambiguity is the greatest. As you might expect, people seeking coaching are usually dealing with uncertainty and ambiguity. So, language has more potency within a coaching conversation. For example, an affirmation that a client is on their way to resolving their issues, stated by another person in another place, will not have the same impact it does during a coaching session. Words of optimism and encouragement from a friend, while welcome, don't often lead to breakthroughs. But in a coaching conversation these same words reduce the feeling of uncertainty and instill faith in one's ability to address the issue. This belief, in turn, generates greater commitment that will drive positive action. Words of encouragement from a coach keep the client engaged in a process that will ultimately lead to success. But what is *success* in coaching? What's the ultimate objective?

I am aware that some coaches feel that the ultimate objective of a coaching relationship is to put and keep the client in dedicated action. I believe there are steps *beyond* action – the idol we worship on the American alter. I have adopted a 7-step coaching-process model that I use. This simply methodology lets me assess how my client is progressing.

Most coaching relationships begin with an *intention* to make some kind of change, personal and/or professional. This is step #1. From there our conversations move through the remaining seven steps.

COACHING FOR CREATION

#1 – Intending
#2 – Committing
#3 – Focusing
#4 – Speaking
#5 – Doing
#6 – Attracting
#7 - Being
#8 - Manifesting

I believe the first five steps are somewhat conventional in most approaches to coaching, but the last three may be worth exploring.

#6 - Attraction -- Delving a bit into metaphysics, I can say that in my personal and professional experience, I have been able to attract help and support by simply opening myself up to it. It seems that when I am committed to achieving a goal, and I am in action, I can attract additional help and support by simply exploring possible sources of assistance. It is not so much the specific sources of support per se, but rather the *process* of exploring assistance that changes me inside, and ultimately changes the world around me as well. I become open to help, and it comes to me. And so I do likewise with my clients. Once they are in action, I follow-up to explore additional sources of help and support both real and imagined. And then I wait for it to show up.

#7 - Being – It is possible for a humans to move from *having* and acting on a commitment, to *being* a commitment. Every time a

single human being has changed the world, it was because they were able to make this transition. Mahatma Gandhi, Dr. Martin Luther King Jr., Jane Adams, Caesar Chavez, Joan of Arc, John Lennon, Catherine the Great, Nelson Mandela – did not just express and act on a commitment, **they *became* their commitment**. I am not sure coaching alone is a vehicle that enables a person to move from having a commitment to being one. However, I recognize that 'being' – a state of fully aware and focused presence – seems to be a natural state from which the future unfolds, in what feels like, a single synchronous shift.

#8 - Manifesting – As fey as this topic might seem to you I know that you have experienced the power to manifest. We have all had experiences, big and small, where through our thoughts and attention, we impacted the physical and material world. We think of someone, and they call on the phone. We pray, and our prayers are quickly answered. I suspect we tend to discount these experiences because this idea doesn't fit in a modern cause-and-effect paradigm.

I can say, without hesitation, that I manifest on a regular basis – bringing something into material existence through my thoughts and feelings alone. In some cases there may have been small action on my part, but in many circumstances I did nothing but focus on what I needed, or made a clear request to the universe. In my case talking to the trees.

I recognize manifestation as the ultimate creative force in our world. If nothing else, coaching can introduce human beings to this possibility – as I am now.

"When are we going to begin the coaching?" "Soon... soon."

Fred had made the mistake that many clients make (and even some coaches) when a coaching conversation is different from what they expect. Coaching conversations occasionally employ a process or technique that departs from what might be termed "a normal conversation." But as I practice it, coaching appears like any serious conversation that you might have with a friend or colleague. A coaching conversation differentiates itself from typical conversations in the quality of listening, the elegance of the questions, and the fact that it is an *ongoing* conversation. It is part of a four-part process (described earlier) that includes preparation, reflection and integration.

Coaching also differentiates itself from other conversations in that there is a spoken or unspoken agreement that the client is willing to explore ideas and options outside “the box.” This agreement, while not always explicit, is contained in any desire to dramatically and fundamentally alter our personal effectiveness.

If a dramatic leap in effectiveness were available within a person’s current knowledge or view, they would not need coaching. All that might be needed is a little time and reflection. In almost all cases, any quantum leap in personal and professional growth comes from exploring outside of our box. The first step is seeing that we’re in a box. This realization is at the heart of coaching.

It seems that we can best come to know and understand ourselves in our interaction with another. This is because every other human being has a different perspective, viewpoint and worldview. When we interact with another person, the differences in perspective are revealed. As that happens, we begin to see the “box” *we* exist within. Only then can we consciously choose to explore outside our “box.” Until that clash in perspectives occurs, we are trapped in a belief that “this is the way life is.”

My informal work with Fred focused on enabling him to see his box, thus supporting exploration outside of it. In our almost weekly conversations Fred began to give the clues that he was close to bumping into the walls or edges of his paradigm. He displayed:

- Increasing indecision about next steps
- A visible emotional response to your conversation
- Feeling challenged or defensive

- Occasional excitement about the future
- Unprovoked denial that he can change his life
- Reticence when possibilities are presented

I continued to support his exploration outside the box by:

- Withholding judgment
- Slowing down the rush to action
- Withholding problem-solving
- Sharing my own vulnerabilities as an opening for him to share his truth
- Deepening our relationship
- Avoiding any surface politeness or trivial conversation

My conversations with Fred supported out-of-the box exploration and much more. Shortly after our conversations, Fred ran for the school board. He did not seem suited for politics, and did not win; but the fact that he went for it told me he had seen his "box" and he was committed to exploring and moving beyond it.

Today, when I meet Fred on the street, he often remarks, "I'm going to take you up on that coaching one of these days."

VIII

"The greatest discovery of my generation is that a human being can alter his life by altering his attitudes of mind."

William James

June 6, 1997

Dear Bill and Marilyn,

I'd been asking around town for people willing to do day-work. Yesterday evening I got a call from Eddie. "How much you pay?"

"Ten an hour," I say.

"I'm making twelve now," came the reply.

I may be engaged in a Trinidadian ritual called "hustle the out-of-towner." This is only one of many cultural conversations I've come to recognize. There's the "Why would anyone move *here* routine," in which your intentions are probed for signs that you might bring change to the community. I also frequently encounter the "So you think you have what it takes" process where local tradesmen test my technical skill or physical stamina. Such social games are common everywhere.

I grew up in Chicago and I've noticed that the characteristics of the folks at 92nd and Lake Shore Drive, and some in Trinidad, are surprising similar - namely that there's a bit of larceny in many transactions. It's part of the survivor mentality which dominates the inner city, and as I have come to learn, many struggling small towns. In places where it's an accomplishment to survive 'til the end of the month, the future is fugitive. The modus operandi is "Get it NOW!"

But upon reflection, it's not that different than the rest of our western culture – just more obvious.

I am, no doubt, currently prey to this fear as well. Am I also chanting the capitalistic mantra? I suspect so. And, if so, I will find my way through and out. For if there is anything I am certain of, this project is not the end of my journey, but rather a way station.

Coaching Principles & Practices

"In places where it's an accomplishment to survive 'til the end of the month, the future is fugitive."

No matter how expert we might become at facilitating future-focused conversations, our efforts will fail if the person we are coaching does not choose to let go of the past. The most important assessment a coach performs, is assessing the client's willingness and ability to let go of yesterday.

The past shows up in our thoughts and language, but it exists within us as patterns -- patterns of behavior, thinking and ultimately being. Patterns are a defense against the randomness that seems to threaten our survival. In reality patterns do not make us more secure, but they do create an addictive illusion of safety.

If a person is in a physical or emotional survival mode, the coaching process will be more difficult and possibly lengthy. This is because patterns take on more power when people are at the lower end of Maslow's hierarchy. We find it difficult to let go of the patterns forged in the past when our physical or psychological existence is challenged. Of course, if an individual is in or approaching a breakdown, there is an opening for coaching because what wants to break down are the patterns of thinking, acting and believing. The jig is up, so to speak. The patterns that we thought were saving and protecting us are seen for what they are -- superstitions. They work in our life solely because we believe they work.

People often leverage "imposed breakdowns" -- wars, natural disasters, disease, death, divorce, accidents and the like, as tools for renewal. When the past is no longer possible, then we find it easier to cleave to the future.

There are also breakdowns of our own making. This is a little better, but still fundamentally the same. I have engaged in life-changing workshops and experiential programs with varying degrees of success. However, I have learned that a committed relationship can provide one of the most powerful catalysts for growth -- assuming both parties in the relationship are committed to their own development, and supporting that in their partner.

Workshops, experiential programs, coaching and committed relationships have at least one important thing in common -- friction. Friction is the resistance encountered by a person moving relative to another person or process. This resistance causes a momentary stop in action and (hopefully) opens the door to reflection, awareness, learning and change. A committed relationship has two additional pluses. First, it is constant and ongoing; and second, game playing is minimized because both individuals have a perspective that enables them to more easily see the thinking and behavioral patterns within the other.

I am fortunate to have such a relationship -- a committed relationship. I tend to be on the receiving end of many of the benefits, and I am working to balance this process. Changing our most defended behaviors is turning out to be the most difficult work I have ever undertaken -- much more difficult than building a home and center.

You will meet my wonderful partner Sara in future chapters, but it seemed appropriate to bring our process into the book now because much of the awareness that bubbles up in me at this stage of my journey is a product of my relationship with Sara. She is a loving force who keeps me blundering toward heaven on earth.

"For if there is anything I am certain of, this center is not the end of my journey, but only a way station."

Coaching is one stop on a longer journey. Coaching addresses *current* issues and problems. . It is good to remind your clients of this periodically. The choices they are seeking to make are simply the "next step," and not the end of the journey.

High quality coaching elevates a client's overall level of awareness and consciousness. This equips the client to more effectively deal with future issues and problems. Coaches might be reminded of this as well. This realization necessitates that as much energy and attention is placed on facilitating sustainable personal growth as is placed on problem solving.

IX

"Do you see now how you are in a prison created by the beliefs and traditions of your society and culture, and by the ideas, prejudices, attachments and fears of your past experiences."

Anthony DeMello

June 19, 1997

Dear Bill and Marilyn,

Falling behind schedule, I've hired Eddie and Victor. Eddie is in his early 20's with long black hair in a pony tale. He is talkative – extremely so. Vic, Eddie's cousin, is older with a bushy reddish-brown mustache. They showed up late. They arrive in an iridescent orange low-rider, explaining that they are late because they had to take the graveled country roads slowly. The three-mile drive from the highway is treacherous for this "work of art" masquerading as a car. I've heard a lot of excuses for being late, but this was a new one for my book.

I have never understood low-riders. Maybe that's because I think of them in terms of driving. But driving isn't the point is it? Low-riders are for cru-u-u-uising, a skill I might do well to learn. I'll start off slowly with fifteen-inch chrome wheels with spinners for my pick-up. I've recently been told I might have some Mexican blood. When my work boots started to come apart, I strapped them together with duct tape. A Mexican coworker saw my taped up boot and remarked, "Bro... you look like a Chicano. Alright!"

I feel at ease and comfortable with most Trinidadians. Only once, when Eddie and Vic were comparing tattoos, did I feel awkward or out of place. Tattoos are an artful personal journal. Each comes with a story. "Now this one I got for my second wife," Vic says pointing to a bluish banner laying over a red heart -- a ribbon with "Theresa" on it. He's on girlfriend (and tattoo) number four now, "... an Indian - a tough mean mama," is how he describes her. Is that a compliment?

I found that Eddie and Victor had both been in prison -- Vic a couple times. The last time was for stabbing his uncle. I was curious about prison life. "Back then I'd fight anyone for the hell of it," Vic boasts, "just for pissing in the wrong toilet. Bongo, a friend of mine and I, took over the whole cellblock. We sometimes kicked everyone out of the day room and the toilet next door. The other twenty guys in the block had to use the downstairs bathroom."

This revelation took some of the mystery out of prison life. It's not all that dissimilar to family life at home . . . everyone fights over the bathroom.

Here is a sample of what my days are like, taken from my journal:

June 9... 10... 11 ... 12... 13...

The days plod on as Eddie, Vic and I grade the slab, lay plastic and insulation and then wire together rebar to make a web on fourteen-inch centers. 320 twenty-foot-sticks of steel wrapped together. We work ten or twelve hours a day. When it rains we cut holes in plastic trash bags and make makeshift ponchos. Many nights I'm too tired to cook or wash. I eat a can of tuna and a can of beans and go to bed.

June 14 ... 15 ... 16 ... 17

The rebar web is done. Now for the flexible plastic tubing for the in-floor radiant heat. I installed the manifolds and main lines earlier. We strapped down more than a mile of tubing to the rebar mat with nylon ties. We've been working on our knees for two weeks now. My knees are raw from balancing on rebar. I wrap duct tape around them before I dress to provide some protection. At night I pour peroxide on my kneecaps and watch them sizzle. My body is taking a beating. My arms ache at night despite the Advil I pop regularly. My right foot is numb. My fingers swell up during the night so I can't hold a glass of water.

June 18

I only worked half a day because it rained and the guys called. “Hey man, it’s raining. You know we lost those neat plastic raincoats you gave us. We can’t afford to buy another until payday. Hey . . . wait a minute man . . . this is payday.” I told them I would drive into town and deliver their checks. Now THAT’S SERVICE.

I trust this explains the recent decline in letters. Monotonous work, measured progress, tired body.

Coaching Principles & Practices

"I found that Eddie and Victor had been in prison . . ."

I thought that Eddie and Victor's prison experience was something we didn't share. But upon reflection I know that is not true. Prison deprives people of the joys of life. If we accept that definition, then many of us are in prison. Our walls are not physical but mental, emotional and perceptual. It is the job of a coach to breach these walls and allow people the opportunity to escape. It's a tricky undertaking because most people do not realize that they are in prison. Anthony DeMello often uses the prison metaphor in his writings and I'd like to build on his concepts.

A coach is sometimes called upon to facilitate a change in behavior, in particular, patterns or habits. But it doesn't take long before other "prison bars" appear. Limiting beliefs, core assessments about life, and deep fears, often become visible to a coach and beg for attention. I understand that some coaching schools and coaches might say that exploring personal beliefs is off-limits, but I don't share that opinion. If you go deeper with a client there must be an explicit understanding of what is involved. There must be a clear invitation to explore non-behavioral domains such as beliefs, attitudes, values, traditions, norms, expectations, cultural morays, ideals, principles, ideologies, etc. These are the "building blocks" which create the walls of our prison cells.

My commitment as a coach is to the total wellbeing and happiness of the person I am coaching. I suspect that many first-world human beings are so deeply programmed that happiness becomes fugitive. At times it almost seems that unhappiness is the purpose of our conditioning.

For example, the consumer culture that surrounds us teaches that we need to be something other than what we are, and need something more than what we have, to be happy. That belief puts us in an almost continual state of anxiety and fear. Driven by a sense of lack and scarcity we go after what we are told is *missing* and, when we attain it, we fear losing it. There may be momentary exhilaration and pleasure when we first attain something we are told we need -- a person, thing or circumstance -- but it never lasts.

Add to this the padlock on our prison door -- the belief that if we do not get what we need to be happy it's *our fault.* This belief creates guilt, doubt, self-hatred, despair, anger, and a host of other feelings that make us miserable.

So, inside my commitment to a person's total well being, I offer clients the opportunity to go deeper, to go beyond just managing limiting behavioral patterns. Let me give you an example.

I recently coached a leader who wanted to improve her ability to give candid, balanced feedback to the people she leads. For the most part she avoids giving feedback that may be difficult to hear for fear it will hurt someone or create conflict. As a consequence she finds herself dealing with poor performers, and fairness issues that come from the better performing members on her team.

We had been working together for a couple weeks dealing with this issue and she was having limited success giving effective feedback using some tools and processes we created together. What we soon realized was that we must explore a different arena if we are to have a breakthrough around this issue. I asked her if she would like to explore what might be behind her difficulty giving candid feedback. I make it clear that we would be looking at experiences and ideas she may have picked up along the way that shaped her relationship to feedback. If she agreed we would move on, but not before I reminded her that she was in control and could stop the exploration at any time. She elected to move on.

One brick at a time we dismantled the prison walls. We explored beliefs, core assessments about life, and deep fears. Here are a few examples of exploratory questions I shared with her.

Beliefs

- Tell me what feedback means to you -- distinguish it for me.
- How do you feel when you know you are going to get some candid feedback? Why do you feel this way?
- What kind of feedback did you get from your parents? What did that teach you about feedback?
- Can you recall an occasion when you received feedback that hurt you in some way? Tell me about it.

Core Assessments About Life

- Can you give me your philosophy about people? What have you learned about people in general?
- Tell me how you feel about yourself.
- If you were the guru on the mountaintop, and a seeker came to you and asked what the meaning of life is, what would you tell them?

Deep Fears

- We all have some common fears, but each of us also has some fears that may be unique to us. Can you think of one or more fears that might be unique to you?
- You said that you feel __________ (*insert emotion*) when you are about to get feedback. Tell me more about that feeling and other feelings that sometimes come up.
- What are a couple of the most important things in the world to you? (The loss or possible loss of these things generates fear.)

As she explored these three arenas, the "walls" came tumbling down.

The mere *observation* and reflection on our inner thoughts, feelings and beliefs begins the demolition process. Once the walls are crumbling, we can see things as they are. We are able to see something like *feedback* as a take-it-or-leave-it assessment that is shaped and received based upon the intention behind it. However, this new way of seeing cannot take hold *until* we give up the old way of seeing. This is one of the basic tenants of coaching.

"Sometimes I sits and thinks and sometimes I just sits."

From <u>*Do It*</u>
by John and Peter Mc Williams

June 24, 1997

Dear Bill and Marilyn,

We finish pouring the foundation this week. In preparation I picked up a camper trailer in Taos New Mexico this week, and moved out of my rented room to the property. I have no electricity and, thanks to a rusted out water heater I didn't know about, no hot water - but I'm finally living on my land.

I should probably comment on the beauty of the place, but what continues to strike me is the quiet. I've never known quiet like this. I can hear a car or truck approaching when they are two or three miles off. At night I hear my own breathing and my heart clanging away.

And the stars . . . like a million tiny keyholes peeking into heaven. My worry and frustration can get lost in the midnight sky. When that happens, all that remains is silent gratitude.

I had almost forgotten why I'm doing this . . . almost.

I'm finally here. I feel imbedded in this landscape. I am now a part of it. I suspect that over time I will feel no separation at all.

I'm out of words.

Coaching Principles & Practices

"I should probably comment on the beauty of the place, but what continues to strike me is the quiet."

We've already begun to explore silence as a coaching tool. I'd like to take that inquiry further by focusing on what we find *within* the silence and quiet. For me, quiet does one important thing. It allows me to experience "the observer."

Quiet brings me to a place where I observe my self and my thoughts. In the silence of my new trailer home I was able to observe, without judgment, the workings of my mind -- much as I would watch the red-tailed hawks gliding on the thermals in the canyon, or the native ants scurrying around the huge gravel anthills that dot this land.

This observer inside is part of me . . . and yet not. Focusing on the observer inside is how I have come to distinguish spiritual coaching. I never had this distinction for coaching until I met Marilyn. Since then I have met another spiritual coach – Tom.

A while back I engaged Tom in a dialogue to distinguish spiritual coaching. In our second conversation Tom remarked that he thought I may already be doing spiritual coaching. When I asked why he thought that, he asked me about the *spectator*, which I had referred to in a prior conversation. "Who is the spectator?" he asked. I said that the spectator was something other than me. But then I was struck with a curious afterthought. I said, "No, the spectator is me – but it's not?" Tom replied, "I think you've got it."

That coaching session was a mind-opener for me. I might label the observer *en theos* -- the God within. Tom might say that the observer -- the God within -- is our true nature. Spiritual coaching puts us in touch with our true nature in a way that allows us to manifest it more completely. There may be little chance of improving ourselves, others or the world, if our actions are not driven from the God within.

But if the observer is the real me, then who is it I am observing? In a word, it is the persona we explored earlier. It is the story about us that we confuse with ourselves. So, when I ask the classic coaching question, "Who are you?" I am sending my client on a spiritual journey because I am helping them distinguish between who they *truly* are versus who they currently *believe* they are. This can only be done in a gentle and caring manner.

When we tell the same old story of who we are -- over and over and over again – it becomes hollow and unreal. We eventually begin to suspect that it may not be the truth. A coach can accelerate this phenomenon, not with an in-your-face confrontation – which I confess I sometimes used in my early years – but rather by expressing a gentle and loving skepticism.

Whenever you put someone in the observer role and ask them to observe themselves and their thoughts -- you are bringing them closer to en theos. Over time, they will observe that their thoughts create a world. They think it is THE world, but it's not. By continually observing their thoughts, they will begin to see the difference. Over time, clients may begin to identify more with the observer than the observed and, without any effort on your part, or theirs, they will begin acting out of the God within them. When this happens, everything is possible.

" I feel imbedded in this landscape. I am now a part of it. I suspect that over time I will feel no separation at all."

Being closer to Nature was a large part of the reason I chose to live in the foothills of the Rockies. Nature always takes us beyond what we know, and past what we've been taught to believe.

The natural world is a gentle coach bringing me into the present moment again and again. The wind whispering to the treetops, the vanilla smell of Ponderosa Pine bark after a rain, the caress of the scarlet-grass as I lay in the pasture. My senses ground me in the present. Indeed, I take advantage of this reclaimed relationship with nature in my coaching.

It's easy to be in our heads during a coaching conversation because that's where we spend so much of our time. Calling on the *senses* of the client brings them into the present moment. For example, if I suspect the client is not aware of what is happening in their body during a coaching conversation, I might ask (as an aside) "Are you comfortable?" or, "Are you too warm?" Such remarks tend to bring us back into the present moment while making the client aware of what is transpiring in his or her body. Our bodies have a lot to teach us, they never second-guess themselves.

We need to grow better at being in the present moment. While I have for many years, touted the virtues of what Mihaly Csikszentmihalyi calls "present perfect," but only recently have I come to fully appreciate what it means.

The characteristics of the present perfect include:

- Extemporization --- being without time
- Lack of judgment
- Sensory awareness and joy
- No reaction, panic, blame or stress
- The world seems to come to you
- Awareness and acceptance of all parts of yourself
- You speak the truth to yourself

When I am in the present moment, nothing else exists but what is in my awareness. My total attention and all my thoughts come together in one exquisite moment. I am totally alive. Living does not impinge on being.

Once we experience this we immediately want to recreate the experience. Interestingly, many people are introduced to the "present perfect" in unusual, if not bizarre, ways. For example, when people describe a split second car accident where everything seems to be happening in slow motion. This is the description of a present perfect experience. Likewise, I recall reading descriptions of present-perfect experiences in letters from friends in Viet Nam. These mens' mesmerizing descriptions of fierce firefights came through as ethereal, almost mystical experiences. Speaking personally, my goal is to have these "mystical" experiences in the course of everyday life.

The main obstacle to being in the present moment is the mind's relentless effort to know, change, or avoid the future or the past. In short, we seldom live in the present. So you might understand why I find it difficult to reconcile my current beliefs with earlier notions that advocated managing our conversations and focusing them more in the future. This very act takes us away from the present perfect. Indeed, what if this mental and verbal time-travel I once advocated is nothing more than an exploitation of our mind's need to flee the present?

It seems true that future-focused attention and conversation is necessary to create and accomplish something in the physical world. This need to create and explore appears to be fundamental to our human nature. But if human beings have an innate need to create something new, is it the accomplishment that brings the greatest joy? No. We have the momentary exhilaration and excitement that comes with accomplishment, but it doesn't last. However, when we are consciously in *the process of creation* . . . ah-h-h.

There is only one world, one reality, that only exists in your present moment. Paradoxically, however, we operate and tend to live in two worlds. One world is comprised of the future and past, and the other is comprised of the present moment. Our lives are filled with words, ideas, and actions driven by a response to the past, or the desire to create a future. But when we become totally engaged and absorbed *within* our actions, we can enter the realm of the present perfect, and there we can fully experience the joy of being. If we do not bring this awareness to all of our endeavors, we are quickly and easily seduced by the sirens calling us to do the next (oh-so-important) thing. When we worship the idol of action, we are not able to rest within the experience of the present perfect. Coaching can develop this fundamental awareness.

XI

"Power can be seen as power with, rather than power over, and it can be used for competence and cooperation, rather than dominance and control."

Anne L. Barstow

June 25, 1997

Dear Bill and Marilyn,

The old yellow trestle bridge over the Purgatorie River is still broken down and restricted to cars only. All traffic to my place has to take the long way around -- an extra 13 miles. You may recall my telling you about a back road that goes through a private development. The road is normally open, but with the new flood of traffic, people who live along the road are becoming concerned. One owner put up a gate. Eddie, the excavator, had the combination to the gates because he maintains the road. However, after I cut the chain on the gate to get my concrete trucks through, Eddie is reticent to give me the new combination.

I paid for a new chain and apologized for cutting it – explaining my dilemma at the time. I listened to his concerns and asked if we could reach and agreement whereby I could bring my materials and workers through the private road until the bridge was fixed. The owner agreed . . . partially. "I'll have someone open the gates two more times between 9 and 5 for you if you call ahead." "Thanks," I say. "What if we need to come earlier or need a third trip?" I ask.

"You'll have to work within those limits," he states. I'm disappointed. I suspect I will need more than two deliveries before the bridge is fixed. It will hold up the project. "Can you think of a way whereby I can make more trips, while still keeping you informed?" I ask. No luck. I can tell Wally was still upset about the chain cutting, even though he said he understood my motives. But there may be another reason he was imposing an arbitrary limit -- he had power and control, and he intended use it. The power to restrict or stop the flow of traffic created a higher status for him.

Since I work with business leaders, this is not the first time I've encountered a person who wields power just because they have it. I'm reminded of a scene from one of my favorite movies - _Head Office_ where the president of the company, at a prayer breakfast, leans over to his aid and points to a member of the team who has incurred his wrath and says, “Have that man killed.” His aid is startled and whispers back, “We can't do that sir.” Dismayed, the president responds, "Well, what's the use of having all this power if you can't have someone killed.” I guess Wally says, “What's the use of having a gate key if you can't lock people out.” If the gate owner is like most human beings, he may be doing this in other areas of his life as well.

I know I am upset and angry and I know I will move beyond these feelings. [DEEP BREATH]

I will try to work within his constraints and pray for a quick repair on the bridge.

Coaching Principles & Practices

"Since I work with business leaders, this is not the first time I've encountered a person who wields power just because they have it."

After two decades designing and facilitating leadership development programs for businesses, I have come to believe that the mostly unconscious use of power and rank may be the root cause of many common organizational breakdowns and workplace dysfunction.

Exploring the domain of power, and confronting the "big kahuna" inside each of us, is a rich, new frontier in coaching.

Friedrich Nietzsche believed that power is the primary driving force behind all human actions. Indeed, nearly every philosopher from Plato to Bertrand Russell had something to say about the use and abuse of power. Alvin Toffler helped to mainstream the exploration of power in the business arena in his book *Powershift*. Toffler defined power as using information, wealth or violence to get people to do what you want. Toffler's definition undoubtedly resonates with many business leaders. When I ask executives to define power, it is common to hear that it's about controlling limited resources and directing people in order to achieve desired goals. While this distinction for power may seem reasonable, it has within it beliefs that can lead to the conscious and unconscious *abuse* of power and rank.

If we believe that power is about controlling limited resources, we create a scarcity mindset that limits cooperation, puts the priority on dollars, and treats people as a commodity.

As coaches we can help our clients learn to distinguish power in a broader and more realistic way, such as the ability to influence the flow of energy and information in an organization. If we hold to this definition, which is inspired by consultant Herb Stokes, we can tap vast human resources that often lie dormant. If we see power as influencing the flow of energy and information, we will tend to act in ways that enable people to offer all they have to give, rather than just what we ask of them.

A new distinction for power, and **increased consciousness around how we use power, can be the genesis of an organizational transformation**. The top down, control-over mentality runs deep within most organizations, and is embedded in everything from work processes to the design and layout of offices. It shows up in everything form the way we run meetings, to the language we use. Take the word "leader" for example.

The term "leadership" implies someone to be led. Immediately a dichotomy is created, a separation, a class distinction. When I ask a coaching client, "Who are the leaders in this company," how do you think they answer? They tell me about people on the top floor. They seldom include themselves. No wonder most empowerment efforts fail. This notion that leadership is synonymous with authority (power granted by an organization) is but one example of our deep seeded beliefs about power.

David Kipnis, a noteworthy social psychologist, did a watershed study which revealed that the more power a manager had, the more likely he or she was to devalue the workers they were supervising. Kipnis reported, "Subjects with power thought less of their subordinate's performance, viewed them as objects of manipulation, and expressed the desire to maintain social distance from them." Despite this, these same leaders, who are struggling to deal with the fallout from their unconscious use of power and rank, often launch well-intentioned leadership development or culture change initiatives.

Many coaching and leadership development programs instituted within organizations ostensibly focus on cultivating behaviors intended to improve the quality of relationship by treating people in a more egalitarian manner. They focus on listening skills, encourage feedback, mentoring, managing diversity, etc. However, if underneath those behaviors there is a belief that "I am fundamentally superior," learned behaviors, such as active listening, have little lasting impact. Indeed, such unconsciously insincere efforts may have the opposite effect.

When power and rank are routinely abused within an organization, inspired action -- a vital life force -- is not present. This deficiency is often difficult to see because the illusion of personal choice and responsibility is usually maintained. Lip service is given to collaboration, quality feedback, teamwork, brainstorming, etc.

Power is a juicy area to explore with our clients, because the unconscious use and conscious abuse of power often create the problems or issues clients often say they wish to address – such as . . .

- **Diminished personal accountability and responsibility within team members**, because of over reliance on authority -- power granted by the organization.
- **Restricted flow of information**, the lifeblood of an organization, because controlling information is one of the primary ways power is exercised.
- **Competitive and adversarial relationships** rather than cooperative ones, since people are vying for limited, high status "power positions."
- **The presence of guilt and blame**, because the power to reward and punish are key tenants of the control-over paradigm.
- **Less creativity and innovation,** because power dynamics restrict expression of viewpoints and opinions that radically differ from that of the "power holders."
- **Limited collaboration and teamwork**, because artificial distinctions between leaders and followers, thinkers and doers, exist.
- **Breakdowns in relationship**, because pulling rank creates separation and fosters anger and revenge.
- **Ineffective communication**, because the messages from power holders are structured, and later interpreted, in ways that causes their meaning to be lost.

This list only touches the tip of the iceberg that floats above the murky waters of most enterprises. Below the serene organizational surface lay the less obvious and more treacherous shoals of misused power and rank . . .

- **Problems are not publicly noted as soon as they become apparent**. This occurs because an early declaration of problems is often interpreted by those holding power as resistance, or a lack of cooperation. In reality, the declaration of potential problems, the moment they are perceived, is a courageous and useful leadership act.
- **Diminishing commitment**, lack of wholehearted action, is the result of limited personal choices. There can be no commitment without choice.
- **Turnover, absenteeism and illness** increase because oppression creates enormous stress on everyone.
- **Revenge** subtly shows up within business organizations as inaction and is often mistaken as lack of motivation or miscommunication. The passive-aggressive phenomenon where team members seemingly agree during a meeting, and later withdraw support, is one example of how revenge manifests.
- **Pseudo-loyalty** is created when people trade personal power and freedom of choice with the expectation that their lives will become safer and less chaotic. When organizations need the commitment of people the most -- when they are struggling, cutting budgets and downsizing -- people bail out physically and emotionally because they feel swindled. They've traded their personal power for an unspoken promise. This phenomenon creates a lot of business for change management consultants and lawyers.

Having identified the negative impact of abusive power, it hardly needs mentioning that power, defined as influencing the flow of energy and information, is absolutely essential in business organizations. We all need power to get things done. So the question for our client leaders becomes, "What can organizations do to ensure that power is consciously used in healthy and beneficial ways?" This inquiry can be approached through a variety of topics:

- Self-worth -- Poor self-esteem or self-perception encourages power abuses.
- Values -- Differences in values or differences between professed values and real values can give rise to "power games."

- Locus of Control -- What each of us believes about what we can and cannot control, or influence, shapes how we use and abuse power and rank.
- Scarcity /Abundance Paradigms – Which of the two camps we fall into drives our power norms. As noted earlier, a scarcity mindset underlies control-over behavior.
- Accountability-Responsibility–Authority -- These three domains of power often get confused. Distinguishing them in a pragmatic way encourages reliance on legitimate personal power.

Inquiries into personal and organizational power dynamics have in themselves a transformational effect because they are not simply a conversation about power, but a process that reduces and, over time, eliminates abusive power. This happens because power games lose their effectiveness when they are exposed. I can recall a conversation with one of my clients who, after telling his power-abuse story, added, "I guess I'll never be able play that game again."

If the inquiry into power goes deeper, we will often discover that many of our traditional beliefs about power are myths. All too often, I hear these seemingly "powerful people" express feelings of powerlessness. These feelings likely contribute to the depression and anxiety that runs rampant today in boardrooms and executive suites.

The feeling that many executives have about a lack of control is a valid one. When they seek power, they need support. In the process of moving into a powerful position, they become beholding to others and subject to their control. They give up personal power and freedom to gain their position.

An inquiry into power dynamics and games might be a priority when we coach leaders because an individual or organization cannot fundamentally change without changing its power patterns and structures. A bold exploration of the use and abuse of power is the next frontier for leadership development, organizational transformation and human consciousness.

"I suspect he may be doing that in other areas of his life as well."

It is a well-known fact that much, if not most, of our behavior runs within a series of patterns. It is this "patterning," among other things, that makes behavior so difficult to change. Often times, the moment we are not fully present and aware, we slip into our automatic way of behaving. Indeed, the primary benefit of coaching is that it makes us more aware, and thus able to recognize and avoid, our old behavior patterns.

Initially our awareness comes after the fact. In a coaching situation, this is not a problem, but without coaching it can be. In general, behavior change tends to be negatively reinforcing. That is, when we first try to change a behavior, we often only become aware of our troublesome behaviors AFTER we have acted. When this happens, we not only experience "failure," but, along with it, we tend to feel bad and judge ourselves harshly in other ways.

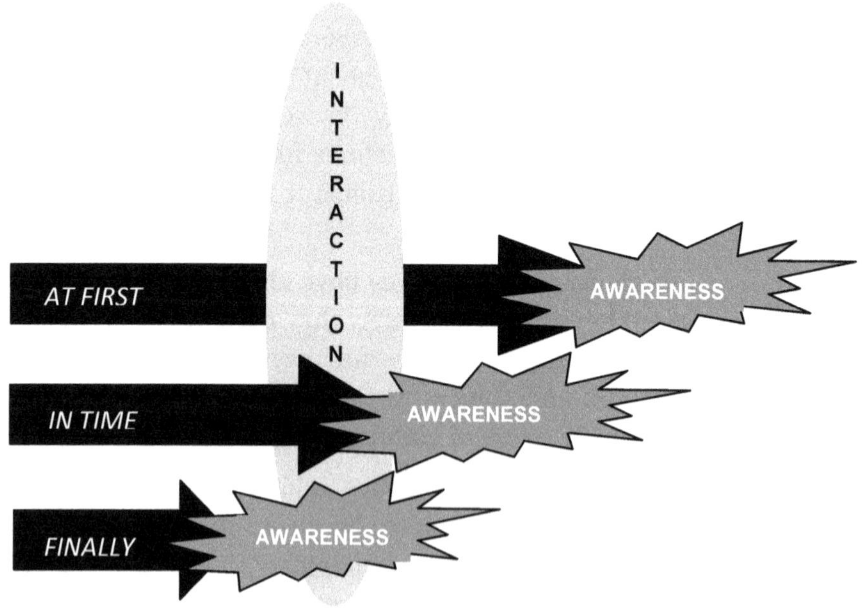

A coach sees this awareness, whether it is before or after an acaction, as a good and positive thing. Indeed, a coach will usually remind the client that, not so long ago, they were not even aware of their troublesome behavior.

Over time, thanks to the positive reinforcement from the coach and others, the client will become aware DURING the behavioral act and eventually BEFORE. Furthermore as we begin to manage and change a particular behavior, there is a tendency to fall back into the old behavior pattern from time to time. However, even when this happens, it becomes easier for the clients to catch themselves and maintain the new behavior. This is because the client is experiencing some success, and is often receiving positive reinforcement from others as well as from their own personal sense of accomplishment.

The positive reinforcement and accountability that coaching brings as a client changes behavior is critical. Of course, there are other ways to get these benefits other than via coaching. For example, small groups or "communities of commitment," and peer mentoring groups, can provide this -- whether it is Weight Watchers or a regular yoga class. A good coach can often motivate their client to seek out and join such communities or groups in order to support their ongoing development. Doing so will help minimize the possibility of co-dependency, and accelerate self-development.

For me, coaching is a short-term engagement. It is meant to help and support, but never become a crutch. Most of my coaching engagements run from three to eight months. They run longer only if the decision to maintain the coaching relationship is given serious thought. This is not to say that some clients will again request coaching a year or two later. When this happens, it is usually a short and powerful engagement because the client already has a clear distinction for coaching and comes with very specific requests.

When a returning client approaches me, I don't immediately jump into their new issue. My first job is to validate that person's interim progress. Indeed, while there is usually a specific need and request by the returning client, the unspoken request is to "validate my progress and accomplishments." It is sad but true, that there are few places in this world where we can declare and share our true accomplishment and evolution as human beings. This is a central role for coaches.

XII

"Every man has the right to risk his own life in order to save it."

Jean-Jacques Rousseau

June 26, 1997

Dear Bill and Marilyn,

Thursday morning the sun seems to sneak over Fisher's Peak with trepidation, or possibly it's my imagination. I've decided to "crash" the back road gate and violate the "two-trip rule." I need to bring in a crane to set up my 20-foot high spine-walls. Of course, the crane operator could only do it at dusk on the weekend. It has something to do with avoiding a permit needed to take the crane down the state highway.

The evening before I asked Eddie out for a beer. I was up front, saying I need the new combination to the lock on the gate. Eddie was reluctant, but I had on my side what often passes for a good reason -- he's being a jerk.

I claimed the rules of western hospitality were violated, which created a moral dilemma. One of the first written and unwritten rules of the West is respect for a neighbor's fences. Eddie agonized about the situation over his third beer.

Some people feel that drinking makes things less clear, but there are exceptions. Looking out through blood-shot eyes, things can look hazy. However, sometimes you can see inside your heart with amazing clarity. Such was the case with Eddie.

The combination to the lock is 1-8-5-4.

The crane was brought in without incident – at least in the external world. I broke the law. I rationalized that law and justice are two different things. I have come to points in my life where I had to make a decision – clearly knowing what was right and wrong. In most cases I did the right thing. In some cases the wrong thing.

That evening I reflected on my actions and attitudes. I regretted violating another's boundaries. I was surprised at my actions, but maybe I shouldn't be. My life to this point saw compromises and desperate moves, but now I seem to be living a different way.

If I could characterize this new life, I might say that I intend to live without regret. At this stage of my life, I am haunted by it. I suspect that, if there is a hell, it is the ghostly regrets that taunt our spirit as it leaves the body.

I'm a ghost-buster now. I'm making conscious choices and taking responsibility for those choices. I have read about, and advocated this way of life. It's a bit ironic that I am only now taking my own advice to heart. If this keeps up, my words and actions might end up being consistent. However, I suspect I have a long ways to go (stop nodding in agreement).

Coaching Principles & Practices

"I've decided to "crash" the back road gate again."

It's embarrassing to read this letter now. I suspect that, had I been in a coaching relationship at the time, I might have made a different choice. But at that time I had adopted a kind of "don't think, just do" approach to the world. Much of the time, when I "just do it," I end up in do-do. Instead of doing *it,* I should have done something about my thinking, and a coach would have helped me with that.

I acted. Action has value regardless of the result because action always leads to learning -- especially when we make mistakes. So, what have I learned? What prompted me to do what I did? By the way, it is not advisable to ask oneself, or a client, *why* they did something, because the word "why" often harbors a judgment. Judgment is the antithesis of coaching.

Not only does a good coach avoid judgment, but coaches also help their clients avoid self-denigration. Judgment keeps us and others focused in the past. It would seem that we spend too much time there already. About eighty percent of our conversations are past-focused and it seems one-half of our thoughts. We human beings spend a lot of time and energy dwelling on what is unfinished -- on regret and sadness about the past.

While coaching is often distinguished by its future focus, it's equally important to help clients let go of the past and forgive.

Forgiveness, particularly self-forgiveness, is absolutely necessary for a happy life. Forgiveness does not mean condoning or pardoning. We can forgive ourselves while knowing that what we have done is not okay. Such may have been the case with my crashing that gate, although I am still able to rationalize that choice to this day.

For me the process of forgiveness always begins with something I was taught in psych class, "We're always doing our best." This seems true even when it appears we were not because most judgment and self-criticism comes from hindsight, with knowing the outcome. It also comes from comparing ourselves to others. We will not always do as well as someone else in a similar circumstance, and it seems we will not rest until we can find that someone who would have done better. We don't have to look very far. There is usually someone nearby who will gladly point out how they, or someone else, would have done it better. A coach does the opposite.

When a client brings a poor choice or failure to a session, a coach can facilitate self-forgiveness using six steps:

1) Remind the client that hindsight makes their choice appear poorer than it seemed at the time – they had diminished awareness in that moment.

2) At the same time, help the client take responsibility for the subsequent outcome. This is responsibility not as blame, but as a simple fact. Even thinly veiled denial will make forgiveness difficult, if not impossible.

3) Extract the learning – What prompted them to make this choice and/or take this action? How do they better understand about themselves now as a result of this event?

4) Ask them what they might do today if faced with the same situation or circumstance? Point out that they have changed, grown and evolved since that time and that they are a fundamentally different person today.

5) Ask them to use this new perspective on themselves now. Hold that "old self" in their minds eye and reach out to comfort and love that "old self" as they might to a friend who had made the same mistake. Point out that they are simply showing the same love for themselves that they would show another human being. They are not making themselves an exception.

6) Finally, reorient them to the future to keep them from squandering too much energy in the past. Remember the learning, accept the love and compassion they are offering

themselves, and move on. Leave them with the affirmation that this past event will probably surface again in their awareness, but that they can dismiss it quickly.

The second point, ensuring that the client is "at cause," is critical because that premise makes coaching work. We don't always get a choice about "the hand we are dealt" in life; but we always have a choice about our attitude and response. When I think about this, I am reminded of a story about a friend of mine who is a member of a Buddhist learning and meditation group in Santa Fe. He and his wife recently had a late-life child who was born with Downs Syndrome. As they were coming to grips with their situation, my friend requested some time with the teacher who facilitated their Buddhist gathering. When he told his teacher about his child the teacher surprised my friend by saying, "A child is a wonderful gift. And this one has shown you your path."

We don't always get a choice about the hand we are dealt, but we always have a choice about our attitude and response. This Buddhist teacher reminded my buddy of this life affirming truth. My friend and his wife knew there was a risk associated with having a late-life child. Now he felt bad for the child, his wife and himself. He was aware enough to know he had begun to rationalize the situation, blaming himself and God. This teacher helped him face the facts and own the situation, thus putting him squarely on a healing path. At the same time, the teacher reoriented him to the future by reframing the situation as an opportunity for personal growth.

All action contains risk. And because steadfast action is the desired outcome of coaching, there is risk involved in coaching -- necessary risk.

The Risk in Coaching

I think that most coaches are aware of the inherent risks associated with their practice. These risks are minimized by ensuring that the awareness, possibilities and actions come from the client. This approach might eliminate blame, but only minimizes risk. More and more these days, clients are seeking breakthroughs. One recent prospect said, "I want to go deep. Don't hold back. Get in my face." How would you respond?

Initially I approached this situation by assessing the capacity of the individual to cope with change. Part of their capacity has to do with physical and emotional health. It also has to do with their current circumstances, relationships and responsibilities. I don't want to make the mistake of focusing solely on the individual, assuming that what is best for the individual is best for all. This learning comes at a price.

More than a decade ago I was working with a team of coaches to provide intensive coaching to an executive team as part of a weeklong leadership development program. Each of these leaders came to the experience with a written request indicating where they wanted changes in their lives. Most of them walked away having had a powerful experience. One leader, Michael, left the program committed to a total and fundamental change in his life. It seemed like a wonderful result until the follow-up coaching ensued.

Michael went home from his workshop and immediately shared his experience with his wife and family. This sharing scared the hell out of everyone, especially Michael's wife of 23 years. He was talking about a totally new direction in his life's work, dramatically scaling down economically, etc. I will spare you the details, but what initially seemed like a breakthrough for this leader, turned out to bring chaos, pain and suffering for him and many other people -- including Michael's employer. He quit three months later.

The coaching team, being human, initially greeted this situation with a rationalization that Michael's actions were inevitable and, if anything, we only accelerated his process. However I knew, and I think we all knew, that we were in large part at cause and we had to take responsibility, not so much for what happened, but the way it happened.

As his coach I was so focused on helping Michael achieve a breakthrough, I did not devote adequate attention to the ripple-effect of his "new future." I took responsibility for this error in judgment. My team and I provided pro bono coaching to Michael and his wife, invited spouses to participate in future programs at no additional cost, and we began to do more thorough assessments of participants prior to going into a program. Our assessment included the physical and emotional condition of the leader, the quality of key relationships, recent performance at work, etc.

I walked away from that coaching experience highly tuned to the potential risks associated with coaching. This is an extreme example, but the point is valid in any setting and with any client. Risk always plays a role in change. Using thorough assessments, proper techniques and processes, we can minimize the risks associated with coaching, but we cannot eliminate them.

XIII

"He who is not busy being born, is busy dying."

Bob Dylan

July 5, 1997

Dear Bill and Marilyn,

I celebrated a construction milestone, completion of the center spine wall, by driving to Dallas to visit my daughter Jennifer, Pamela and other friends. I got my teeth cleaned, hair cut, and bought some new clothes. I acted in all ways like the stereotypical man coming out of the wilderness, or the cowboy after the cattle drive. And like both, I did not tarry long. I drove back on the 3rd of July. On the way up my road I got a call from a new friend Dick and his wife Tracy. He took me up on my "if your ever in this area" offer I had made in the past.

I met Dick on a plane flying from Chicago to Dallas. We immediately hit it off. We had a delightful freewheeling conversation. I believe Dick is one of those people you meet knowing that you have some part to play in his life. Sound familiar?

When they arrived that evening, I gave them an abbreviated tour knowing that he would be back soon. I spent the next day at a benefit picnic lunch at the Baca House, a historic home and local museum. It was to raise money for all the museums in town. The festivities embodied the small-town virtues I discovered in Trinidad -- simple and fun loving. The fabric of this community is homespun -- and a bit raggedy.

The meal was choice of hamburger or hot dog, beans and potato salad on the side, and Kool-aid. We sat under the umbrella of hundred-foot trees, enjoyed each other's company and the entertainment . . . the entertainment!

After obligatory acknowledgements and short remarks by the mayor and museum directors, the sing-a-long began. Lyrics were passed out -- a medley of patriotic songs. Greta, an older woman with a strong German accent, led the songs accompanied by her guitar. She was recently naturalized (what a strange word). Her appreciation for this country is strong and clear, but not just in her words. She had researched each song and gave a little history. We sang America the Beautiful, Yankee Doodle Dandy, The Star Spangled Banner, God Bless America, Home on the Range, etc. Everybody sang along, many with hands on their hearts.

Uncle Sam was there too. A 92 year-old resident who had white hair and pointed beard. The locals provided his red, white and blue-stripped suit. An amazing new friend Sara and I got our picture taken with him, standing against a large American flag that was flying when he was born. It had 36 stars.

The fire chief and his teenage son, dressed as New York Yankees, did Abbott and Costello's famous "Who's on first" routine. Of course, there was an apple pie baking contest with the winning pies being auctioned off, if you can call it an auction.

The auctioneer called "The Colonel" was the real thing. He was just a bit over zealous. He did warn the audience that ANY movement - even breathing, could be taken as a bid - and so it was. He taunted the husbands of the pie bakers, "A brave man aren't you . . . you really mean to say that you're not up the bid on you wife's pie?" And the minute they began to open their mouth in rebuttal they found that they upped the bid. Inevitably he would stick the mayor, or the fire chief or some other local celebrity with a fifty-dollar pie.

The high point was the announcement of the slogan contest sponsored by the Chamber of Commerce. Evidently the tourists had demanded a slogan. The townspeople had fun with it. *The Chronicle* printed some of the more whimsical ones. For example, since it's located on the Purgatoirie River (pronounced PUR-GA-TOR-Y), I submitted. "It's not heaven, but it's not hell either."

A week or so ago, while drinking beer in celebration of the last concrete pour, the crew and I came up with what, at the time, seemed like the spectacular a submission . . . "Trinidad. Wow." However, it seemed to miss the mark with the judges. The winner was:

TRINIDAD: TOWN OF THE PAST, PLACE OF THE FUTURE.

It seems to fit the town, and me also. I'm not so much building a house, as creating a future. I stumbled into Trinidad almost exactly a year ago today. While the days seem to grind on, I am reminded that my life is moving and changing quickly.

Trinidad. Wow.

Life. Wow.

Kim. Wow.

Love and warm regards,

Coaching Principles & Practices

"I believe Dick is one of those people you meet knowing that you have some part to play in his life."

The truth is that we are connected to everything and everyone. However, my experience is that sometimes we feel that connection more with certain people, and with certain places. This phenomenon, which I suspect we all experience, is most noteworthy with regard to strangers. Over the years I have developed theories about how and why this happens. Certainly, exploring what connects human beings, and how to facilitate that connection, is a useful inquiry for any coach.

I used to hold that what connects most people are common problems. A more positive spin might be that what connects most people are common commitments. Indeed, a good definition of "problem" is a perceived barrier to act on a commitment or need. However, our clients tend to focus on problems because they don't always see or share commitments as readily.

When a client describes a problem a coach hears the commitment or need that makes their situation a problem. Usually the coach will reflect that need or commitment back to help the client get in touch with it. This is standard operating procedure since, as we discussed earlier, coaching is commitment driven.

While sharing common problems or commitments seems to be a natural bonding agent, I have discovered that I am also attracted to people who engage in free-flowing conversations I call *improvisational conversation.*

This is a distinction for conversation that I learned in an acting class that I took in college. The instructor took a Zen-like approach to teaching and, on the very first day, asked us to try some one-on-one improvisations. Of course, we failed -- the main difficulty being an inability to sustain our impromptu scenes. Any pretense and ego was immediately stripped away. We were ready to listen and learn.

Dr. Gerard then shared the "Five Rules of Improvisation," which I have adapted for my coaching practice.

THE FIVE RULES FOR IMPROVISATIONAL CONVERSATION

1) Hold no preconceived idea about what the scene is about or where it is going.
2) Pay attention to others.
3) Accept all "offers."
4) Always advance the action.
5) Support others in looking good.

If we followed all these rules, two or three actors could sustain an improvisational scene seemingly forever. If the scene broke down, we could usually trace it back to a failure to follow the rules. As you might suspect, Rules #1 and #5 were the sticklers -- hold no preconceived idea about where the scene is going, and support others in looking good. To this day I am convinced that I could teach coaching using just these five principles alone. However, I might have to add one more rule: Pay attention to what's happening *inside* of you.

"I'm not so much building a house, as creating a future."

As noted earlier, the idea that creating the future is the cornerstone of leadership and coaching is far from a novel idea. I can go further and assert that creating the future is fundamental to being human. This too is a mainstream thought today. But what might seem true today was not always seen as such. Indeed, the idea that creation is fundamental to being human has its roots in Kantian philosophy. Kant distinguished between a future that is *invented* versus one that is *discovered.* The next major contribution to this fundamental belief came with J.L. Austin and John Searle, mid-sixties pioneers in a newly emerging field called the philosophy of language. J.L. Austin, in particular, deepened the distinction for what he called illocutionary acts, which I have already mentioned in a prior chapter.

Illocutionary acts, later termed "speech acts" by John Searle, are speech actions that impact the thoughts, actions, and beliefs of the listener. They include assertions, warnings, commands, orders, requests, criticisms, censure, promise, objections, demands, etc. Austin identified hundreds of illocutionary and perlocutionary acts.

I learned a lot about how to generate action from these and other thought leaders. When I wrote my last book, I believed that creating action was the most important thing for a coach to do. That was fine, but incomplete. Now I engage a conversation about *change* before any conversation intended to generate action.

At some level all human beings are aware that most actions, by their very nature, create change. However, relatively few people put this awareness into play in a way that begs them to thoroughly explore the change they desire *before* they focus on action. This shift in priorities and attention has transformed my coaching practice.

In the past, when I focused primarily on generating action within a coaching conversation, I made an assumption that change happens *after* the coaching conversation – as a consequence of actions emanating from the coaching session. Now I believe that by focusing on the subject of change during the coaching conversation, and using perlocutionary questions, the change the client is seeking actually begins to happen *within* the coaching conversation. This is because focusing on *change* creates a crucial shift in perception and attitude. It is the shift in perception and attitude that becomes the catalyst for action, and the foundation upon which any viable plan is built.

Examples of people consciously using perlocutionary speaking to create change are not difficult to find. We see it in great leaders. We can also see it in shamans, writers, filmmakers, songwriters, and many, many others. Some of us articulate, assert, communicate, convey, declare, express, pronounce, state and tell. Others of us blab, chat, chin, gab, jaw, yak, spiel and spill. It all has the power to create change, but that change begins inside of us. Conversation creates change *out there*, but there is an inner process that takes place even before action is discussed.

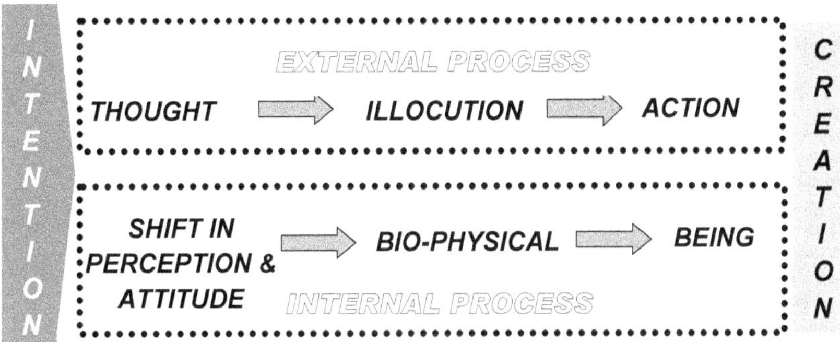

Again, the process of human creation *begins* with a shift in perception. Even if one is not aware of the inner process, it happens. There are external and internal processes that *together* create change – not just external actions. Furthermore, these outer and inner elements must be in alignment in order to manifest a new creation.

Human beings tend to focus on the external process, either being unaware of, or maybe just expecting the internal process to simply happen automatically. While this can happen, the possibility for change dramatically improves, and change itself is accelerated, when we consciously understand and support our internal processes. So let's take a closer look at these internal processes.

Internal Processes that Support Creation

Every book or program on coaching I have encountered mentions, if not highlights, the role of commitment in the coaching process. Every coaching conversation surfaces, generates and supports commitment. But not all coaches understand what lies behind and within commitment.

Commitment is characterized in many different ways – as energy, emotion, an elemental power, etc. My ongoing inquiry into the nature of commitment has brought me to an appreciation of the bio-chemical processes inside every human being, and ultimately to the power of being. I acknowledge that I am standing on the shoulders of those who have pioneered ontological coaching. My intention here is simply to advance their work.

The term *ontology* comes from the Greeks. Ontology literally translates "the study of being." And if you delve into the original meaning further, you will find that the Greeks more accurately meant, "the study of Reality." It was an inquiry into the nature of Reality and Being that continues to this day.

When I speak of the internal human processes that accompany the act of creation, it is an ontological, but also a somatic inquiry. There are bio-chemical processes that take place in the body-mind that produce a physical changes. These changes play a key role in driving and supporting the more obvious thought-speech-action processes that lay within creative action.

The inner processes are triggered by a shift in perception – how a person *sees* the world and, more importantly, their relationship to the world. As I said earlier, this shift happens within the coaching conversation itself – not afterwards. It is important to keep in mind that this shift in perception and attitude manifests as, not just a change in feelings and emotions, but lasting physical changes within our bodies.

Our brains contain neuronets that connect to duct and ductless glands that produce bio-chemicals such as ACTH and adrenalin, influencing how we feel and ultimately how we act. Shifts in perception and attitude not only show up in our neuronet and glandular systems, but actually *change* the physical structures within those pathways and systems. Coaches, at some level, must be aware of these bio-chemical processes because they are part of the unseen coaching dynamics. This may seem farfetched until we realize most coaches already do this when they work with emotions. After all, emotions are also a product of processes occurring within our neuronet and glandular systems. Most coaches know this, and to one degree or another they deal with emotions as both allies and barriers to change. Indeed, some coaching disciplines excel at working with emotional information.

While I have never had Newfield training, many colleagues in that network have shared how Newfield has made some wonderful contributions to the field of somatic coaching, and working with emotions in the body-mind. Likewise, *integral coaching* embraces the body-mind process. However, our inner bio-physical processes involve more than our emotions.

Our very *thoughts* are physically imprinted within our bodies via the same bio-chemical processes that generate emotions. Every thought we have, and every bit of learning and experience, is stored away inside of us, and has emotions associated with it. I am suggesting that coaches can move *beyond* working with externalized emotions by including an awareness of the bio-physical processes that drive emotions – and ultimately creation. As our client's emotions surface, we can encourage acceptance and exploration. In so doing, emotions can be transformed and transcended, producing higher quality thoughts and actions. This same process also changes the client in a fundamental way that we can call "elevating the quality of being." As Mahatma Gandhi said, "Don't try to change, be the change." A shift in the quality of our being puts us closer to the actual creative force or source. In addition to the Greeks, these ontological and somatic concepts are based upon the work of pioneers like Abraham Maslow and Candace Pert, as well as from my own experience.

In chapter three I related my experience with a Buddhist monk who was *being* love. I have had other encounters with the power of being, but only recently have begun to recognize this power in my own life. One noteworthy experience of mine was with a lawyer who was taking a deposition from me in a lawsuit that had popped into my life.

My research into the company going after me told me that they were an aggressive organization that used lengthy and expensive legal maneuvers to get what they wanted. I was told to expect a long and difficult session and I should be well prepared. Since I was committed to speaking the truth, my preparation took the form of internal work designed to bring my truth clearly into the deposition process.

For two weeks prior to the deposition, my partner Sara and I methodically engaged in daily dialogues, visualization and guided meditations all focused on helping me *be* INTEGRITY and LOVE.

The deposition process was brutal -- five hours straight with only one toilet break. I was bombarded with hundreds of questions and malicious “off the record” accusations and allegations in an attempt to stir emotional responses. All the while, I was consciously BEING integrity and love. I continually blessed the attorney and listened deeply, staying fully engaged in my own internal process.

For the entire five hours we were on opposite sides of the table. But at the conclusion I got up and came around to where the attorney was sitting to shake his hand. As I approached him, his body impulsively moved away from me. He leaned so far back in his chair that he nearly tipped over. I looked him in the face and held out my hand. As he took my hand, he said the strangest thing, “You have the bluest eyes.” I simply replied, “Good luck.” And, as I walked out of the room, I could feel his gaze. I was initially puzzled by his behavior, and even more so by his parting words.

As I debriefed the experience with Sara, I was left with the possibility that who I was being had possibly caused the strange behavior in this unfriendly attorney. This was a breakthrough for me. I had chosen to avoid meeting aggression with aggression. Armed only with the ability to cultivate and bring forth my authentic being moment to moment, I projected my intention in a powerful way. It was this state of being, and not my verbal responses, that defused the situation and created a positive result.

While I am more conscious of the role that my internal processes play in the act of creation, I have only reached an elemental understanding. This ongoing exploration will inevitably lead to a new coaching paradigm.

"Trinidad. Wow. Life. Wow. Kim. Wow."

The experience of building our home and center brought me much closer to consistently living in the present moment. I lived in a state of WOW a lot of the time – although I didn't realize it then. My time was mostly spent setting rafters, framing walls, stuffing insulation, etc. These were sometimes flow experiences for me. In the evenings, I wrote, read, hiked, and did a lot of sitting and watching. I watched the sun go down most evenings. I watched the seasons change. And when I went to town I watched the people who often seemed to be going a hundred miles and hour, even in Trinidad.

When I was able to watch and observe, I was often in a state of awe. I watched my dog Phantom tracking a scent in the pines and I marveled at her process. I watched for what I called the "golden moment" as the sunlight hit the canyon walls turning everything a pulsating yellow-orange. I watched myself as well. And when I did, I was also in awe -- and in love.

People I see and interact with amaze me. I suspect that is true for most coaches. My love and compassion for others grows as I become more aware of, and compassionate about, myself.

XIV

*"Nothing makes us so lonely
as our secrets."*
Paul Tournier

August 10, 1997

Dear Bill and Marilyn,

More than ever this glimpse of my life illustrates the yin and yang dynamic. I am happy to have such caring and loving friends as you in my life. There are but handful of people with whom I could share this journey. The sharing seems to help. There is something about being witnessed that satisfies a deep need.

This morning I slid open the window of my trailer just as the rain was ending. The air was so sweet it made me cry. But it wasn't the cleansing fragrance that rung my heart. Today is my x-wedding anniversary.

Long ago someone distinguished anniversaries by ascribing elements such as paper, wood, silver, gold, etc. Today would have been almost silver. I know that Pam's choice made sense in most ways - for her, and for me. But the sadness I feel is not of the mind.

When we were first dating I told her, "I feel comfortable with you." I'm certain this is something all lovers say to one another . . . a precursor to "I love you." Feeling you can be yourself - reveal your tarnished self -- to another and still be accepted, liked, loved and cherished is part of the bargain we call love . . . the intimate bartering wherein love of another and love of self is woven together.

I am developing some good friends in Trinidad. I especially enjoy the brief times I share with Sara, my former landlady – now my good friend. She has a boyfriend and seems happy, and I don't wish my friendship to impinge on that relationship. As I write this I know that this is not completely true.

Sara mentioned a workshop being held in a spiritual community in Loveland. I am thinking of going – in part hoping to be with her there.

While I miss intimacy, I also fear it. However, the isolation and hard labor is softening my protective shell. I'm cracking open. I'm sometimes afraid, if people look too closely, they will see my secrets pouring out of me.

Coaching Principles & Practices

"There is something in witnessing another's journey that satisfies a primal need."

One of the most fulfilling aspects of being a coach is that I am, if nothing else, a witness. In doing so, I know for certain that I am meeting a useful need. It seems to me that we all live in an almost constant tug-of-war between wanting change and, in the same moment, not wanting change.

If we are conscious, we are aware of being continually presented with new ideas, possibilities and realities. We do not see or accept all these invitations to explore beyond what we already know, want or believe. In a way, it's as if we are in a continual state of cognitive dissonance. A coach can help here by making us more aware of this tug-of-war that mostly happens in the "background."

Cognitive dissonance, as you probably know, produces the discomfort we feel when we are caught between what seems, in the moment, to be two diametrically opposed concepts or ideas. It is discomfort that we feel because there is a discrepancy between what you already know or believe and some new information that seems to contradict it. It usually occurs when there is an invitation to accommodate new ideas. Cognitive dissonance is the open doorway to a new reality. So as a coach, you can see how and why cognitive dissonance is not only okay, but also an absolutely necessary condition for human evolution.

Carl Rogers recognized that if someone were called upon to learn something that contradicts what they think they know — particularly if they are deeply committed to that existing knowledge -- they would likely resist the new learning. Coaching can help overcome this innate, internal resistance.

I have noticed that many of my clients come to coaching feeling cognitive dissonance. True, this state often shows up as a breakdown of some sort, but whatever the motivation, they begin to question what they "know" – often what they have been taught. They are caught between an existing reality that doesn't seem to be working, and some new reality that is not yet clear. They stand at the doorway to a new way – possibly a new world. A coach throws them a line or tether and promises to hold on as they explore this new territory.

Belayed by the coach, the client begins to explore this alternate option, idea or reality much like an astronaut on a spacewalk. As the exploration deepens, there is a need for validation. I will validate an idea or insight from a client if it is within my own experience. If it is not, I simply encourage them to "try on" the newly discovered "truth," idea or interpretation. Providing support is not as important as the fact that I am *witnessing* their journey. Holding tight to the other end of the line, a coach is the anchor that allows others to step away from their known world to explore "outer space" -- a new reality.

Without a coach in some form most people, when confronted with new options, ideas, and perceptions, will not walk through the new doorway that lies ahead of them. They usually retreat back into their known world. They "revalidate" their current experience, and thus do not respond to their most recent invitation to grow and evolve.

My own recent shift away from a single-minded focus on creating a new future has dramatically impacted my approach to coaching. My focus on coaching as a way to facilitate a change in *perception* helps the client find a new, more *meaningful reality*. This shift is significant for my more recent clients who usually begin to experience a higher quality of life because they are no longer completely preoccupied with the future.

You see, when we talk of the future we typically frame it as some goal, objective or "place-to-get-to." It can show up as anything from an elaborate wish that goes nowhere, to an obsessive preoccupation with an objective. Either way, it keeps them from experiencing and living their life more fully.

A meaningful reality is completely grounded in the present moment. It exists now in the moment our mind and heart seizes upon it. It is from this new reality, a new way of perceiving the world, that human transformation takes place.

And so, to summarize this inquiry -- a coach is a witness that guides an individual through a state of cognitive dissonance to a new reality they experience in the present moment—not as a goal to achieve. At the moment this new reality manifests for the individual, the *important change* has occurred. What will follow are the actions that will automatically flow out of this person's new reality – out of their change in perception. There is no need to create a detailed blueprint for the future. If an individual is fully grounded in a meaningful new reality, their behavior will change, more or less, without effort. A new future will emerge naturally and organically.

". . . the intimate bartering wherein love of another and love of self is woven together."

I have been pondering this thing called LOVE, trying to separate fact from fiction, and the pragmatic from the programming. I believe that coaching is a form of love. Not just a loving act -- but love itself. This might make more sense if I share my distinction for love.

Thanks to some "coaching" from one of my angels – Anthony DeMello, I have come to better understand what love is. In a word, love is "seeing" – seeing people and the world we live in as they truly are without judgment or expectation. We don't "fall in love," we are in love when we are observing our world and ourselves without judgment. What I had been programmed to believe about love was just the opposite.

In the past when I fell in love, I was focused on some ideal. I went out into the world with my shopping list. When I met a person who met most of the criteria on my list, I began to fall in love. But what was I loving?

Lovers often have or carry pictures of one another. This seems most appropriate because, in most cases, we are in love with a "picture" of that person, not the person themselves. Over time a dissonance begins to reverberate inside us. What we initially believed about the person does not jive with who they actually are in our growing experience of them. As the saying goes, "the honeymoon is over." Love ceases to be an idea or ideal. As some might say, "reality sets in." Ironically, the moment we are closest to true love, we tend to think love is no longer there.

One of my favorite stories comes from a movie I saw many decades ago. I no longer recall the name, but one scene still lingers in my heart. The scene is set on the beach of a Mediterranean Greek island. A young man is strolling on the edge of the surf deep in thought. He is sad. He spies an old fisherman mending nets a short way off and walks toward him. The old fisherman is the boy's uncle and welcomes him warmly, and then noting his nephews mood asks, "Why so sad?"

The young man, who was married just three months before, shakes his head. "I am worried Bala that I may be falling out of love."

Bala looks worried. "Why do you say this Maksimos?"

"Because the fire is gone. I no longer feel fire in my heart for Lalla," he remarks.

The old man smiles and puts both his hands on the young man's shoulders and looks him squarely in the eyes. As the young man raises his head to catch the gaze of his uncle, Bala says, "My son, do not worry. Love is what remains *after* the fire is gone."

I must have remembered that scene because it resonated deeply with a truth I was learning. Real love is not blind. Just the opposite – love is fully sighted as sees what is *really* there. Love comes from knowledge.

Hopefully you can begin to see what all this has to do with coaching. A good coach in grounded in reality. They see their client as they are. As much as possible, a good coach withholds assessments and judgments, internally and externally. I myself cannot seem to stop making internal assessments, but I am usually aware when I am doing so. And that may be as good as it gets for most human beings. The good news is that the more we practice observing our judgments, the less frequently they will arise.

I see my clients as they are, and accept them as they are. That is love. At some level, they feel it and know it. I know this is true because, within a few coaching sessions, my clients no longer posture or try to project a false image. They withhold less and less. They are comfortable being themselves. This may be one of the greatest gifts coaches give. For by allowing "spontaneous ordinariness," clients learn self-acceptance. They harbor less anxiety about their self-image. They begin to love and appreciate themselves.

"I'm sometimes afraid, if people look too closely, they will see my secrets pouring out of me."

You cannot practice coaching very long before you encounter someone who is struggling with a secret. There are many reasons why people keep secrets – positive and negative. In most all cases, a person holding a secret has made an assumption or prediction that sharing certain information will yield a result that they do not want. Thus, the "locking mechanism" for secrets is the unpredictability of how another person will respond to the revealed secret. And, to a lesser degree, the unpredictability around how they – the secret keeper – will feel after a secret is revealed. Typically a client will "test" the coach before revealing a secret.

"I have something I might share with you . . . but I am not sure that it's relevant," could be something a client might say. There is a tendency for most coaches to encourage the telling of secrets, but I have learned that doing so is not always the best practice.

I have had clients end our session, and even the entire coaching agreement, after revealing a secret. Why? The first thought might be that they did not get the response they had hoped for; but there are other reasons this might happen. For example, the client felt bad after telling the secret and held the coach responsible for their negative feelings. I could continue to conjecture about the reasons why revelation of a secret might adversely impact a coaching relationship, but suffice it to say that encouraging a client to reveal secrets is not automatically a good thing. Some thought and preparation is required before secrets can safely be revealed.

There are a series of questions I ask any client before they reveal a secret. First I try to determine how big and deep the secret is. Next, I help my client explore *their* expectations upon sharing their secret. Finally, I get them to consider the consequences of not sharing, or delaying the sharing of their secret with me so that they can make a well-informed choice.

Depth and Importance of the Secret

How long have you been keeping this secret?

Does this secret often surface in your consciousness? Do you think of it once a week?

How do you feel when you become aware of this secret?

Expected Responses

Have you ever told anyone else this secret? If so who? What was their response, etc.?

Why do you want to share your secret with me now?

What do you think my reaction might be? (Probe deeper here.)

What do you think your reaction will be after you tell me? How will you feel?

Impact of Delaying or Not Sharing a Secret with Coach

If you don't tell your secret to me now, what do you think might happen?

Why are you considering sharing this secret with me – your coach – rather than someone else? Who else might you explore this secret with?

Determining the depth of the secret is important. If it is a "big secret" you will want to be prepared to spend significant time exploring it. Indeed, it might change the whole direction and plan for coaching. You must also begin to shape *their* expectations – particularly with regard to how they might feel afterwards. Finally, you want them to consider the possibility of not sharing, or at least delaying the telling of a secret. This puts the choice about whether nor not to share the secret clearly with them – where it needs to be.

Having said all this, my experience is that sharing a secret is oftentimes good for clients. They usually feel better, and it has the potential to improve the quality of the relationship I have with them. However, holding on to secrets is not *always* a bad thing. If holding onto the secret is not causing much anguish, it might be okay. But if the withheld secret is causing stress and suffering, then it must be dealt with sooner or later in some fashion and venue. The moment the secret comes up in awareness may *not* be the optimal moment to reveal it. More importantly, YOU – the coach – may not be the right person to deal with it. They may need to seek help from other professional or non-professional people.

Here we approach a line between coaching and counseling or therapy. We do not wish to cross that line, but at times we dance on the edge. One of the best ways to ensure that we don't cross over the line is to conduct a brief inquiry similar to the one described earlier, *before* a client shares their secret(s).

XV

"The most difficult thing is the decision to act, the rest is merely tenacity. The fears are paper tigers. You can do anything you decide to do. You can act to change and control your life, and the procedure; the process is its own reward."

- Amelia Earhart

December 26,1997

Dear Bill & Marilyn,

Christmas is quiet, hushed by the snow that's been falling for three days now. An iridescent carpet of milky crystals covers the brick streets of Trinidad. On this quiet morning I am able to see and appreciate the beauty around me. For the last three months the snow and cold have been adversaries — daunting my relentless efforts to close my home and center in the mountains. We've had over 58 inches of snow so far this year --20 inches more than usual. I'm getting to dislike this El Nino kid.

If I relied upon how I feel, I wouldn't be getting much done. I would stay warm at home. I made a promise to myself when I noticed I was beginning to make excuses for not working on any particular day. I promised that if it were humanly possible to get to the jobsite, I would show up EVERY DAY. I may only work a few hours, but I would show up. Thank God I know enough about human nature and myself to declare this commitment and create this behavioral structure for myself.

I still have a long way to go, but I must take time to generate some funds before I can continue. In my initial journal entry, when I began this project in April I wrote, "this process would likely strip me down to the essential Kim." This feeling was more accurate than I could have imagined.

It has been a labor of the heart and a test of the spirit from the start. It has challenged me physically, emotionally and spiritually. I'm seventeen pounds lighter, have muscles where I had none, practice yoga and write most days — words and feelings endlessly pouring through me, although I'm sometimes too weary to write them down. I regret that I have recently ignored my daily journal. I've been too tired lately. I have a new appreciation for people who have to work in the cold every day. It's twice as difficult to do something at thirty degrees as when it's sixty degrees. The shear energy needed to keep warm is draining.

I moved back to town and I'm living with Sara. When I come home, she runs a hot bath for me in her turn of the century claw foot bathtub -- adding Mr. Bubble to keep the bathtub ring from forming. All manner of dirt and sawdust finds its way onto me these days. My feet are always cold and the water seems to burn as I step into the tub. Eventually I am able to soak up the heat from the water, lying back so the cool bubbles form a collar around my neck. It's there my workday ends.

Sara and I attended a candlelight service at one of the local churches last evening. She has become a hub around which my life turns these days — my yoga teacher, counselor, sweet friend and playmate. I'm aware that living with me is difficult for her at times. Unlike me, she lived alone for many years. I try to respect her quiet time, as she does mine.

I've enclosed an outline for a proposed workshop I sent to a potential client. Any thoughts and suggestions you have will be appreciated. I know that it will take some time for these efforts to become money in the bank. For that reason I have begun to look for odd jobs around town. Recently, Sara shared the secrets of waiting on tables with me. She was a waitress for several years as she worked her way through college getting her degree in occupational therapy. I could tell it was work she enjoyed. Strangely enough it sounded like work I might enjoy also. I like serving others and plan to do it the rest of my life – in part as a coach. Which brings me to *my* coach.

I have only been able to call my coach a few times this year. I had prepared him for a separation that was driven more by expense than lack of time, and thankfully he offered a pro bono arrangement if I ever felt the "strong need" for coaching. I have developed a rich distinction for when I need coaching – in this case, when I re-e-e-ally need coaching. I am so grateful my coach is there for me.

Any possibilities, leads, ideas, coaching and prayers you can offer will be appreciated. I'm on *my* path. I've reconnected with Nature in a way that is transforming my life. I no longer care if I make a lot of money. I don't even care if I am able to make our center a long-term business success. However, I do want to finish it. I'm at a critical stage of development — personally, and in terms of the physical structure. Ancient fears and familiar ghosts taunt and tug at me, calling on me to walk my talk, and live in faith. I intend to see it through. I'll find the funds, renew my physical self, and go on to finish the center. I know you understand.

I've enclosed a few pictures to give you an idea of how the place is shaping up. It would be nice to see you again. Maybe when spring comes. Until then, continue to take care of each other. You are in my thoughts and prayers always.

Love and warmest regards,

Coaching Principles & Practices

"If I relied upon how I feel, I wouldn't be getting much done."

There is a tendency, when coaching, to approach behavior change in a methodical and logical manner. This can cause both the coach and client to overlook what may have *motivated* the client's past choices and decisions. The exploration of past choices, and the emotions driving them, opens the door to addressing a pattern of behavior rather than an isolated situation.

One juicy area of inquiry has to do with the fact that human behavior is most often directed by how a person *feels* rather than what they think. We often take action based upon how we feel and, as we are doing so, we create an intellectual rationale. This makes it appear we made a logical choice. So, any exploration of current problems and difficulties must begin with an inquiry into the emotions associated with the client's past decisions. There are other dynamics that may also need to be explored.

For example, what reinforced or supported a client's past decisions? Was it positive or negative reinforcement? By that I mean was their decision motivated by inspiration or fear? And even if the motivation was seemingly positive in nature, it may not have been based in reality. Their decision may have been made in a state of denial or wishful thinking.

All behavior change begins with awareness, and the broader and more complete one's awareness is, the greater the possibility for lasting change. A coach can facilitate greater awareness in ways few individuals can muster for themselves.

"Fortunately, I have developed a rich distinction for when I need coaching."

One of most useful distinctions we can instill in a client is recognizing when coaching is needed. It is part of the first conversation I have with my clients. The conversation begins with a simple questions – "What brings you here? Why are you seeking coaching?"

One of the ways that I cultivate awareness about when coaching is needed is to invite clients to call me *anytime* between our scheduled coaching sessions -- whenever they feel a strong need for coaching. When a client calls me between sessions, I know they are learning to recognize when they need coaching. I am not always available in the moment, but I respond as quickly as possible in order to reinforce their behavior.

Initially clients may be apologetic when they initiate an unscheduled call. I quickly reassure them and inquire into their issue. At the conclusion of the session, I thank them for calling me. I like to leave them with an understanding that coaching is most useful in the moment you feel the need for it. More importantly, I help them understand that their felt need for coaching, and the momentary stop in action or thinking that their awareness created, is central to their development.

In-the-moment awareness that prompts a stop in action or thinking is not just a cornerstone of coaching, but the pathway to self-sufficiency. It is this process that will serve the client long after formal coaching ends. It is what prevents coaching from becoming co-dependent.

I began coaching in the late 80's when coaching was new in the personal and business arenas, and the practice was not officially recognized in most enterprises. But as it emerged and grew into a recognized discipline, I saw this as a wonderful sign. The growth of the coaching profession became the symbol of a new paradigm -- a shift from where the individual is controlled, to one where individuals are driven from their own commitment.

In organizations that embrace the coaching disicpline, you have but to utter the word "coaching" and a rich context surfaces. While each organization I have worked with has a slightly different distinction for coaching, it is clear that a coaching conversation is different than a leadership or management conversation. The latter are focused on what the enterprise needs, and the former on what the individual needs. This change represents an enormous shift in organizational focus.

THE COACHING SUPPORTED ORGANIZATIONAL SHIFT

OLD FOCUS	***NEW FOCUS***
Goal is CONVENTIONALITY	Goal is CREATIVITY
COMPLIANCE	INVOLVEMENT
Seeking KNOWLEDGE	Seeking WISDOM
Attention to WHAT IS HAPPENING	Focus on WHAT COULD BE
Want to find ANSWERS	Want to explore POSSIBILITIES first
People are RESOURCES	People are THE MEANS

The American culture, it has been said, is a culture of the individual – respecting the dignity of the individual, the rights of the individual, etc. However, in my experience, support and nourishment for human beings is limited to ways that focus on keeping society, and the economic engine that drives it, going. This is true of most societies. However, my hope is that the presence of coaching, particularly within business enterprises, is the harbinger of a more generative world.

If we truly focused on supporting and nurturing individuals, helping them grow their talents and express their passions, we will create a society far beyond what we can imagine.

Our current social, economic and political structures do not seem to support the evolution of human beings individually and collectively. Personal growth must be systematically pursued. I see this happening. One recent manifestation includes eco-villages and intentional communities that are popping up across the world. People are creating social and economic communities that allow individuals to prosper and generate *true* wealth, the things that human beings genuinely need.

So, coaches can weave the threads of transformation into the fabric of humanity. You are supporting the evolution of Homo sapiens to Homo sapiens sapiens – a *truly* wise being.

THE SECOND YEAR

XVI

"The difference between school and life? In school, you're taught a lesson and then given a test. In life, you're given a test that teaches you a lesson."

Tom Bodett

March 18, 1998

Dear Bill and Marilyn,

I'd been asking around town again for people willing to do day work. Someone gave me a name – Terry Baldwin. When I called him he was anxious to find work. We immediately jumped into wage negotiations. When we reach an agreement I asked, "Do you want to know the work we'll be doing?" He said it didn't matter. This told me he was living on the edge – surviving week to week.

Terry differed from other people I encounter in his ability to be honest -- all that he seemingly cared about was making money. Abraham Maslow explained this phenomenon, and also why it exists in our country where most people are *not* living at a survival level.

Our culture equates money and material gain with happiness. I've learned, as you may have also, that this notion is largely false -- indeed almost 180 degrees from the truth. I suppose some might say, "I'm suffering anyway, I may as well suffer in comfort." But if you are acquainted with psychic pain and suffering, you know that it robs you of joy. I'm not sure Terry was aware of this intellectually, but I would guess that he feels it at some level.

During our first break on the job, Terry began to tell me his story. It was a bad country western song. It seems like life has been giving Terry a lot of hard hits. I couldn't be sure, but I wondered if he was getting life's messages. If not, I fear that he would get another cosmic dope-slap in the not too distant future.

I also wondered if his story was true. But in the end, it didn't matter. Sometimes the stories we tell about ourselves and our lives are made-up – a myth. Terry seemed trapped in a mythology of his own making, as I am in mine. I have to remind myself that I'm here in the mountains because I want to *rewrite* my story -- make it read less like fiction.

Love,

Coaching Principles & Practices

"Our culture equates money and material gain with happiness."

In America, there has been a 5% net drop in adjusted income since 1979. At the same time, average hours worked per week have increased 9%. We are working harder and getting less. This direction is not sustainable. At some level people realize this. As a consequence, there is an underlying insecurity in the workplace. We live in a more fearful environment. This feeling is clearly manifesting in our current (2008-11m) recession.

One of the most unfortunate outcomes is that people, in a survival mentality, typically become more "me-focused." This philosophy is also exacerbated by our business-driven culture. We try to apply market principles to living. Each company looks out for #1, and now, so do most people.

The focus on self is understandable, especially in rough times. However, it is not sustainable. When an individual focuses primarily on what they need, they may become a little bit sociopathic. They build their lives on a feeling of deficiency. "I don't have enough – power, money, status, etc." One of the most enlightening statements that Abraham Maslow uttered was, **"All extrinsic goals and values are deficiency motivated."** Thus, if we build our lives on extrinsic needs, we constantly feel deficient. In this mental and emotional environment, there is no way we ever know true and lasting joy.

We have *happiness moments,* and continue deluding ourselves with the notion that, if only I resolve this or get that, then I will be happy. As a coach, I attempt to get my clients to see the bigger picture. Oftentimes the way we do this is to ask a simple question, "Are you happy?" When you ask this question, it is important to note body language as well as verbal responses, since the non-verbal information is usually more revealing.

Another way to initiate an inquiry into happiness is to ask clients to make a long list of what they want and need right now

– what they are striving to achieve. Give them plenty of time to make a good long list.

After they are finished, look at the list and notice how many of the things on the list are *extrinsic* and how many are *intrinsic*. If proportionally, there are far more extrinsic items, then there is a high probability that the individual is unhappy. If there are roughly equal parts of intrinsic and extrinsic items, then you may have to probe further by asking them to prioritize their list – identify the top four or five most important items. If the top wants and needs are mostly intrinsic, then that person has a good shot at happiness.

An interesting thing about extrinsic wants and needs as they relate to deficiency motivation, is that you never get to a place where you have enough. For example, even if I get a raise and more money, I want still more because I still *feel* deficient. Enough is never enough. On the contrary, with intrinsic wants and needs, we can feel accomplished without ever having achieved a specific goal. Simply being *in action* on our intrinsic goals, values and needs is usually enough to create joy and a sense of fulfillment.

An interesting way I explore this phenomenon is to use a simple graph.

I ask my clients to put X's on each of two lines. One on the success-failure line that describes how successful they feel they are, the other along the fulfillment line to show how fulfilled they feel. In most cases clients put an X close to the *success* end of the graph, and near the middle of the *fulfillment* line.

I point out that the ideal trajectory is to have success and fulfillment move in tandem so that as we become more successful, we become more fulfilled. I sometimes combine their two lines to make a graph to illustrate this point.

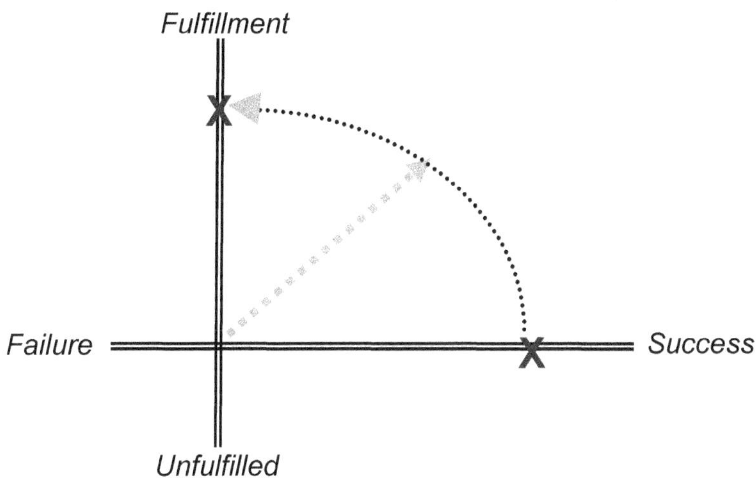

When I share this graph, the obvious question comes to mind. "Why aren't success and fulfillment moving together in my life?"

This inquiry often leads to the realization that clients are not spending their time doing things that bring them joy and fulfillment. From there the exploration usually leads to what would offer fulfillment. The answer usually points to (you guessed it) intrinsic values, needs and goals.

For most people in the U.S., success is defined *for* them. It is defined primarily in extrinsic terms – big office, nice car, home in a great neighborhood, financial investments, etc. This is part of our programming that began almost the moment we are born. The primary focus of socialization and education is to make us productive workers, able to contribute the economy.

Think about it, what's the first lesson you learned in school? Answer: to be controlled. You are taught to sit quietly, raise your hand before you speak, do this assignment, turn in your papers now, etc. To be a good worker, you must be able to take direction – be controllable. And because all human behavior must be reinforced in order to persist, our behavior is rewarded. Unfortunately for us, "reward" is also defined for us.

In most schools we are not allowed to explore what makes us happy. Indeed, given our programming, it is a wonder anyone is happy. The first step on the path to fulfillment then, lies in awareness. There is nothing you do can make someone happy or fulfilled. The most we can do is to make them aware if they are or are not. And that is no small thing.

"I couldn't be sure, so I wondered if he was getting life's messages."

I've heard it said that we're all on a spiritual journey whether we know it or not. A spiritual journey is our evolution as human beings toward a higher level of consciousness. It allows us to live within our true interconnected and interdependent nature.

I've lived long enough to see what I call "the evolutionary hammer." That is, the "whacks" that we continually get throughout our lives. It works like this:

Almost everything that happens to us has a directional message in it. But we do not always get Nature's GPS signals. If not, it or something like it happens again. Life gives us another "slap on the cheek," and a little more pain associated with it this time. If we're conscious at all, we recognize the message. We say, "I've been taught a lesson." However, if we are still not getting the message, life seems to escalate the intensity of the process.

When the evolutionary hammer comes out again and again, it gives us a *good hard whack*. We now have a major breakdown -- a "big problem." We will keep getting whacked, harder and harder, until we get it. Some people never do. This is why, when a client brings a problem, one of the first questions I ask is, "Has anything like this happened before?" In other words, is there a pattern here? There often is. When life delivers a *big* whack, there have probably been smaller "slaps" in the not too distant past.

Coaches are not just there to help someone solve a predicament. Coaching is not just about solving problems. It is also be about increasing awareness so that our clients understand life's messages as soon as they are delivered. As a coach, I must help my clients move beyond a specific problem toward the bigger message – the lesson. In this way the evolutionary hammer might be avoided – at least for a while.

Pain is the compass that keeps us oriented in the right evolutionary direction. We cannot live without pain. However, we can avoid suffering – defined as being in pain longer than we need to be. A coach's job is not necessarily to help a client eliminate pain, but rather to avoid suffering. To do this, we must move beyond problem solving to the patterns and messages behind the problem or issue -- the lesson learned. Coaching can help a person read life's messages. The rest is up to them – as it always is.

XVII

"Being an actor is the loneliest thing in the world. You are all alone with your concentration and imagination, and that's all you have. Being a good actor isn't easy. Being a man is even harder. I want to be both before I'm done."

James Dean

April 13, 1998

Dear Barry,

It is Sara's birthday. I am writing to you today because it was in a conversation with you, almost a year ago, that I came to the realization that I was in love with her.

Your call last April, and subsequent visit, was a real treat for me -- connecting my past with my future. You came to look at a piece of property near Sara's parcel on the North Fork River. I asked her to meet us and show you around, since she knew the area so well. When I mentioned her name you asked, "Who's Sara?"

I can't recall my exact words, but I described her as a new friend – a woman who follows her heart, loves adventure, and has an awesome innate honesty and beauty. Then I added, "She was my landlady for a month or two."

You gave me your signature silly grin and simply said, "Sounds like you're in love with Sara." Your comment caught me by surprise then, but later I saw the truth in it.

As you and I were traipsing around on the vacant parcel on County Road 21.6, Sara came along -- flowered dress, big straw hat, and a galloping roan-colored Australian Border Collie running ahead. You said, "This HAS to be Sara." Indeed it was. My Sara.

We had a great time that afternoon. Sara brought some refreshments and we sat on the little porch of her camper trailer by the river, and we all chatted for hours. It was great to have you there because it allowed me to sit back and observe her. Your words were spinning around in my head – "sounds like you're in love with Sara."

I was not wrestling with the truth of it, but rather what it was about her that was so attractive. To be sure, she was a pretty woman, but it was something deeper. I can't recall if I put my finger on it then, but now I know now what it is. Sara is completely authentic. There is no pretense. Despite her sometimes square-peg manner and impulsive nature, she knows who she is, what she wants, and she seems to be comfortable in her own skin. By comparison I often catch myself playing a character in a play – the intrepid pioneer, or the alienated writer, or the sad man in mid-life crisis. I can see myself slip into these roles. I suppose I do it to cover up some part of myself that I am ashamed of -- or some part of me that I don't want others to see.

In the early days on the land I recall lying on the narrow bed in my trailer under a small aluminum window. As I wondered how I got here, fear loomed up inside and all around me. I felt alone – maybe because I was. In a cold sweat I would yell at the top of my lungs into the nearby forest of ponderosa pines. "Help me ple-e-e-ease. Where are the angels!" Crazy things like that.

I envisioned the vibrations from my shouted words penetrating the forest, striking and rattling the great pines and then transmitting my S.O.S. through their roots deep into the earth and around the world. It must have worked, because help began arriving in many forms.

I recently hooked up with two great guys, Bob and Al. After going through countless helpers I found two that work hard, have fun, and show up every day. I know now that my cries for help brought Sara too.

Our relationship seems solid, but I am reminded that I am still with Sara on a "trial basis." When she agreed to take me in as the winter closed in, she said in a matter of fact manner, "Let's see how it goes until spring. If it doesn't work out, the weather will be warm and you can move back to your trailer."

It's spring and neither of us has said anything about this agreement. It seems to be working, although some unexpected legal problems for me have put a strain on us both. I imagine Sara may be wrestling with a few "what ifs."

I have come to loath "what-ifs." They suck the joy out of life – or rather, they can if I let them. What-ifs are simply my old friend fear dressed up.

If I am going to deal with "what-ifs" I intend to create some that are filled with promise, rather than paralysis. What if . . . Sara and I fall more deeply in love? What if . . . the very best of both of us emerges when we're together? What if . . . she can love me because of who I am, rather than in spite of who I am?

I am tired of "what ifs." I am tired of being scared half to death. We all know what happens if we're scared half to death twice . . .

We don't die. We simply stop taking risks, and then we're as good as dead.

I need to get beyond my what-ifs – another in my seemingly endless list of needs. I sometimes feel as though I am being buried by my needs. In this building process I expect to come to understand what is really important in my life, and what I can let go of. I know that I will always need good friends – soul friends like you.

So, once again . . . thank you. I would like to think that the vibrations emanating from the tall ponderosas brought you, but I suspect it was love. Stay close my dear friend.

Jim

Coaching Principles & Practices

"Sara was completely authentic. There was no pretense . . . she knew who she was . . ."

Human beings tend to habitually compensate for some real or perceived inadequacy by making themselves "special" in some way. While we may each have some unique abilities, the need to *feel* special often covers up these mostly self-generated feelings of inadequacy.

We are programmed to believe that, while we are good at *some* things, we have *many* deficiencies. Our family of origin is responsible for much of this programming. Recent research into messages parents send to pre-school children revealed that a pre-school child, on average, gets 27 corrective or negative messages for every 1 complimentary or positive message. As a consequence of this conditioning we make our initial appearance in our "life's autobiography" as a character written by other people. Additional characterizations happen in school and in our relationships. We begin spending a lot of our time and energy covering up the "bad parts" and only revealing the "good parts." We lose our authentic selves in the process.

So, how do we break out of this life of pretense?

A good start is to question the need to be "exceptional" at something. By allowing ourselves to be "ordinary" or "average" we learn self-acceptance that leads to self-love. In this way we can lessen our underlying anxiety about our self-image and ourselves. This is not to say that we are not *unique.* On the contrary, we are each totally unique. We do not need to be expert or accomplished at anything in order to join the human race. The truth is we are fine, okay and lovable "as is."

This notion does not seem to jive with our culture of performance in which we are encouraged, and rewarded, for being special, accomplished, expert, etc. However, there is a mental framework that can enable us to function in the culture of performance and still maintain our authenticity. This framework has to do with the idea that we are required to play many roles – much as an actor on stage or in a movie would. Sociologist Erving Goffman did some brilliant work in what might be termed "social performance."

It is Goffman's view that we are all actors playing a role on various stages with other people simultaneously being fellow actors and our audience. This notion begs the question, "Why are we acting rather than being ourselves?" Goffman's answer is that we do it to be perceived well by others, and accepted. He does not elaborate here, but it's easy to see that acceptance becomes imperative because, by nature, human beings need one another to survive. If you doubt this, try to imagine a human baby or child managing on it's own -- even ten years after birth.

In addition, we learn that being well perceived and accepted by others helps us to be more effective in our interactions and endeavors. For most of us, acceptance is the food upon which the ego thrives.

Inspired by Goffman's ideas I developed a model that I use in my coaching practice.

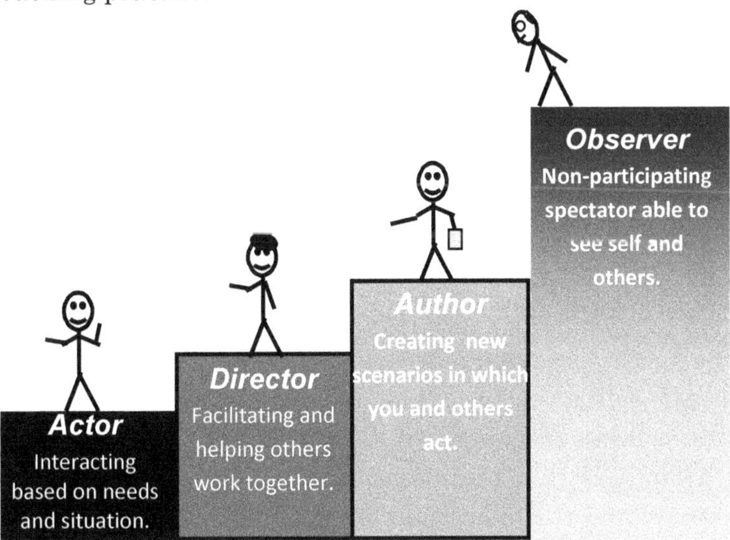

Even though most of us continually shift from one level or step to the next in the course of a day, we tend to spend most of our time on the bottom step – as the actor. We get caught up in the day-to-day drama, and the roles we play in that drama. It is important to balance the time and energy we spend on all four levels of this model.

When a client is caught up in a specific situation, I often draw a simplified version of the 4-step model on a piece of paper and point to the "actor" step, noting that this is the place from which they are operating now. Then I point out that it may be useful to get a new perspective on their situation by looking at it from a higher perspective.

For example, if they could rewrite the "scene" or situation they are exploring, how would they do that? If they were to step into a "director role" and tell each of the actors in the "drama" what to do, how might that look? I especially endeavor to elevate them into what I consider the most powerful level – that of the observer.

It is my opinion that the observer level is unlike the other three because it is NOT A ROLE. It is on this level that you can get in touch with your authentic self. And here I am speaking about authenticity at the deepest level. When we are observing, we are experiencing our essential self.

We can change roles and climb up and down the bottom three steps at will. Changing roles is like changing clothes, our essential self -- the observer -- remains unchanged. The observer watches us shift from being an actor, to a director or writer. This practice is transformative, because we can see the whole autobiographical drama unfold without getting tangled up in it.

Being the observer may be as close as we get to being our authentic selves because, when we do this, we connect with the greater collective consciousness. It is this state of consciousness and awareness that the monks and mystics tell us is the true Reality. From this place we can see and react appropriately to the continual drama unfolding all around us.

"I have come to loath "what-ifs." They suck the joy out of life – or rather, they can if I let them.

What ifs are the harbingers of fear and doubt. They often masquerade as reasoning. As coaches we must be vigilant when they surface.

When a client says "what if . . ." I ask them what they are feeling in that moment – "What do you think is hiding in that *what if*?" I might ask. If a client has a pattern of using what-if, I often go a step further. I play a game with them by revealing the flipside of their what-if. I might say, "What if . . . you don't do what you love?" or What if . . . you don't take this risk?" It is the all too familiar "what-if" way of thinking that, as Thoreau said, leads human beings to lead "lives of quiet desperation."

It was no accident that *Walden* was one of the books I took with me to Colorado. It is a bit ponderous at times, but it was a great companion. I would not compare myself to Henry David Thoreau, but he did built a cabin in the woods and used it as a vantage point from which to look at the "modern" world around him.

Thoreau's observations about American economics seem just as valid today as they were then. He created an elegant distinction for "true economics" by contrasting it with commercialism. One of his most memorable metaphors was the ice business. People had made a business of harvesting and storing ice. While ice was used to store meat, Thoreau wrote of the emerging use of ice to cool a gentlemen's drink. He noted that ice costs nothing in raw materials, adds no value, and soon melts into nothing. How much of today's products and services fit that description?

"In this building process I expect to come to understand what is really important in my life."

Clients come with a goal – something they wish to achieve. I have found it useful in many situations to facilitate an exploration of the need behind the goal before I take up a conversation intended to help them achieve it.

For example, a client of mine initially came with a stated desire to find a new career path within the company she worked for. She wanted something "more challenging and fulfilling." On the surface, this appears to be a simple request. However, let me add another bit of information. My client's business was "network television news promotion." Think about this for a moment. Don't get confused by the word "news," because what passes for news today strays pretty far from Webster's definition.

My opinion of TV network news is that it is mostly unsupported opinions and fear-based entertainment masquerading as information. Now take it a step further – my client's profession was *promoting* network news. *"What are the five things that can kill you in your kitchen? Find out at 6:00 on KBUM News Tonight."*

My client is a smart person. In her heart she knew that the ethics and morality of her profession were suspect. My intuition was that this knowledge might well be at the source of her lack of challenge and fulfillment. I wanted to open the door to exploring this possibility. I know this would violate what some see as "boundaries" for coaches, but my own approach to coaching causes me to use my intuition.

I didn't share my assessments or confront my client in any way. Rather, I took a circuitous route toward my client's goal. I facilitated an exploration of my client's *need* – i.e. "What aspects of your job make you feel unfulfilled?" By letting true needs become the basis for our coaching conversations, we elevated the exploration beyond a simple search for a new position or job.

The challenge here was coaching without sharing my personal assessments and prejudice. What enables me to do this is *awareness* of my assessments in the moment, and some awareness of my non-verbal demeanor as well.

As a coach, I cannot avoid having opinions or making judgments. I am a human being. It's part of my make-up. It is only when "my stuff" – opinions, values, prejudices, etc. -- come up during a coaching session, and I am <u>not</u> aware of them, that I can get into trouble.

Awareness, awareness, awareness . . . I cannot say it enough. Your degree of self-awareness in the moment, is what distinguishes good coaches from great coaches.

XVIII

"One advantage of talking to yourself is that you know at least somebody's listening."

Franklin P. Jones

JOURNAL ENTRY -- August 27, 1998

Payday. I paid Bob and Al yesterday and included a paid day off. I think they were a little upset that I brought in a special five-man team this week to help us get all of the windows and doors set. From their viewpoint it takes work away from them. But I felt winter approaching last week – the first cold night in a while, and I wanted to be sure the house was closed in tight. I also wanted to be ready for the stucco crew who, although I cannot get them to commit to a date, say they might be here next month.

Waiting on the stucco crew is wearing on me. The biggest frustration is keeping the heavy black plastic on the straw walls in order to keep them dry. A big wind comes up and tears the plastic to shreds. I don't know what there is about the wind, but it can drive you nuts. It's a constant irritating assault on all the senses – blowing dust in your eyes and mouth, howling in your ears, and buffeting your body. As I run around pinning new plastic to the straw, I am often cursing at the top of my lungs.

When I become aware of how emotionally out of control I am, I get embarrassed. I want to be more aware, more vigilant. If nothing else, my obnoxious behavior will keep me humble, and that is not only helpful, but also necessary for a coach. The worst thing that can happen to a coach is to feel, in any way, superior to your client. After all, I've always prided myself on being modest. Ha!

The wind usually dies down at night, but I find myself still muttering away. Spending so much time alone, I have begun talking to myself more and more. I've been told it's okay . . . as long as I know I'm doing the talking.

It seems conversation is often the best way to gain access to issues and problems. We think at nearly the speed of light, but conversation travels at the speed of sound. Talking slows things down so we can grasp them more easily. But it also suggests there are at least two entities there – the observer is one of them. That's good --right?

Coaching Principles & Practices

"The worst thing that can happen to a coach is to feel superior to your client."

One of the ways a coach can be distinguished from counselors and the like, is that a coach operates as an equal partner with the client. The coach does not have greater rank or status. If the client grants a special status their coach this situation must be remedied. Equal status is necessary in order to create a context for self-disclosure, client responsibility for outcomes, and most importantly, higher client self-esteem. It is essential that the client completely own their accomplishment.

Egalitarian status is not hard to establish, or reestablish. For example, asking a client for help in understanding, or inviting the client to teach, signals that a coach is seeking equal status. Whenever I have caught myself "pulling rank" on a client it was usually unintentional. I was unconsciousness. This happens when I cut off a client, or when I do not fully engage an offer the client makes.

As I noted earlier, I believe that the conscious and unconscious abuse of rank, power and status is the root cause for many breakdowns in relationships and dysfunction within organizations. This is especially true in today's organizations that are dominated by white males who are often only vaguely aware of their innate rank and status. As the saying goes: "White men were born on third base, and they think they hit a triple." Even those who are aware of their lucky advantage, often rationalize that they earned it and deserve it. Given this assertion, it is easy to see how the misuse of rank and status might be the source of many problems that business leaders struggle to manage. In so many cases, it is not people that need to be managed, but the leaders who need to manage themselves.

"Spending so much time alone, I have begun talking to myself more and more."

Contrary to popular belief, talking to oneself may be one of the healthiest things we can do. The most useful solo conversations revolve around questions.

There are different levels of questions. There are "the big questions" such as: Who am I? What most important to me? What are my gifts and passions? Then there are the everyday questions that usually revolve around "problems."

A coach deals with all kinds of questions, and many kinds of problems. How effective a coach is depends, to a large degree, on the quality and creativity of the questions asked. Over the years I have gathered a number of useful questions – ones that help people to break out-of-the-box. When I am creating possible questions to prepare for a coaching session, I find that the best questions have one thing in common. They facilitate a shift in perspective.

The genesis of human transformation is a shift in perspective. There are many ways to create this shift using perlocutionary questions.

You can change your perspective by getting *elevation* – a "higher" or larger view -- as when an astronaut sees the earth from space. Examples of "larger view questions" include:

What is the larger issue of which this is only a part?

Is this situation a problem of the system? If so, how might you bypass it?

You can change perspective by facilitating a deeper, less superficial look. Examples of this type of question are:

What does the person creating this situation really want?

What might be the root cause of this situation?

One of the most interesting ways to shift perspective is a 180-degree turn. Here you get in touch with the underlying assessment and reverse it. Examples of this include:

What would happen if this situation meant exactly the opposite of what you think it means?

What would you do if this problem were an opportunity? What would make it an opportunity?

Then there are my personal favorite ways to facilitate a shift in perspective – off-the-wall questions:

If this situation were funny, what would we be laughing at?

How would you resolve this problem if you were 20 years younger?

So in addition to using questions to provide greater focus, consider that the most potent types of questions – perlocutionary questions -- facilitate a shift in perspective. A change in perspective seems to give a client the equivalent of 80 additional IQ points. A new perspective transforms people into "geniuses."

THE THIRD YEAR

XIX

"There can be no knowledge without emotion. We may be aware of a truth, yet until we have felt its force, it is not ours. To the cognition of the brain must be added the experience of the soul."

Arnold Bennett

February 7, 1999

Dear Bill and Marilyn,

Sunday – a day of rest -- but only physically. My mind is spinning. I am rapidly moving beyond the point of no return. I have so much money sunk in this effort it will be difficult to pull out. When I came here my total life savings added up to a little less than $34,000. I parlayed that into the purchase of 35 acres, and then used the land as collateral for a $120,000 construction loan. I've used up the construction loan and I've been operating out of pocket for the last couple years. My personal funds are dwindling fast.

I'm anxious – can you tell? I can feel it in my bones as I write these words. As someone once remarked, anxiety is merely fear without enthusiasm. I'm afraid. I told myself it didn't matter if I couldn't pull this off. I didn't have much money to start, so it wouldn't be a big loss. Obviously, I was thinking financially, and not emotionally. I probably wouldn't be talking this way if it were not Sunday. The demands of this building project keep me distracted during the week.

The Metile roofing from California finally arrived – almost. The recent snowstorm closed Raton pass and the trucking company said they couldn't get here and couldn't wait. They had to find a place to make a drop in Raton and I would have to pick it up from there. I already talked to Al and I have arranged for him to pull it up the mountain on a rented trailer using his new truck next week.

Bob and Al have been great. They have been steady on with me for almost two years now. I wait for them at the bottom of my drive these days because their vehicles can't make it up my drive in the heavy snow. They hop in and I put the peddle to the metal. We fishtail up the 1,300-foot driveway. I know that if I hesitate or stop at all, I will get stuck or slip into a ditch -- a fitting metaphor for my current situation.

The center at Longs Canyon looks well planned on the surface. I developed drawings, arranged for loans, created a building schedule, etc. In reality I am ad-libbing. I'm making it up as I go – improvising. It's my own strange concoction of creativity and denial.

If I can conquer my fear and doubt, it will be a great way to live my life. Improvising allows for almost limitless possibilities and spontaneity. I am not spontaneous by nature, or by nurture. Many people in my life have pointed this out to me. And so, as strange as it sounds, I planned to become more spontaneous! And that intention helped to bring me here to Colorado – to this undertaking. So I will continue this reckless improvisation.

And so on this Sunday, I find myself trapped between success and failure. However, Sara recently reminded me that this feeling is an illusion. I think she picked up on my anxiety as we talked about our situation. It was one of those great coaching conversations where I didn't know I was being coached. Sara is a natural coach. Indeed, her friends, knowing this at some level, talk with her on a regular basis.

Sara helped me realize that I have already achieved a great deal in terms of skill building and personal growth. There is a lot that lies between success and failure. Especially since success and failure are usually defined within our programming. I tend to live in a black and white world. I'm good or bad, right or wrong, etc. But, I'm waking up. It's not easy. And its not always fun.

Sara made me aware that I have been creating a scenario where I will be happy *if* I finish this project. And that thought ferments my fear and anxiety. But even this fretfulness is a good thing in a strange way. In trying to shed it, I am becoming more aware. These painful emotions serve a purpose.

I am learning a lot, but more importantly, I am unlearning a lot too.

Writing these letters is enabling me to become clearer and more aware. Thank you for your generous listening. You are an important part of the process.

Love,

Coaching Principles & Practices

"I'm anxious – can you tell? I can feel it in my bones as I write these words."

In the past I have tended to focus on speaking, listening, and conscious conversation. But there is another profound aspect to language. Language influences and shapes another's *thoughts* and *emotions.*

You might take issue with this assertion, however, as I have noted earlier, it is my belief that people first have an emotional reaction to something, and then rationalize their feelings intellectually. Obviously this dynamic can create obstacles for a coach.

Coaching is typically "billed" as a rational process. However, since thought and emotion are so closely linked, it is impossible to take emotions out of the coaching process. Once again, let's deepen our distinctions for the role emotions play in coaching.

As noted in previous chapters, it is important to bring feelings into the light of awareness as part of the coaching process. Surfacing, identifying and exploring the emotions that accompany assessments, thoughts, possibilities and the like, help to diminish the overpowering role they can play in choices and decisions. But does not mean a coach should be a cheerleader either.

As much as humanly possible I try to provide a neutral emotional context for my clients. I am positive and affirming without "cheering." Can you get that distinction? It is a line coaches need to walk.

Coaches know better than to give advice, yet we come close to doing that when we non-verbally react to a particular assessment or idea. This requires that we be aware, at all times, of our emotional state and accompanying body language. If you are having an emotional reaction to something a client shares, then it's often *your* stuff that is coming up. And like every other human being, your emotional reactions will tend to drive what you say and do. In other words, your emotions can diminish your coaching proficiency if you do not mange them.

If we are not aware of what is going on inside of us, then emotions control us. If we are aware of what is going on inside of us, then we can manage our emotions. The same is true for our clients. So a necessary part of coaching is observing the emotions that surface when needs, issues, assessments, possibilities and the like are being explored. This whole arena of emotional awareness may represent one of the biggest breakthroughs in my coaching practice.

I was taught, a long time ago, that emotions usually got in the way of coaching, that they were something to rise above or get beyond. Now I realize the folly of that approach. I honor them now. I continue to inquire into the role emotions play in our evolution, seeking and developing new tools and process that offer greater access to human emotions.

"So I will continue this reckless improvisation."

As I shared earlier, I learned how to have more effective interactions during in acting class I took in college. You may recall the *Five Rules of Improvisation*:

1) Hold no preconceived ideas about what this is about or where it is going.
2) Accept all offers.
3) Pay attention to others.
4) Always advance the action.
5) Support others in looking good.

I walked away from that acting class, not ready for Second City in Chicago, but with a greater capacity to engage others in a truly creative conversation. Indeed, I may have learned as much about coaching from my improv class as I have from any formal coaching workshop. I certainly learned a lot about myself.

Interactions offer the greatest opportunities to learn, know and understand ourselves. This is especially true when you are acting. Being allowed to be different than "yourself" opens up new possibilities for behavior, attitude, and ways of being. When the improv or acting scene is over, there is a moment when the imagined self stands next to the real self. This is certainly grist for self-development, but more importantly it provides a peek into a new reality that was just invented a moment ago on stage. This is one of the things that gives coaching its power.

Coaching deconstructs existing modes of thought and behavior, moving the client beyond their self-defining, self-reinforcing limitations to a new reality. Again, coaching is less about creating a new future and more about creating a *change in perception* that leads to a new reality. When you can fully appreciate that difference you will find yourself operating at a whole new level – personally and professionally.

"I tend to live in a black and white world. I'm good or bad, right or wrong, etc."

One of the primary tools for coaches is language. Therefore I find myself returning again and again to explore language. I often focus on tapping the full power that language holds for human beings. Yet language has *limitations*, especially in the ways in which it limits our ability to think and fully perceive.

One example relates to what seems to be our innate sense of separateness. This illusion has permeated the philosophical underpinnings of language. All languages are filled with duality – up-down, right-wrong, in-out, you-me, etc. Not only does this create polarized thinking, but it also keeps us from true Reality. As coaches we must be aware of this and other limitations of language. But, how do we do this?

The ability to minimize the limitations of language begins when we observe yourselves, or our clients, engaging in polarized thinking. The most common and insidious form of polarized speaking and thinking is "right-or-wrong."

Clients want to make the "right choices," and you wish to help them. A good way to begin is to abandon the right-or-wrong modality. You can do this in many different ways. The easiest way is to create a new, broader perspective that negates polarized thinking. For example:

Client: I'm at a critical juncture in my career. I've been offered a new position – a promotion, but it would mean a lot more travel and time on the job. I'm concerned I will make the wrong decision.

Coach: (*Rephrasing and expanding*) I understand that you feel the need to make the right decision. So let's take a moment to explore what "right" and "wrong" means to you in this context. Maybe we'll discover a new way to frame your question.

Another way to overcome, or at least expand the limitations of language is to "re-distinguish" an existing word – give it new, deeper meaning. For example, *wealth* in our culture is thought of as a form of capital, money, property, etc. However, it can and should be redefined to include intellectual, spiritual and physical resources and reserves.

Another word that coaches need to re-distinguish for themselves and others is "future" since that seems to be in the background of most coaching conversations. For many people *Future = Plan*. If I have a plan, then I have a future. It sounds a bit silly when we say it out loud, but this is how most people think. For them the future is a place they have to get to, and the plan is the way to get there. If this were so, coaching would be merely planning.

There is nothing wrong with planning unless we become obsessed with it. As Alan Watts said, "Unless one is able to live fully in the present, the future is a hoax." But if we re-distinguish "the future" as the place I will be as a consequence of my choices *now*, then I am in the heart of the future – in the present moment awareness of myself, and the choices that I am making. This shifts the focus from somewhere else to hear and now. This is helpful because this moment is all that we have access to and can utilize.

Have you ever found yourself in a place or situation and asked, "How in the heck did I get in this crummy situation?" We often say or think this as though it's some kind of mystery. The answer is usually, I got here by way of the choices I made, or didn't make in the past. I may not have made the choice to be in this situation, but typically I usually made choices that brought me here.

In hindsight, most people can see this. The key is to have that same awareness *now*, when they are making decisions. A coach can and must bring the client into the present moment – again and again.

XX

"Knowing your own darkness is the best method for dealing with the darkness's of other people."

Carl Jung

JOURNAL ENTRY -- September 19, 1999

Had another phone call from my publisher. The accusations around some of the terms and phrases I used in my last book are getting uglier – dark shadows gathering over me. It's difficult to make plans and move ahead. The past can hold us hostage. I should hire a lawyer, but I don't have the money to do so. All I can do is tell the truth, but that doesn't seem to go far in our legal system. I told the publishing company I wanted to sit down and talk with these people, but I was told it might be a mistake. As the publisher's attorney put it, "These people are not your friends." The worst part is that these shadows have cast a pall over my relationship with Sara. She doesn't talk about it much, but her doubts and fear occasionally show up in what she does not say. This is compounded by our financial situation.

Last Saturday I noticed that I only have $1,476 in the bank. This prompted me to ask Sara how she stands. About the same. I'm going to have to find some work soon. I've made calls to former clients, sent letters, but my network is crumbling because I have been disconnected for so long. One client recently called back (though I missed their call) and remarked that they heard I had left the country. I am disconnected from my old network and professional communities.

I already told Bob and Al we're going to have to take some time off and I think they are okay with it. They both have other work they can take up. I still go up to Longs Canyon most every day to keep the promise to myself. I always find a little something to do, but without additional materials there is little real progress. The possibility of a coaching center and home for Sara and I seems a long way off. I'm dangling between the cloudy past and a dim future. All of this is keeping me up at night. Consequently I can tell you that it's *not* always darkest before the dawn. There's actually quit a bit of light before the sun peeks over the horizon. I'm looking for a bit of that pre-dawn light right now.

Coaching Principles & Practices

"It's difficult to make plans and move ahead. The past can hold us hostage."

Getting someone to imagine a different future is relatively easy. The harder part is getting them to let go of the past – who they think they are, where they think they are going, what they wished they did or didn't do. The metaphor I use around this notion is a small child learning to use what I call "monkey bars" – a metal ladder stretched out about seven feet off the ground. The idea, you may recall, is to move across the ladder from one end to the other, hand over hand.

You typically help the child up the ladder so that they can grasp the first rung with both hands. Then you say, "Okay now, swing out and grab the next rung with one hand." And they do! But then they often get stuck -- frozen in place between two bars.

"Okay now, let go of the bar behind you and swing out again to grab the bar in front." Still no movement. They cannot move forward unless they let go of what is behind them. Then you hold them even more securely around the waist, "I've got you now. You won't fall. Now grab the next bar in front of you." And there it is . . . success. They begin to move forward.

That's the picture of a coach. Giving someone increasing confidence in his or her ability to move forward. It is always a choice. The hard part is *not* reaching forward, it is letting go of what lies behind.

In my experience, people spend up to one-half their time thinking about the past. In order to help someone move forward we often have to help him or her delve into their past before they can let go. This process involves helping a client generate understanding and compassion for themselves. I do this by making some assertions and asking them to react to them. Things like:

- Regret is not rational. We judge our past actions from our present circumstances. We usually have information now that was not available in the past, but we forget that.

- You are here *now*, yet you seem to be spending so much time and energy in the past. Are you aware that you have a choice to make with regard to how you hold your past?

The process continues by asking them to explore one or more of their "regrets" from a higher perspective. As they do, you are watching their body, for this is not an intellectual inquiry. It requires somatic processing. We have to deal with past events by surfacing the emotion initially generated by that past event and releasing it from our body-mind. Release is initiated with forgiveness -- loving your old self

We may touch on forgiveness again, but it is sufficient to note that forgiveness is a *choice.* We simply choose to let understanding and compassion take the place of anger and regret. Forgiveness is one of the purest forms of love.

It is enormously helpful to include a coach, or any other person, when dealing with the past. There is power in witnessing a person – particularly when they declare their forgiveness of themselves and others.

The regretted past does not totally disappear, but when it surfaces, it has less power. It's like a visit from an old ghost. It's no longer a monstrous poltergeist, but more like Casper the friendly ghost.

"The possibility of a coaching center and home for Sara and I seems a long way off now. I'm dangling between the shadowy past and a dim future."

Present moment living is the key to happiness. We know this. And living in the present moment requires some deep and continual explorations in every domain of time. A coach's goal is to leave their client poised to act. Some would say, to act on a future possibility. Within the American culture in particular, we focus on the future, and quest after action as though it was the "golden fleece." But what is often behind this obsession?

The future may pull, but the past freezes, holds and directs us. The sad truth is that many of our actions are driven from the past. Nowhere is this clearer than with patterned behavior. Much of our day-to-day behavior is repeated, in the same way, oftentimes using the same words and identical activities. We tend to do today what we did the day before.

A good coach understands and honors the interrelationship between the past, the present and the future. Indeed, my typical coaching conversation almost always touches on these three areas of time within a single coaching session. You can think of it as shifting, and eventually balancing, the conversation on a teeter-tauter.

BALANCING THE COACHING CONVERSATION

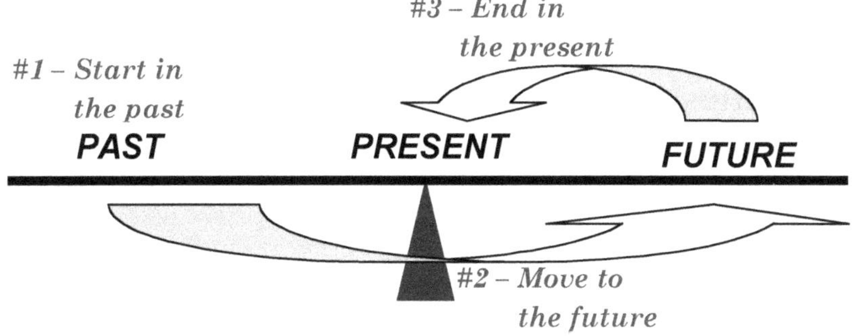

I begin the conversation in the past, move to the future and wind up in the present:

Past - What happened? Has this happened before? What have you tried? What was the result?

Future - What are some other ideas and options you have not explored? What if you did that?

Present - Of these possibilities, which ones seem the most appealing? What are you going to do next?

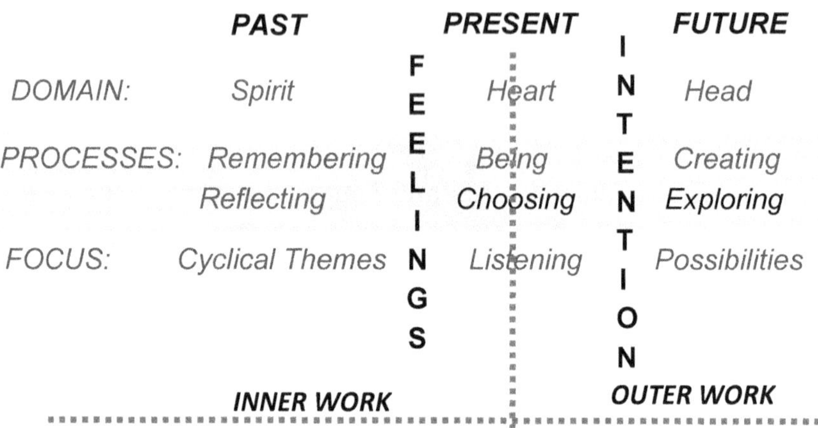

Coaches are time travelers of a sort. We move back and forth in time. And, as we do, we need to be conscious of the processes that guide our conversations – as the picture above points out.

Of particular importance is the "connective tissue" that bridges each arena of time. Most *feelings* have their genesis in the past and live in the present. Likewise, *intentions* manifest in the future but also exist in the present.

I understand that some coaches focus almost entirely on the future and present. But I cannot see how to separate these arenas, or ignore one. While interacting with a client, I spend a fair amount of time exploring the present and future. This is what I label "outer work." And it can also be a catalyst for "inner work" – explorations of the past and how they relate to the present. Obviously, the clients themselves must do the inner work. We can only stimulate and support the desire to it. Inner work is a solo journey. That said, my opinion is that no human being can achieve fundamental and lasting change in the world – their outer life -- without doing their inner work.

If coaches only focus on a client's outer work, we are colluding with them. We may be able to bring momentary emotional relief, but the client will be in a breakdown again in the near future. Good for business, terrible for everyone's integrity.

One last point here. If you haven't started already, begin your inner work. It's not a one shot deal, so even if you have done some, there is usually more to do. Reading books and attending coaching workshops and seminars will not help unless, and until, you've dealt with past issues. It is this belief that brought me to Colorado.

As you may recall, when I took on the building of this home and center, I invited the process to "strip me down to my essential self." It seems to be working. Much of what is in this book has flowed from ongoing inner work, and this is now allowing me to do more elegant outer work. So we circle back again to the key premise of this book -- mastery in coaching relies primarily on your own personal development and evolution.

"The only thing you live to regret are the risks you didn't take."

Unknown

October 5, 1999

Dear Bill and Marilyn,

Something wonderful is happening – actually several things. On a pragmatic note, the stucco crew is back and hard at work for three weeks! Yeah! And I even have the money to pay them! This gives us a whole new perspective on our project.

I wish I could say that they are as happy as we are. Everyday they drive in from out of town in a beat-up extended van – usually about 9:30 am. The van door slides opens and they pile out toward the house, looking like a gang of sad dwarfs. As Steve passes me he remarks, "I beginning to hate this place." I'm tempted to go to my trailer and get my copy of The Power of Positive Thinking, but I don't think these guys are big readers.

Putting stucco on straw walls is extremely hard work. If you don't think so, just try holding your arms above your shoulders for 20 minutes. The men on this crew are slapping stucco on the wall for six or seven hours every day.

I help where I can, but I stay clear of the finishing action along the walls. This gives me the opportunity to observe these men at work. They grumble a lot. And beneath their complaints I can see what they can't or don't want to see. They are unhappy. I know that they can be happier by changing their attitudes. They're tired of this big job and apparently unable to make it work for them. I can see this so clearly in them. I wish I could see my own resistance as clearly in myself.

I know I have the power to do this. Indeed, I can make this shift on many occasions. My guess is that, right now, I don't want to see my situation because my expectations are like a house of cards. If I begin to see the truth, it may all come tumbling down. Maybe I would discover that all of my efforts over the last two years don't mean anything. I'm not ready to go there yet, and I don't have to – which brings me to my next bit of good news. More angels have arrived!

I recently received a call from a training company wanting to meet to discuss the possibility of developing a new training program. When I ask whether or not they can pay my travel expenses for the meeting, they are stunned. "Normally prospective contractors pay their expenses during negotiations," they say. They don't know that I am not being obstinate, but rather I'm just broke. However, they relented. They agreed to pay travel expenses for Sara and me.

When they picked us up at the airport they seemed surprised that I was not wearing a suit or tie. Again, not out of eccentricity, but rather because most of my clothes are in storage five hundred miles away. So they take me to the nearby mall on the way to their offices and buy me a tie.

When I get to their office the whole team is assembled in a large conference room. I am told that they include their whole staff as part of the decision making process. I ask for a flip chart and marker and I begin to answer questions. After a while, I begin to do a presentation of sorts. Three hours pass. No one leaves – a good sign.

Finally, the VP of development asks me to wrap up so we can go to lunch. I'll spare you the lunch conversations. When we finished lunch, Sara, the VP, and I went back to her office. She said, "It may take some time for us to decide on whether or not we wish to develop some of your ideas into a training program, but I have a more immediate need."

She went on to explain that they have another project that is behind schedule because the writer/developer can't seem to grasp the subject matter – which is about fostering innovation within an enterprise. This is a subject matter is new for me. "I'm convinced that you are a good writer and developer," the VP said.

"Would you be willing to take this project on? And, if so, what would you want to produce a finished product in four weeks?"

My mind was spinning. I needed to think. I asked if I could have a moment to consult with Sara. We ducked out of the office. Sara asks me what it will take in terms of time, and what a fair market value is for this project might be?

I scratch around on a piece of paper and come up with a figure -- a big figure. Sara looks at it and says, "Okay, but I think they are going to want to whittle down your asking price. I would ask for more. I'd add 50% more." I only hesitate a moment.

We head back into the VP's office and, with a little couching, I lay the big number on her. She hesitates for a moment. My heart sinks. I begin to dig my heels in, prepared to negotiate and . . . "Okay, that will work," is her answer.

Sara and I are both stunned.

I've since worked full time on developing their training program for the last three weeks. I write an average of ten hours a day. Sara brings me food and drink. I am definitely surrounded by angels. We have money again. The building can go on.

We needed this. Not just the money but the cosmic support. The construction project had almost been at a dead stop. Doubts were creeping in. I wondered if I'd crossed the line between taking a risk and being reckless (again). The universe spoke and shattered these doubts. Or, at least that's how I have interpreted recent events.

Thanks gain for your kind thoughts and support. I count you two among the choir of angelic beings that are blessing us.

Stay well,

Coaching Principles & Practices

"I wondered if I'd crossed the line between taking a risk and being reckless."

Any action or inaction contains a risk. The familiar doesn't look risky, but that assessment is based upon a primordial feeling, not logical thinking.

By definition the familiar is composed of patterns. There is a pattern to how we drive to work everyday, a pattern to when we eat and sleep, a pattern to how we spend our free time, etc. Patterns are a defense against the randomness that our animal brains tell us threatens our survival. A coach must expect some emotional resistance as clients begin to explore out-of-the-box possibilities and actions.

When you see a somatic response to new ideas, concepts, directions, and/or actions, make sure your client notices it too. "What's going on inside of you right now?" Let them use their own words to describe what they are experiencing. Encourage and reassure them. Fear and stress must be relieved, for these are the "shackles" keeping your client chained to the status quo.

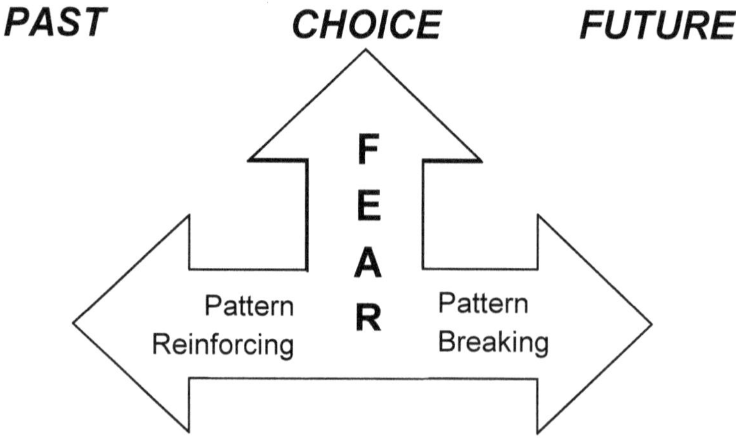

Fear and comfort keep us trapped in old patterns – the past. Once this fear and comfort is identified, two things happen: First, the fear loses its' emotional power. Second, the door is opened to exploring our patterned behavior. Remember, fear of the unknown is more *emotionally* than rationally based. It doesn't usually stand up well to reasoning.

As you facilitate this exploration of the unknown with a client, there are many directions you can go. For example:

- Explore the risks the client may have taken in the past.
- Recall a time when taking a risk turned out to be a good thing.
- Think of situations where *not* taking action was risky, or created a problem.

Another direction is to pull the "distinguishing tool" out of your coach's toolbox and distinguish *risk.* There is a difference between taking risks and being reckless or impulsive. You want them to make that distinction. What you are after here is a higher level of thinking.

When confronting a risk, the normal impulse of human beings is to seek more information. And, while there may be a little more information available, in most situations there is not enough . . . that's what makes it a risk – the lack of information. One of the most common stalling tactics is "waiting for a more information." It's a game we play with ourselves, part of the "getting ready to act" game. Your task, as a coach, is to move through the innate emotional response a client may have to a higher-level of thinking.

"I'm tempted to go to my trailer and get my copy of The Power of Positive Thinking.*"*

Norman Vincent Peale wrote *The Power of Positive Thinking* in 1952. Since then many millions of copies have been sold. It was a landmark book because it got people to become aware of their thoughts. This was not a new concept. The Greek philosophers touched on this principle when they inquired into the nature of thought. More recently, William James, a pioneer of modern psychology (and brother of author Henry James), stated, "The greatest revolution of our generation is the discovery that human beings, by changing the inner attitudes of their minds, can change the outer aspects of their lives."

Our attitudes determine our behavior and especially the way we interact with others. In turn, the way we interact with others determines how they listen and respond. And the way they respond ultimately determines the possibilities and results being created. It's a chain reaction that begins with awareness of our thoughts and attitude.

If you could only be aware of one thing – your thoughts might be it. Of course, positive thinking alone will not accomplish much. We must act.

If we held a race between a purely positive thinker, a gung-ho doer, and conscious doer, who do you think would win? The outcome is not a sure thing, but let me conjecture.

The positive thinker may still be thinking when the race is ended. It is possible the gung ho doer might win . . . or the conscious doer. They may even tie. But here's the big difference. The conscious doer *enjoyed* the race and can't wait for another one. The gung-ho doer is often exhausted and not certain if they want to enter the next race. Consciousness allows us to enjoy the journey.

One of my favorite stories about unconscious doing happened when I took a long weekend to one of my favorite places – El Porvenir west of Las Vegas, New Mexico. I was hiking up Hermits Peak. It's an all day trek if you do it right. I left in the morning. After a three-plus hour hike I reached the top. I was pleased to see I was the only one at the summit. I sat on the edge of a ledge and broke out the lunch -- peanut butter and jelly, an apple, and a banana. It was unusually clear and I could see three states from where I sat. After an hour or so, I reckoned I needed to head back. It could take up to three hours to get down and I wanted to be back before it got dark.

As I headed down the trail I spied a man bouncing up the path in yellow and black running gear. He had on a red sweatband, and he was bounding in large strides up the trail, coming toward me. When he saw me, he jogged in place and asked, "What do you think the record is for hiking Hermit's Peak?"

I had to say I didn't know.

"I'm at just under two hours, think that's a record?"

I offered some advice, "You might try the ranger station at the entrance, they may know."

"Okay, he said as he clicked a button on his watch. I'm going to time my way down too. Thanks."

And off he scampered back down the mountain. The interesting thing was that he didn't stop for even a moment to look at the spectacular view from the summit. I was totally amazed, but probably shouldn't have been. That is how many of us spend our lives. Achieving one goal after another, but never enjoying the journey. We are in action, but operate in a hypnotic state. We go through life "sleep-running," an eyes-open slumber induced by our culture and media. It's time to wake up. Unplug from the Matrix!

THE FOURTH YEAR

XXII

"When out on a picnic, the Master said, 'Do you want to know what Enlightened is like? Look at those birds flying over the lake.' While everyone watched, the Master exclaimed: 'They cast a reflection on the water that they have no awareness of and the lake has no attachment to."

- Father Anthony De Mello, SJ -

January 6, 2000

Dear Bill and Marilyn,

The course development work I've been doing, coupled with the holidays and bad weather, have given me the first real break from building I have had in almost three years. I have time now for a proper letter.

The stucco crew came again just before Christmas to put the first two coats of plaster on the inside. I bought a second hand gas heater and hooked it up to a 100 lb. propane tank to keep the plaster from freezing. I go up every day to crack open the windows, let the dampness out, and check the propane level. I checked on Christmas Day too.

It snowed the day before so the canyon was beautiful. I could smell wood fires in the air. I wondered if Sara and I might be living there by next Christmas. It looked possible with the new influx of cash.

We've overcome many problems. "Problems" may not be the right word. At the moment we are not so much pushed by our problems as led by our dreams. When a problem shows up it simply becomes next thing to do. To be sure, there is anxiety and fear, but it seems to pass quickly these days.

I do see a new problem in the not too distant future. It was not apparent until now because I was never certain we would ever finish this place. Now that it appears we will, I can foresee the day will come when I will have to leave this home and center.

I was recently reading an essay by the Dalai Lama. He was writing about evil in the world, noting that evil is based in fear. He noted that aside from the economic, military, and health fears that dominate the headlines today, the real fear many people harbor is the fear of losing the stuff they have accumulated. Our home and center is the biggest amount of stuff I've ever had. And if I am honest with myself, I am afraid to lose it. I know I must let go – intellectually. I have a long, long way to go emotionally.

I think my attachment to the center is so strong because I have identified with it. MY center – MY project – MY place – MY accomplishment, etc. Again, I know intellectually that this is not true. Our home and center is no more part of me than the clothes I am wearing. I am also aware that many, many people, in addition to myself, made it happen. Chief among them is Sara. I think it is safe to say that much of the success of this undertaking goes to my lovely helpmeet.

You may recall that when I began this process I hoped it would strip me down to my essential self. I wonder again what I meant by that. What is the "essential self?"

I am not my stuff. I am not my clothes. I am not my body. I am not my accomplishments. Maybe if I eliminate everything else I will arrive at what I am.

Some people call it the soul, or spirit – that part that is unchanging. Rene DuBos calls it the God within. I might be able to label it . . . but can I experience it?

I apologize for these philosophical monologues masquerading as a letter. Let me shift gears and answer your recent questions about Trinidad. My personal saga is getting boring – even to me, so let me tell you what I learned about my new home town.

I have been gathering books and articles about this area that abounds with history and legends. Trinidad was a main post on the Santa Fe Trail. It is said that several famous gunslingers came through Trinidad at some point. Bat Masterson was a sheriff here.

This is coalmining territory. There are no mines operating now, but it was one of the richest coalfields in the country for more than six decades. Labor unions took root here with the coal mine workers. The location of the infamous Ludlow massacre is just ten miles from here.

The cultural diversity here is a result of the coal mining business. It was one of the few jobs an immigrant could get at the turn of the century. Coal companies recruited workers overseas and out east to replace striking workers, part of a strategy to keep unions from being able to organize. In some coal camps ten different languages were spoken, making it difficult for union organizers to work.

Today, Trinidad has large Hispanic and Italian populations, but some western European groups are represented here as well. These demographics have helped to foster cultural tolerance that you don't always find in other small towns.

I hope this answers your questions about this western town – so different from your community in northern California.

I think about you often and wonder how you're doing. I hope there is some way you can see our home when it is complete. It’s nice be able to say those words – attachment and all.

Coaching Principles & Practices

> ***"Problems" may not be the right word. Right now we are not so much pushed by our problems, as led by our dreams."***

Often coaching engagements focus on a "problem." We know problems only exist within an individual's assessment. However this truth provides little consolation or help for a client.

Problems carry such a stigma and negative connotation that people oftentimes use euphemisms – challenge, barrier, issue, concern, etc. I tend to use whatever term a client uses for their problem and then, right away, do some work to re-distinguish problems in a more useful way. For example, I often say to a client that I can hear the *commitment* inside of their description of the problem. Of course, this is true because there cannot be a problem without a commitment. And, since coaching is commitment driven, problems can be seen as a "good thing."

Problems are most often a perceived need for change that the client is committed to achieve. When I reframe problems in this manner most clients resonate positively, indicating that they are taking responsibility for the situation. They are motivated to change.

Once again, there is a coaching model I use that helps me focus efforts in ways that will help the client address and solve the problem.

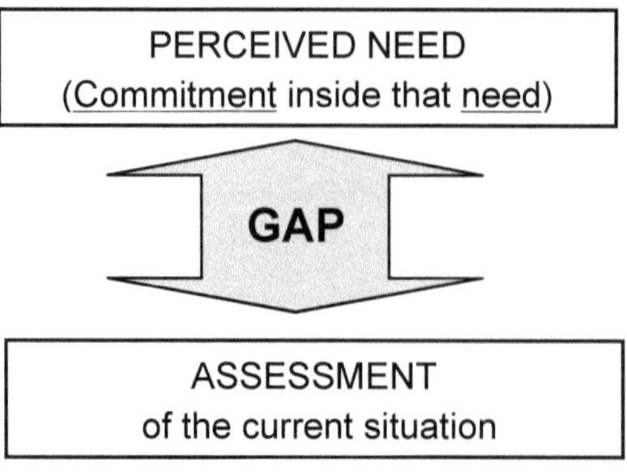

This model illustrates a gap that is the difference between what a client needs/wants, and his/her assessment of where they are with regard to getting what they want. The larger the gap between their need and their assessment, the bigger the problem. Our task, as coaches, is to close the gap, or make it smaller.

I close the gap by focusing on *both ends* of this model. I help them clarify their need, and also explore the accuracy of their assessment. An example probably serves best here. This occurred during a period when I was working on the center and almost broke.

My daughter was going through a rough time emotionally. During our periodic phone conversations I could tell that she was stressed out, depressed, and anxious. I did my best to coach and provide support during my calls, but I wanted to do more. I was increasingly feeling like I needed to spend some time with her. However, I didn't have the money for the airfare to New York City and other related expenses.

During one of my calls with my coach, I mentioned this dilemma with regard to my daughter . . .

"You remember my daughter. We'll she's going through a tough patch right now and I feel I should be there to support and help her. However, I don't have the money to be there. I feel like I'm letting her down."

My coach began by immediately supporting my commitment to my daughter. Then he facilitated an exploration of this commitment, as well as my assessment of my current situation. His intention was to help me find new ways to honor and act on my commitment. Our conversation went something like this:

Coach: I hear your love for your daughter clearly. My guess is she loves you too. And you want to help and support her – is that right?"

Me: Right. I want to be there for her.

Coach: When you say "be there for her" I assume you mean physically?

Me: Exactly. I don't have the money for the trip.

Coach: I got that. It sounds like you think that *you're physical* presence is the best way to help your daughter. *(A moment of SILENCE to signal attention.)* My question is, besides flying there and talking on the phone, what are some other ways you can be there for her?

Me: *(I was momentarily puzzled.)* Let me see. . . .

I went on to find some new ways to support my daughter and show my love. I selected a of couple options and shared my intentions for taking action.

Using the "problem solving" model offered earlier, you can see that my coach first validated my commitment.

He did not say, "Your daughter is an adult. She can take care of herself." On the contrary, he said, "I hear your love for your daughter and, I hear that you want to help and support her." He confirmed and upheld my commitment.

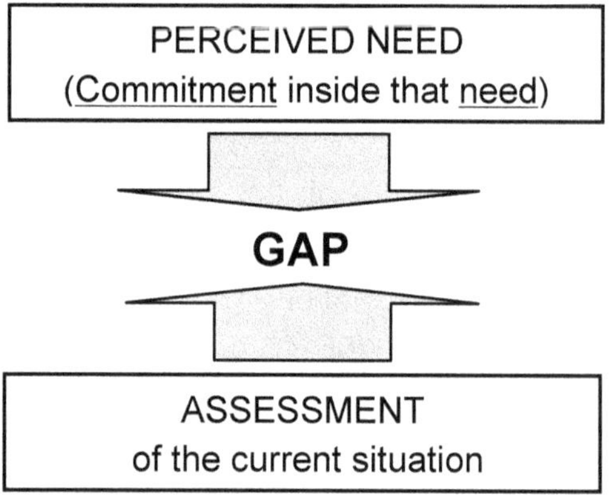

Next, he focused on my limited assessment – adding a little slap to my ego by pointing out that my *physical presence* may not be necessary to help my daughter.

The net effect of our conversation was that the gap became much smaller. The difference between my commitment to support my daughter, and my assessment of my ability to do that, was much less after my coaching conversation. To be sure, there was still a small gap because, being a father, I still would like to hold her in my arms -- to show up for her.

In summary: A coach's job is to identify, support and strengthen the commitment behind a client's problem. Human commitment provides the energy that will be needed to act and change-- call it motivation.

Next a coach facilitates an exploration of the client's *assessment* of the situation. Most initial assessments are limited because they rely primarily on past experience for possibilities. The objective is to generate *new* options and opportunities for action, and leave the client poised to act.

Once someone is in action to meet his or her need, the problem immediately becomes less oppressive. It's as if the client has set down a huge burden. This is because the oppression felt from problems is mostly generated within an individual's interpretation of their circumstances. Indeed, you can see this in a client's emotional state at the end of a coaching session. The tension and anxiety that were present when the "problem" was first described, is usually greatly diminished at the conclusion of the coaching session.

XXIII

"We cannot think of being acceptable to others until we have first proven acceptable to ourselves."

Malcolm X

JOURNAL ENTRY -- August 20, 2000

When I talk about my essential self I do so as though it were something I have lost. So, my question is, when did I have it, or have access to it?

Maybe the only moment I was my essential self was at conception, or the first moment of my birth. Since then I have been covering it up with layer after layer of personality, beliefs, false feelings, ideals, etc. -- until now, when I have little or no connection with my unique essence.

Our whole society seems to conspire to keep us from knowing our true selves. Our consumer and entertainment culture keeps us distracted. Television, alcohol, and drugs anesthetize us. Even the more socially acceptable forms of escape like excessive work, exercise, and even relaxation, can be a distraction.

This is why this search for the essential self is so difficult. It is not supported by our culture and way of life. On the contrary, when you reject the ongoing distractions and programming, YOU are rejected and ostracized. And this is the ultimate punishment for the human animal.

I am getting better at not seeking acceptance and approval from others. But I still enjoy it when it comes my way. Progress?

I have a ways to go. I'm not in a hurry. It would be nice if I woke up one morning knowing who I really am; but I don't think it happens that way. Poco a poco.

Coaching Principles & Practices

"Our whole society conspires to keep us from knowing our essential selves."

I have distinguished a coach in many ways – guide, appreciator, trickster, etc. One role I have not yet touched on is *context creator*. One of the more important things a coach does is create a caring, non-judgmental environment wherein an individual can safely explore.

So much of our thinking and behavior is driven by the need to be accepted, approved of, liked and loved. I can often see this desire surface when a client pauses as they are speaking. When they may appear lost in thought my intuition tells me that they are censoring themselves. I like to use those occasions to build trust, and a more nurturing context.

"You have paused . . ." is a good way to intervene in possible self-censoring. Usually they are caught short and pause long enough for me to add, "What's behind that pause? What's on the tip of your tongue?"

Almost any response opens up a rich field of inquiry. Sometimes they will come to the realization that they were indeed censoring themselves in order to be more pleasing and acceptable. Other times, it's something else. If they are withholding something, you can probe further into the whole realm of judging oneself and/or fear of being judged.

Without making a big deal about it, I simply tell them that being acceptable or pleasing is not necessary in coaching sessions – indeed, it can even slow down the process. You can go on from there if there's interest or energy to do so, but either way, your point is made.

A recent example was with a female client – a high-level executive. She was exploring a self-proclaimed bind between her work and your family – namely caring for her children. I caught her self-censoring and intervened.

I asked, "You seem to be struggling for the right words. What's happening right now?"

She lowered her head and said, "The truth is I don't enjoy being a mother – not as much as I enjoy my work." There was a long pause before she added, "I've never been able to say that to anyone before."

This marked a breakthrough for the client. By revealing her secret she began to replace the grip of guilt and regret with the open hand of the truth. She regained her integrity. From that point on she made rapid progress with regard to what she initially called a "work-life balance issue."

Over time simple interventions like this create a powerful context in which to engage another human being. For many people, a coaching session is the only place they can express themselves freely without regard to how they will be judged. Providing this open, accepting and compassionate context is as important as anything a coach says or does.

THE FIFTH YEAR

XXIV

"Do not worry if you have built your castles in the air. They are where they should be. Now put the foundations under them."

Henry David Thoreau

Easter Sunday

April 15, 2001

Dear Bill and Marilyn,

The finish coat for the stucco is going on next week. I am worried that the freezing nights might be an issue. We had problems with the brown coat two years ago when it went below freezing. The next day when I tapped the wall with a hammer, the stucco would fall off. The chemical bonding didn't take place.

I wonder what is holding me together? Angels have come along on a regular basis, but day-to-day it's Sara that is holding me together. I am so grateful for her presence and love.

We have been together long enough to experience some big ups and downs in our relationship. Aside from the emotional baggage that I dragged with me into this relationship, we have had to deal with group claiming they own a handful of phrases in my last book. And then there is the almost continual worry about money, and the slow grind of the day-to-day physical work that often makes me moody and hard to live with. It's a real rollercoaster ride, and Sara's sitting in the seat right next to me – thank God.

I am also very grateful that I have you and other people available to me as coaches. A good coach seeks coaching. Brother do I need it. When I can, I like to reflect on my experience of being coached in order to gain deeper insights into the coaching process. I notice that after a coaching session there are some subtle ups and downs – mostly emotional – that I do not always notice *during* my sessions. I will be more aware now. This whole process is making me a better coach.

For one thing, I have deepened my distinction for *worry*. I used to be a bit dismissive when a client expressed worries or concerns. In the past I felt that, once the client had greater clarity and was in action, their worry would dissipate and go away. That's how it appeared in my previous years as a coach. However, I have gained new insights into worry now -- being on the other end of the coaching conversation. Even though I am in action, "old ghosts" continue to taunt me -- but not today!

The weather is beautiful. Sara wants to go to North Fork this afternoon. This nearby property represents *her dream* and desire to live in Nature – something we both share. And, being Easter, it seems a good time to resurrect old dreams. I wouldn't be surprised if we saw an Easter bunny or two – and maybe some Easter eggs.

These childlike symbols, you probably know, came from the ancient celebration of the Saxon goddess of fertility called Eastre. And so, as human beings have done for thousands of years, Sara and I will ritualize the coming of spring – renewal.

Thanks for being there. Happy Easter!

Coaching Principles & Practices

"I notice that after a coaching session there are some subtle ups and downs – mostly emotional – that I do not always notice* during *my sessions."

People love roller coasters because they put you in the present moment. The farthest into the future that you can see when you're riding a coaster is over the next hill. And there is also a strange sense of accomplishment as you get off the ride. "I made it." That's what happens when I reflect on my past life. I get the same sense of accomplishment. "I made it," as though it were unexpected.

One advantage to growing older is that when you hit a psychological bump in the road, you more quickly realize that -- somehow -- you will probably make it over this hurdle. This knowledge reduces your anxiety and keeps you in action. However, sometimes it takes a while to come to this realization. And this is where a coach comes in handy.

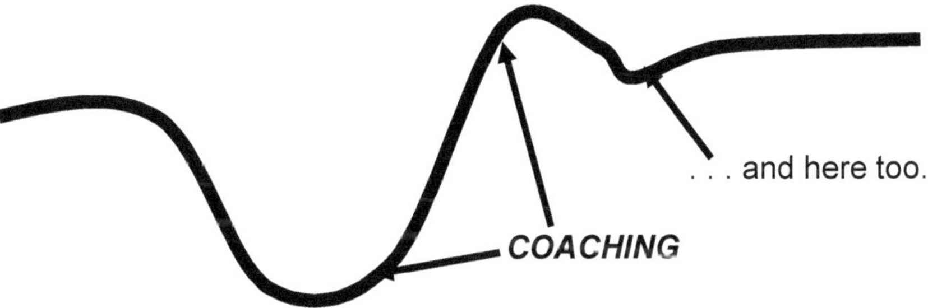

I'm traveling along when I get a kick in the pants. I'm initially caught up in an emotional reaction – sometimes fear and shock. I am psychologically frozen. I seek coaching. With the help of my coach I discover new opportunities for action and new possibilities . . . but there's another smaller, unexpected bump that lies ahead.

A coach must be aware that the original breakdown that created the request for coaching does not magically vanish when the client identifies a new pathway and is poised to take action.

The processing of the emotional content within that breakdown continues and often resurfaces again and again.

While a coach is not on the ride with me, he or she is there at the critical junctures. The first two junctures are familiar. Indeed, they almost define a coach. A coach enters the scene in the aftermath of breakdown and facilitates an exploration of new pathways forward and upward.

The coach's job might seem complete, but there is at least one more subtle bump on the ride. It occurs almost immediately after the client commits to moving forward. In the space between seeing and choosing a novel possibility and taking action, there is another smaller "psychological speed-bump." It's usually unexpressed but it may sound something like, "Oh shit, what am I going to do now?"

At this third juncture a coach's presence is also necessary. In most cases there is little the coach can or should say or do. You can reflect a client's commitment back to them, and show your confidence in their ability to act and succeed. But it is enough that the client knows that you will be there to support them. For it is in this "community of two" that people can more easily accomplish what they could not otherwise accomplish alone. A coach and the client are a small but mighty community.

There are often additional bumps along the way as the client takes action on the new plan or strategy. When a client is in the process of implementing their action plan, and they hit a snag or run into resistance, old emotions generated in the original breakdown usually surface. Once again the coach is there, a symbol of the client's commitment. And so the client continues to move on, no longer blocked by the emotions that resurface on the road to change.

"I have deepened my distinction for worry."

Clients often come to us with concerns. Let's call them "worries." I have come to believe that worrying is not always about the future. Sometimes it's about the past.

We come to our current situation, and our worries associated with it, via choices we have made, or didn't make. Often other people, and *their* choices, have also played a role. It is critical that clients realize that if they are to take action to resolve a "problem," they *alone* must take responsibility for addressing it. Certainly their action might engage and involve others, but the client must take full responsibility for addressing and resolving their own problems and worries.

Next it is important to understand that worry is largely shaped by past experience, and the emotional responses associated with that experience. Human beings project past experiences and emotions into the future. So, it is important to help the client distinguish between the lessons learned and the emotions associated with them. Often what is creating worry now is the association with emotions from the past.

Many people do not like to believe that they are greatly influenced by their emotions, but I have a lot of personal and professional evidence to support this assertion. I touched on this issue several times already. Now I would like to offer a pragmatic way to bring *healthy emotions* into the coaching conversation. How do we do this?

Again, it starts with awareness. As you may recall, a coach needs to shine the light of awareness on the situation to reveal the emotion(s) that are present. This is a straightforward process. If worries have their roots in the past, then exploration of the past, as it relates to the current situation, is important to the coaching conversation:

"Has anything like this ever happened before?"

"What happened?" (Watch for emotion.)

"How did you feel then?" and/or "What are you feeling right now?"

"How might what happened in the past be impacting what's going on now?"

Awareness usually works its magic. Once we recognize an emotion, it loses its power. When we are not aware of our emotions, they control us. When we *are* aware of our emotions, we can manage them. It is a sad choice to let the darker emotions of fear, guilt, sadness, etc. determine one's choices in life. It could even be considered irresponsible. When a client becomes alert to the emotional component of a situation, we can proceed.

"And so, as human beings have done for thousands of years, Sara and I will ritualize the coming of spring – renewal."

Renewal – this is something sorely missing in our culture. Sure, we take vacations, but they can be as stressful as our daily work. I have been blessed recently to work with an organization that believes in renewal. Indeed, that is the name they gave their recently instituted employee sabbatical program. I had a part to play in shaping this program, and the privilege to offer orientation sessions for people about to go on "Renewal."

We wisely made the one-day orientation program mandatory because, almost to a person, everyone coming to *Renewal Orientation* does not want to be there. So the person introducing the program always made a request, "Raise your hand if you believe having a *mandatory* day-long program to plan a sabbatical that allows you to do anything you want, is the SUPIDEST thing you ever heard of?

Almost all hands go up, and that's my cue. I say, "I'm going to ask that same question again at the end of the day. And, it's my job to make sure no hands are raised." And that usually proves true.

Indeed, the *Renewal Orientation* program was one of the more highly rated programs ever offered in this wonderful organization. I would like to take the credit for that, but I can't. What makes the *Renewal Orientation* program so popular is *the process* and the *context*.

We systematically guided people to answer the *BIG QUESTIONS* . . . What is most important to me? Am I happy and fulfilled? What do I need now?, etc. Of course, we conduct this inquiry in many different, fun ways. It's not all just conversation and writing exercises.

During the orientation session, people came to realize that they seldom, if ever, explore and reflect on their lives in a deeply meaningful manner. Ultimately they see the renewal orientation process for what it is – a rare gift. More importantly, the four to eight week sabbatical takes on new significance. The sabbatical is transformed from a just a long vacation to an opportunity to get in touch with, and be in action on, those things that are currently most important in their lives. Wow! What a gift. Coaching is that same kind of gift.

I cannot imagine a vocation that is more fulfilling than coaching. A coach gives the gift that every human being needs, not just at challenging junctures in their life, but periodically throughout their life. It's the gift of renewal and, like spring, it's pure magic. When human beings are taking action on those things that are most important to them, something wonderful happens.

XXV

"I find it interesting that the meanest life, the poorest existence, is attributed to God's will, but as human beings become more affluent, as their living standard and style begin to ascend the material scale, God descends the scale of responsibility."

Maya Angelou

July 8, 2001

Dear Bill and Marilyn,

I just completed one of the most gratifying tasks I have had since I began this project more than four years ago. I set 3,200 square feet of tile. It took me more than four weeks not including my training by a master tile setter.

I had done small tile jobs before, but this project was something different. I searched for many weeks to find the best tile setter in the area. Turns out it was a young man who lives in in the high mountains north of here. His name is Tom.

He learned tile setting in Germany. Tom was a former ski bum who landed in the Alps. He found work in the construction industry, and eventually into tile setting trade. He apprenticed for three years before he received his master's certificate. He married German gal and they moved back to the states.

I phoned him and asked if he would teach me tile setting. He was reluctant – to put it mildly. "I set tile for $3.50 a square foot, I don't teach," was his reply. I needed to get face to face with him, so I asked him to give me an on-site quote. He came out to our place, looked around and said, "$13,000 including mop-board – I supply the mud. You supply the tile."

I explained that I didn't have that much money, but that I could pay him to teach me. He held firm. Then my coaching skills came into play.

"How did you learn to set tile? What do you think it would take to develop some basic tile setting skills?"

Then I moved in with a request. "Are you busy all the time? What would you charge per hour to teach me?"

He said he would have to think it over.

"I'll call you tomorrow," I relied.

The next day I called and he told me he wanted $50 an hour, five days minimum work, and gas money, to teach me. I agreed on the price, the five days, and the gas money, but countered with three days now, and two days later. We had a deal.

He was a great teacher. By the end of the third day we were setting tile together, side by side. I paid him and told him I would call after a week or two, when I expected to have more questions and challenges that would again require his expertise.

Turns out I loved setting tile. It was the first time in many years I could work for days on end by myself. I was inside, so there was no sound save that of the scrap of the notched trowel on the concrete slab as I spread the mud.

Piece by piece, foot by foot, I set the tile. It became a meditation. Aside from a walking meditation I experienced many years ago, it was my first in-depth experience with a moving mediation. I was having a "flow" experience. It was magical. Only once was my trance-state broken.

About two weeks into the project, I heard a vehicle pull up. Phantom barked. In came Tom. "I'm not ready for you yet," was my greeting. "I'll be damned," was his reply. By then I was almost half done with the tile setting. I was cranking out about 160 square foot per day.

Tom was flummoxed, "I only taught you because I thought, within a few days you would be begging me to take the job. But you did it!"

"You're a good teacher," I said.

He came back later and made good on the remaining two days. By the time Tom left he had showed me how to grout and how to lay-out a room four different ways. So now the big tile job is complete -- just in time for a break.

A couple of weeks ago Sara and I were invited to visit a Native American community in Bridger, South Dakota, and this might be the perfect getaway. A former Methodist minister and I had struck up a long distance relationship. One thing led to another and he asked if I would come to his community and help him with a new project that blended commercial enterprise with preserving native culture. How could we refuse?

Doug, our host, came to this most recent ministry in stages. As a pastor he took mission groups from his church to spend one or two weeks helping to repair and weatherize Indian homes in Bridger. He struggled with their seeming lack of interest. He initially attributed this lack of interest in the project to a lack of personal motivation -- that they were not interested in improving their circumstances. But as he continued his work, he came to understand that it was, in part, the reservation culture that was a barrier. The culture and atmosphere did not support broad visions and dreams. Quite the opposite.

Doug also realized that the Indian culture, like most, was too big and powerful to take on directly. He was looking for a new approach. It was during this period that he discovered my last book and decided to harness the power of human commitment to improve the lives of the people in Bridger -- one person at a time.

He simply asked himself, "What can I do?"

This was the classic *Out There – In Here* model, inspired by many great thinkers. Like all powerful models, it is deceptively simple. We have no power and little influence over what is *"Out There."* Fundamental change can only happen when I look *"In Here"* -- to myself for a solution.

When Sara and I pulled in we were not only warmly greeted, but honored. The community had set up a buffalo hide teepee by the Cheyenne River as our guest suite. Doug wanted to call a community meeting the next day, but we requested a more gradual introduction.

He shared his vision of a complex that would house an inn and a native culture and craft center. He was having difficulty getting the community, and especially the tribal council, to buy in. He was respected and loved, but he was still an outsider – and so were we.

I asked Doug to take Sara and me to the homes of the formal and informal leaders in Bridger. We drank coffee and talked, not initially about Doug's project, but mostly about their lives.

Sara and I built a fire ring in front of the teepee. At night we lit the fire and people from around the community would come and sit. One night I told a ghost story – Mark Twain's *The Man with the Golden Arm*. Instead of jumping in fright at the exciting climax, they all laughed.

On the Friday before we left, Doug arranged for a potluck in the community center that also served as his lodgings. We knew that if if food were served the people would come. And come they did, young and old.

We ate and talked and laughed. When the cake and coffee was served everything quieted down. We gathered in a circle. One at a time the elders spontaneously walked into the center of the circle and offered stories and teachings to the community. This was unplanned, but it created the perfect context for a conversation about Doug's vision.

Doug spoke about the new inn and cultural center that he envisioned for the community. Then he asked me to say something to the community. I still wasn't sure what to say when I walked into the center of the circle.

I walked up to one of the elders who had just spoken and asked, "What do you see in the new center?" The reply was quick, "I see a wonderful garden where we can grow healthy food."

I walked over to another member of the community, "What do you see?"

"I see a place where the young people can learn to tan buffalo hides."

And so it went, person by person.

After many of the people had spoken, I simply stated the obvious. "You each have a piece of this vision. Doug has but one piece. He needs your piece. We need *all* the pieces together." There were a lot of heads nodding, but I wasn't sure if this fragile unity would last.

In our parting debrief with Doug the next morning, I explained that our ceremony last night was powerful because it made the vision real. I suggested that a possible next step was to gather a few people in the recreation center to build a scale model of the new inn and cultural center on the ping-pong table – which was mostly used as a buffet table for potluck dinners. He said he would do this.

As we left I realized that this experience was the kind of work I most enjoyed. I want to operate in highly leveraged ways. One-on-one coaching is wonderful, but I also feel the need to work at a whole new level of system – with communities of commitment. I know you two understand because you both have been operating at this level for many years now. Indeed, I learned the A-B-C model that describes this principle from you. That model has served me well.

I want you to know that it was, in part, your teaching and coaching that allowed me to comfortably step into the center of that circle and say what seemed to be the right thing. Thank you my friends.

Coaching Principles & Practices

"It was my first real experience with a moving mediation. I was having a flow" experience."

I am just another in a long line of authors who repackage ancient wisdom. The handful of basic truths about human beings, and how to live a rich and fulfilling life, has to be dusted off and expressed in words that new generations and cultures can understand. The evolution of language, and the emergence of new social perspectives, requires a new vernacular to express ancient Truth and Wisdom.

At the heart of ancient wisdom is the assertion that the key to living a joyful life lies in the present moment. Millennia ago you could find this teaching in the Upanishads. Today you can find it translated and updated by Eckhaert Tolle and Mihaly Csikszentmihalyi.

I read Csik's book *Flow: The Psychology of Optimal Experience* (1991) when it first emerged on the literary scene. It deepened my distinction for what present moment living is about. At that point in time, I did not often have "flow" in my experience. However, looking back on the many days and weeks of setting tile by myself, I can now say I have. I could only see this in retrospect, because when you are in the present moment you are not aware that you are.

Rereading Csikszentmihalyi, my assessment of the tile setting experience is validated. I had all the ingredients he outlined for "present moment stew:"

- I knew clearly what I had to do.
- I knew every movement, and was focused on the *movement*, not the goal.
- The challenges perfectly matched my skills.
- There was a gentle focus on what I was doing.
- I felt totally in control of life.
- I was unselfconscious.

• Time seemed non-existent.

Summing it up in a phrase, being and doing collapsed and merged. A flow experience gives us a glimpse of Realty – a life without concern for the past or the future. Total unselfconsciousness.

More and more, I find myself in this place when I am coaching. This is a great feeling because it indicates that I'm moving beyond the methodology of coaching into a more natural way of being. Coaching is becoming a natural extension of myself.

The primary lesson I learned from Csikszentmihalyi's translation of ancient knowledge is that we need to find and use our innate gifts, because nothing else will enable us to live a "present-perfect" existence.

"This was the classic "Out There – In Here" model, inspired by many great thinkers. Like all-powerful models, it is deceptively simple."

Many years ago a met a fellow consultant who specialized in Total Quality Management (TQM). He had written several books, had a lot of notoriety, and was making the big bucks for speaking engagements. When we were introduced he asked, "So Kim, what do you do?"

"I work primarily in the area of leadership development," was my response. His eyes rolled a bit.

"Listen Kim, we don't know each other, but can I offer a perspective on leadership development?"

"Please," I replied.

"In my experience, the best that we can hope for with leaders today is *benign neglect.* Just tell them to keep their cotton-pickin' hands off the people. From what I have seen of leadership development, it's collusion. You collude with them to make them feel even more powerful, and they gum up the works even more."

I was momentarily stunned and responded defensively. "Some of what you say may have truth in it. But I don't believe I collude with leaders," I asserted.

"How would you know?" he asked.

Fortunately, the "Out There – In Here" model popped to mind. It allowed me to respond to this doubting colleague as follows:

When an issue or problem first begins to reveal itself to a leader, their initial response is often denial – "it's not happening" or it's not my fault' – in other words "Not Here." However, when the problem persists or gets worse, denial does not hold up. They must take action. Ah, but what kind of action?

When I receive an invitation from a leader, they are usually past denial, but they are quick to point a finger "Out There." In other words, the cause of the problem is with our managers, our culture, the stressful business environment, poor work processes, etc. Take your pick. I accept this invitation because it's usually the only open door. I present my work in a manner that guides them to focus on themselves and say, "In Here." Then leaders get to a place where they are willing to explore how *they* are contributing to the problems being addressed. If this does not become a significant part of the plan to address problems, I disengage. Fundamental and lasting organizational change only occurs when leaders take responsibility for the situation, focusing on changing and improving *their* thinking and behavior.

Leaders have total control over themselves, and only a little influence over what is "Out There" – the people, culture, economic environment, etc. I don't expect leaders, or most human beings for that matter, to immediately focus on themselves. Indeed, *Out There – In Here* describes an ontological dynamic that represents the innate reaction most human beings have to problems or calls to change.

Why fight human nature? Go with it -- *initially*. Assuming they are no longer in denial about the problem, begin by focusing out there – on communication systems, work processes, competency gaps, etc. There is always room for improvement in such areas. But if the shift to "In Here" does not happen in a reasonable period of time, then it is best for me to move on – ethically and pragmatically. Ethically because I would be charging for services when I know that I cannot make a lasting difference. Pragmatically because eventually the leaders realize that my efforts are not curing their problems, and boot me out.

So, when you get an invitation from a potential client, don't be surprised if it's couched in a manner that puts the blame on something or someone else. Your coaching can help them shift their perspective and focus in areas that hold greater promise.

"I want to operate in more highly leveraged ways."

If a lifetime is expressed as a bell-curve, I'm on the downhill slope. That awareness causes me to reflect on the need to maximize my time and energy. In the past, this meant doing more – being more productive. Today I have a different perspective.

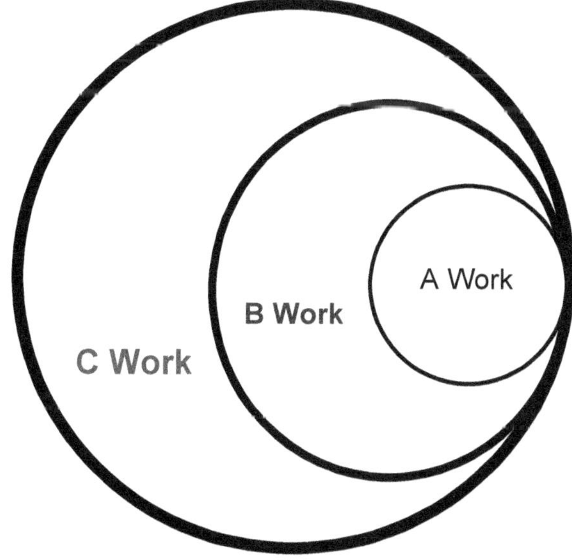

I have a model that helps me focus my time and energy more effectively. As you recall, if you seek greater mastery in any arena, creating and borrowing distinctions is one way to do it. Mastery results from acquiring a vast array of distinctions – often unique distinctions. One of my recent acquisitions came via Doug Engelbart and colleague Bill Veltrop who introduced the A-B-C Work model to me.

A Work – Includes all work that meets day-to-day, quarter-to-quarter stakeholder needs. *Examples include:* planning, executing, administering, communicating, coordinating, decision-making, problem solving, gathering intelligence and data, analyzing, designing, accounting, evaluating, etc.

B Work – Includes all work intended to improve the quality, effectiveness and/or efficiency of A-Work. *Examples include*: redesign of work and meeting processes, process facilitation, getting or giving coaching, training, improving communication channels and structures, systems design, etc.

C Work – Includes all work intended to improve the quality, effectiveness and/or efficiency of A-Work by focusing on the *type, choices, nature* or *effectiveness* of B-Work. Examples include: Gathering intelligence on B/C work options and effectiveness, developing strategies for improving B and C work expertise in or out of house, shaping context and culture to ensure high quality of B and C work, redesigning business models, etc.

This mental model, and these distinctions, point to a greater amount of time and energy being directed at B and C work. The goal is to eventually incorporate B and C work into ongoing A-work.

Many times my coaching clients bring their A-Work to me. For example, how to design and lead a program that creates higher levels of teamwork in their enterprise is A-Work for a team leader.

There is nothing wrong with pursuing A-Work goals, but it would better serve a leader to elevate their thinking and also focus on B-Work or C-Work. In the above example, you might shift the focus from creating a "team-building" program, to exploring ways in which employee performance is shaped and managed – B-Work. Or you might begin to identify the best performance management systems in team-based organizations with the intention of seeking out best practices– C-Work.

An example comes from a recent client leader who was seeking coaching in the wake of a major HR program debacle. This particular organization sought to increase their level of teamwork, particularly across functional boundaries.

They called on a consulting firm that has been doing a lot of work for them. The firm redesigned their annual performance review process to deemphasize individual accomplishment, and turn the focus toward team accomplishment.

Two months after the new performance measures was put in place, the new performance management was breaking down. There were two class-action lawsuits. The union leadership was openly complaining about the new process, and productivity was down, along with customer satisfaction.

They were addressing performance by focusing on B and C work; however, the *quality* of the B-work, and particularly the C-work, was poor. Focusing on the employee performance review process alone (B-work), created breakdowns in other parts of the performance management system. My guess is that they never really identified the larger system. Worse yet, they picked the wrong consulting firm (C-work). The consulting firm was best at business strategy, mergers and acquisitions. Human performance was not their forte.

I am telling this story to make an important point. B-work and C-work are more highly leveraged work. That is, a little bit of time and energy invested in B and C work can pay big dividends. And that leverage works both ways. Poor quality B and C work can quickly and dramatically *reduce* organizational and/or personal effectiveness. Obviously, if a coach shifts the conversation from an A-level to B or C-level, there has to be a simultaneous elevation in the quality of the coaching and thinking.

XXVI

"What is necessary to change a person is to change his awareness of himself."
Abraham Maslow

November 10, 2001

Dear Bill and Marilyn,

We got a call from a colleague in Fort Collins on the morning of September 11th. Our friend knew, since we don't watch TV, get a newspaper, and seldom listen to the news, we knew we would not immediately know about the tragedy in New York City. He knew that there was a chance I had some coaching sessions scheduled, and that I needed to know what was happening so I might be prepared when people called. To this day I have not seen video of the World Trade Center tragedy. I can't see any good coming from seeing it.

On that day Sara and I were on our way to an event at a spiritual community in Loveland. It was a good place to be. The heartbreaking events in NYC have ripped through millions of hearts and I can still see the shock in people's eyes. A sad numbness permeated our lives.

Bush said to go to Disneyland -- keep buying, keep consuming -- keep busy and distracted. The economy was already hitting the skids before 9-11, but this simply expedited and deepened the downturn. My work totally dried up. Instinct tells me that the economy will suffer for quite a while. I am looking over options and possibilities, which are limited in Trinidad.

"What do I know other than how to coach, facilitate and train?" I asked myself. Build. I made up some business cards for my new construction enterprise – TT Builders. I am putting the word out. I may also call on some of the contractors in town this week. I ran into one and when I ask about work he just shook his head and said, "Sorry." I guess 56-year-old carpenters aren't in big demand.

I keep telling myself to think out of the box. Coach and carpenter are both in the box. Sara tries to help me – coach me, but I get irritable when she offers possibilities. I become especially upset when she suggests that I may have to leave here to find work.

The only good news is that our center is totally closed in and the basic infrastructure is in place. As you know, Sara and I had been living in the garage loft, and more recently moved into the main building. It will be a while before we can really say we are finished, but the sense of urgency is no longer there.

I feel stress and anxiety, but I am aware of my feelings and do not get caught up in them as much as I used to. I catch myself sooner. The feeling that everything is okay is more and more present for me.

A couple years ago it would have bothered me to put on a tool belt and go door-to-door looking for work – hoping to get an eighteen-dollar an hour job. I would have felt like a failure – like I didn't make it. Make it? Make what?

I'm not a success. I am not a failure. I am not good. I am not bad. I am not smart. I am not stupid. I'm me. This is *my* life.

I just got off the phone with one of our neighbors. He said he and his family would pray for us. Why does that upset me?

He and his family are good and generous people, but I sometimes wonder about his motivation. He says he does "good things" because the Bible tells him to. He said he's trying to "do what Jesus would do." However, right now I think we need to BE Jesus.

Jesus was a carpenter. So maybe I am on the right track.

I may give you a call. I could use some help breaking out of the box. Sara and I may be too close to coach one another. Look for my call. Until then, love to you and stay well.

Coaching Principles & Practices

"I keep telling myself I have to think out of the box."

James Adams popularized the term "breaking out of the box," and the related 9-dot puzzle, in his book *Conceptual Blockbusting*. Wikipedia notes that management consultant Mike Vance claims that the term stems from the corporate culture at Walt Disney Company, where the 9-dot puzzle was used in-house. But the puzzle itself seems to go back to a time long before the term "breaking out of the box" was mainstreamed. The 9-dot puzzle can be found in the *Cyclopedia of Puzzles* by Sam Loyd, published in 1914. Today the 9-dot puzzle is widely known and used and still doing a great job of distinguishing "patterned thinking."

INSTRUCTIONS: Connect all of the nine dots with four straight lines without lifting your pencil and without retracing lines. Good luck.

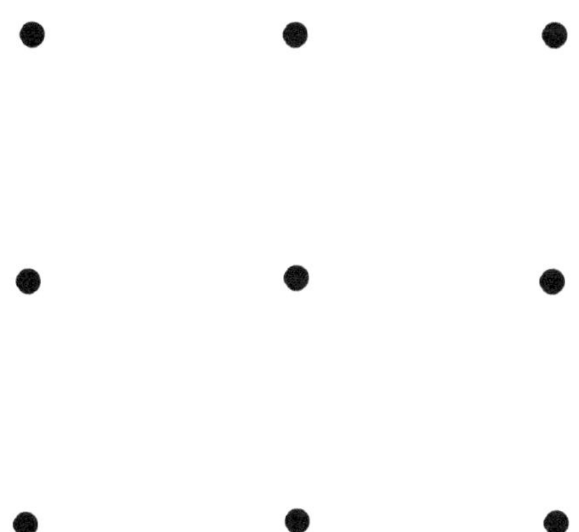

SOLUTION:

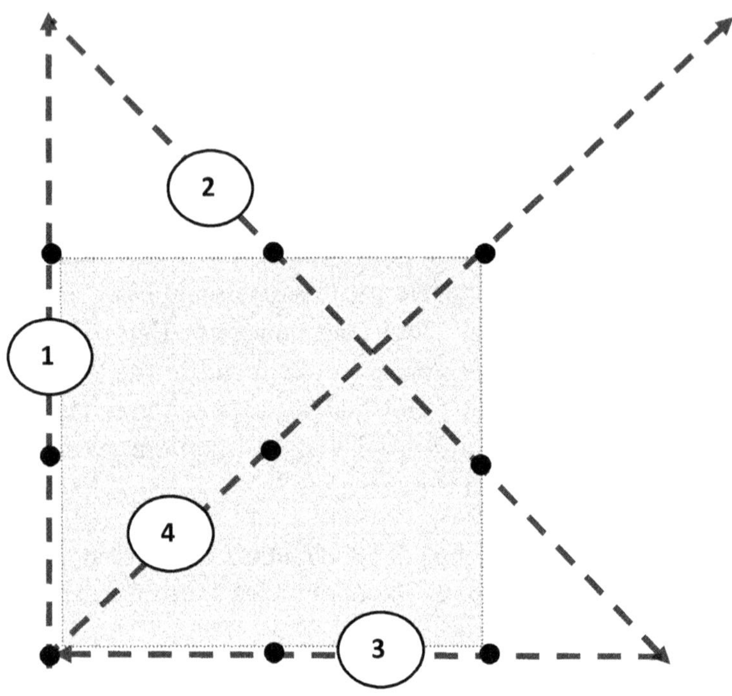

As you can see, the solution requires that you draw lines OUTSIDE "THE BOX." There is no way to solve the puzzle if you stay inside the 9 dots. The interesting thing about this solution is that there is no box at all. We visualize a box formed by the nine dots, but it only exists in our imagination. It's an artificial boundary created in our minds – in our perception.

We all live in a box created by our beliefs, values, education, fears, experience, etc. We don't see the box we live in. We think, "This is the way it is." Our box though is dynamic. It can grow bigger. This happens when we bang into the boundaries of our box. When we begin to question our beliefs, values, judgments, what we have been taught —especially our assessment of ourselves – our box gets bigger. The enlarged box allows for more options and possibilities.

Coaching is about helping clients get out of the box. Helping them make their way into a "bigger world," with fewer limits and more possibilities. A coach can do this because she or he stands outside of a client's box and thus has a different perspective. This allows the coach to better see the boundaries or edges of another person's box. When I coach, I use the term "edge" with my clients. I first distinguish "edge" as I am doing now, early in the coaching relationship. When I notice a client hitting an edge, I simply and quietly note it – "I believe we may have hit an edge here." I leave it to them to determine whether or not to explore it.

For example, I had a client who had a pattern of banging heads with his boss. In various jobs over the years, this person, sooner or later, got into what he called a "power struggle" with his boss. In some cases it led to him being fired, in others it just made for an unpleasant work experience. At one point in our conversation I asked them what his relationship with their father was like. His body froze and he shook his head slightly. Then he replied, "Let's not go there." My response was, "Okay, but I think we may have hit an edge here."

It's likely that this pattern of struggling with authority may go back to his childhood. I left it to him to see this, and more importantly, choose whether or not to bring his childhood experiences into the conversation. It was not just his rational response that tipped me off, but also his emotional reaction. Our emotions provide clearer indicators than our intellect as to when we are hitting the edges of our box.

Some possible indicators that we (or our clients) are banging against the edges of our box include:

- Anxiety/fear
- Feeling attacked
- Defensiveness
- Unnatural excitement
- Quiet caution
- Quick denial
- Physical disengagement
- Anger

Coaches must be alert to these reactions, keeping in mind that these kinds of emotions are harbingers of better things ahead. When an individual rubs up against the walls of their box, we support their exploration.

You can begin by noting the edges of the box, not as an assessment, but as a simple observation. Next get them to surface their discomfort. "What are you experiencing right now? Can you describe it to me?" A common reaction is to deny or minimize it. If this happens, ask the client to withhold his/her judgment.

The drive to explore the self-imposed boundaries of their world will depend on two things: their willingness to do so, and the degree of trust they have in you and the coaching process. It takes a high quality of relationship for a client to explore the boundaries of their box. This is because to do so, an individual must be willing to be wrong. And, as we all know, the need to be right is one of the most powerful imperatives within the human psyche.

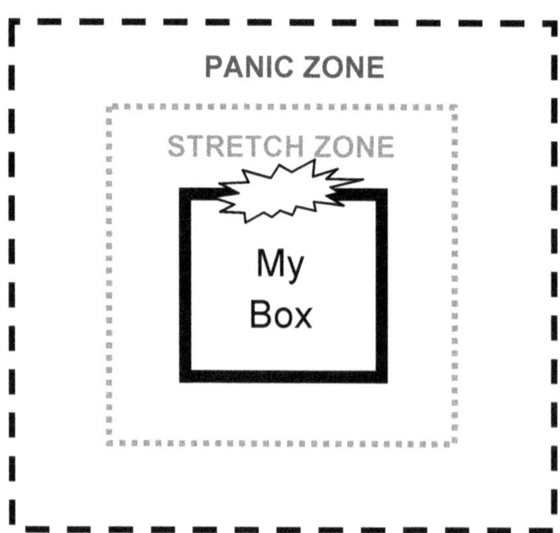

Breaking out of the box does not always happen suddenly and dramatically. As a client begins to get close to the edges of their box, they don't always bang into them. Sometimes they simply feel a "stretch." This often shows up in subtle, less emotional ways such as indecision, a momentary lapse where they cannot think clearly, or nervous laughter.

As a person begins to explore outside their box, you will again become aware of how far out they are by their emotional demeanor. Your job as a coach is one of support. You do not want to *push them* beyond their current perceptual and emotional capacity. You simply support them if and when they begin to stretch their boundaries. Indeed, I prefer it when a client makes a series of incremental moves over time. I can facilitate this by revisiting the box-busting conversation from time to time. If a person has time to integrate their out-of-the-box experience, they are better equipped, rationally and emotionally, to explore more deeply.

"I am aware of my feelings and do not get caught up in them as much as I used to. I catch myself sooner."

Awareness . . . awareness . . . awareness. Awareness is the door to growth and human evolution. I want the greatest awareness around my thoughts. Thoughts create a world – a reality.

The link between our thoughts and our reality is simple.

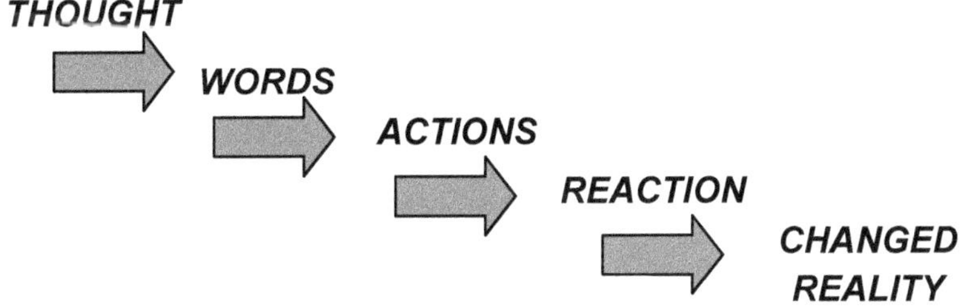

Language is first and foremost a *thinking tool*. I believe that conscious thoughts can only be known as they are expressed in language. Our thoughts show-up in words -- icons of language that manifest in an internal dialogue or conversation. While our bodies hum along thanks the parasympathetic nervous system, our thoughts require language. In this way, word-thoughts become action.

John Searle (mentioned in Chapters 3 and 13) mainstreamed this notion that speaking is an action. He asserted that speaking is an action because it changes people's thoughts and/or creates action. This is easy to see when we focus on illocutionary acts like *requests* and *directions*. But it shows up in many other forms of speaking as perlocutionary acts.

As you may recall, there are hundreds of illocutionary acts according to J.L. Austin. So even when not using forms of speaking intended to create action, we are often changing people's minds. The point is that speaking and words create change, internally and externally – the beginning of a new reality. Upon this simple fact rests the coaching discipline.

Language, not opposable thumbs, is what separates us from other animals. You may recall what Fernando Flores, a Chilean philosopher, said:

> *"In language we build our own identifies, our relationships with others, the countries we live in, the companies we have, the values we hold dear. With language we generate life. Without language we are mostly chimpanzees."*

Coaching primarily intervenes in the thought-to-reality process between thoughts and words. This is the boundary between the individual and the world around them. It's a pivotal boundary for human beings.

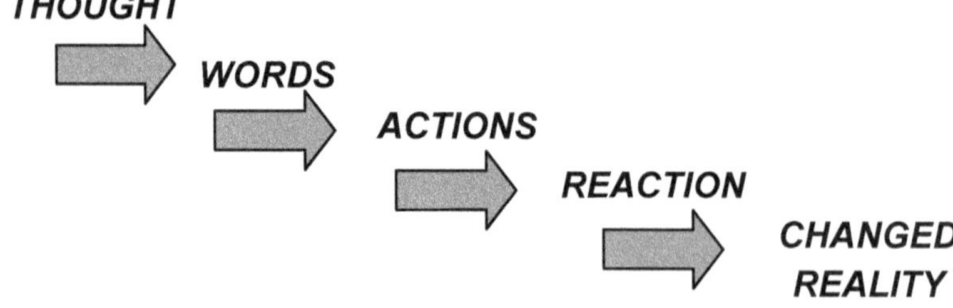

In larger and more complex the systems, interventions to make change must occur farther along the thought-to-reality chain. For example, with a family or team, we tend to intervene to make change between the word and the action stages. With countries and the world at large, there is a greater tendency and necessity to intervene between the action and reaction stages. This is true because as we increase the size and complexity of the system, our ability to intervene to change people's thoughts diminishes. This accounts for the fact that individual change and transformation is relatively easier than changing a social or political system, or transforming the human race for that matter.

The dream of elevating the overall level of consciousness in the world is possible, and it requires that people everywhere change the way they think. The coaching profession can give us some insights into this process. But this process is slow and I am not certain we have the luxury of time. Homo sapiens have been around for about 25,000 years, but we don't have another 25,000 years to wake up. That is why I am exploring and experimenting with technologies that accelerate the evolution of consciousness.

In the past I have squandered time and energy. But that has led me to commit to using my remaining time in more highly leveraged ways. The same commitment and search that led me to coaching is pulling me toward the next adventure.

Decades of interactions with coaching clients seem like a drop of water in the ocean of mass consciousness. It will not dramatically raise the tides of change, but it may enable me to drift toward what might be next. More importantly, I know I am not alone.

You are a drop of water in the ocean of consciousness that we all swim in. And, drops of water, when focused properly, eventually hollow out a stone.

THE SIXTH YEAR

XXVII

"By three methods we may learn wisdom: First, by reflection, which is noblest; second by imitation, which is easiest; and third by experience, which is the bitterest."

Confucius

January 4, 2002

Dear Bill & Marilyn,

A milestone! We just got the occupancy certificate for our place -- though it's not totally finished. Does that make sense?

We were told we can move in. Wonderful news as we've been living here for the last couple years. Many months ago I asked Terry Mason, the building inspector, about the bare minimum needed to get occupancy. You might be surprised to know I didn't need interior doors, kitchen cabinets, finished walls, etc. As a result, I only worked on those elements required to pass the final inspection. So, when you pack to visit, be assured that we now have doors in all of the rooms.

You may recall that the most daunting job to get occupancy was the most fulfilling – tile setting. I mixed the mud, cut and set each tile – one at a time, piece-by-piece, foot by foot. The repetition and quiet were wonderful. That experience made me aware that I can now take pleasure in the simplest tasks. This awareness causes me to reflect on all the crap I used to spout about being present, operating in the zone, being in charge of myself, etc. I was, and largely still am, a pretentious and arrogant jerk – though a lovable one (right?).

I am also aware that I can feel pride when I, or others, talk about this center. A recent visitor said, "You are a special person." My chest swelled up before I could catch it. Turns out they were only half-right. I am a *person.* It was the "special" part that would eventually cause me problems if I believed it.

Some words can get us in trouble. This is a recent awareness for me.

I recall that one of my intentions when I began this project more than five years ago was that it would allow me to answer the big questions. About forty years ago I had an encounter that I might have shared with you at some point.

I was about 14 years old and wandering around Old Town in Chicago. This would have been about 1960. Old town wasn't the yuppy nightspot it is now. There were a lot of strip joints, seedy bars and the like. My friend Marty and I wandered down an ally – beckoned by what sounded like jungle drums.

Turns out we found one of the last beatnik coffee houses in the city. Visions of *Reefer Madness,* which was shown in school the year before, vibrated in my head. I was ready to run but Marty teased me into exploring the place. We sat down in back and ordered a coke. When the waiter returned he asked us what we knew about the beat movement. I told him that watching Maynard G. Krebs on TV was the sum total of my knowledge. But my precocious friend Marty responded in his inimitable way, "So, what's it all about Alfi?" The response was quick, "Felix. My name's Felix."

We got quite an indoctrination talk. When Felix was done, he pointed at me and asked, "So, where are you headed? What do you want to be *if* you grow up?" The "if" was a bit disconcerting, but I responded with a familiar reply, "I want to write – be a writer." Felix looked doubtful. "Do YOU want to be a writer, or is that what your mommy wants you to be?" He went on, "You see, the beat movement is about taking time out and disconnecting so you can answer the big questions. If you don't, you'll end up at fifty with the realization that you've been living your father's life."

Felix was a prophet. It did take me until I was fifty to wake up and realize that I was living my father's life. I don't have all the answers, but at least I'm asking the right questions.

You may recall, in one of my first letters to you, I stated that I wanted to be stripped down to my *essential self.* It was my way of saying that I was seeking my true nature. I talked about this goal as though it was a place I could get to – true understanding, enlightenment, etc.

Many spiritual practices seemed to promise just that – the arrival at some place, the truth, and the answers to our questions. We think we have plumbed the depths of the great mystery. We've arrived. If that is so, then many spiritual practices and religions probably take us *away* from the truth, because we stop searching when we feel we have the answers.

Maybe the most important thing I have learned is what is *not* the right way or direction. This allows me to keep searching and to keep evolving as a human being. I'm not sure I will ever *completely* know and appreciate my true nature. But I believe I know some of the Truth, and I am able to experience it when I'm paying attention.

I don't know *the* way, but I am confident I'm moving in the right direction. That may be as good as it gets.

As I struggle to say what I have learned, I feel illiterate. I need a whole new language. And so, I lift my pen with a combination of hope and regret.

Stay well my friends.

Coaching Principles & Practices

"Some words can get us in trouble. This is a recent awareness for me."

Words – conversations -- are the tools of a coach. The spoken word is "magical." It is an act of creation. But what are we creating when we speak? Words can be white magic or black magic.

In my last book I explored and exalted the power of speaking and listening – the "art of conversation" I called it. My ideas and concepts were incomplete and, in that sense, may not have been helpful. I fear I may have sent readers in the wrong direction because words can only take us so far.

A word is a concept – an idea. A word is a way to describe a thing, but it is not the thing. This seems obvious, but we confuse the two all the time. I have a picture of Sara above my desk because I love her. The picture is not Sara. The love I experience is in me and not Sara – and certainly not the picture. Yet, if Sara were to take her picture off the wall and smash it on the floor, I would be upset, hurt and angry. It would feel like love was being taken away. And that would be an illusion.

We human beings do this all the time. We confuse the concept or word, with the thing it represents. We become slaves to symbols. We fly a flag in place of living a life of freedom. We keep a photo album and believe we are nurturing and enjoying relationships. We go to church believing it makes us holy people.

Words allow us to share our experience, but they are not the experience. They can point us in a general direction, but they cannot take us there. And our confusion about this causes many problems and much human suffering.

People get hurt and depressed when someone doesn't *love* them. Men and women die on the battlefield and kill one another in the name of *America.* People work themselves into poor health and an early grave to be *successful.*

As a coach, when a client speaks, I must be aware of what they are focusing on and striving to have in their life. Is it real or unreal? If it is unreal, then it might be useful to facilitate a deeper exploration of their goal and possibly help them move beyond their illusion.

A familiar example might be a client who comes to you and says, "I want to be a masterful leader." Where do you begin? The possible areas of confusion are many, and you can help to sort them out.

Do they want to be a great leader, or *thought of* as a great leader?

Do they want to be a great leader, or *act like* a great leader?

Do they want to serve others or *only themselves*?

Do they want to be a great leader, or *feel* they are a great leader? etc.

And you might also ask, "Why do you want to be a leader? What does it all mean to you? What will it allow and/or provide that you do not have now?

The latter inquiry is critical because leadership is not a thing; it is a state of being. You have to ensure that your client understands that the thing they seek is not like other things – like good health for example. Leadership is an idea. If we do not distinguish between real and unreal things, we can create unrealistic expectations and pursue the wrong goal in coaching. In the case of seeking to be a more effective leader, there is no universal definition. Each person has to distinguish their quest for leadership in their own unique manner, and embody it in their own special way.

"Maybe the most important thing I learned was what is not the right way or direction. This allowed me to keep searching and to keep evolving as a human being."

For me, coaching is a spiritual practice. I define spirituality as living in Reality, and I will expand on that later. Reality only exists in the present moment. That said, coaching has the potential to bring people in the "present perfect." And so now comes a big question, "*Why* do I coach?"

I coach as a way to grow and evolve myself. Is this self-centered and selfish?

I coach to help others. Am I doing it to feel good about myself?

Ultimately, I coach because it flows from my true interconnected Nature, and my coaching has the potential to touch the True Nature of every human being . . . Ah-h.

Coaching is all of the above for me. But the last idea, that coaching itself is an expression of my authentic Nature . . . that's a more recent awareness. And while this awareness is comforting in its' clarity, I must remain in a state of inquiry about it. Imbedded within my inquiry is my friend doubt.

Doubt is the great sword of freedom. With it I am able to cut through everything I have been taught -- what my culture demands of me, my attachments, fears, desires, and the very words I speak and hear. I trust that, as you read this book, some doubts have been raised. Good!

If you look back to the introduction you will note my caveat. I requested that you treat this book, and everything in it, as an *exploration*. I'm not selling "the truth." If you accept my ideas as the truth, I will simply be adding another layer of programming. On the other hand, if you reject what I say, you do so most likely because of *your* programming. So, this poses a dilemma.

I wrote this book to stimulate insight and understanding about what a coach might be and become. It is intended to stimulate *your* thinking, to deepen *your* distinctions around coaching, and to support this discipline that has the potential to reveal one's True Nature.

XXVIII

"The essential self is innocent, and when it tastes its own innocence knows that it lives for ever."

John Updike

August 4, 2002

Dad,

I am writing to express how very much your recent visit meant to me. Our place in the mountains is not finished, but the bones of our home are firmly in place. As you were circumnavigating our edifice, I stepped back to take pictures of you. As I squinted into the camera viewfinder, a flood of emotions swept over me. Initially pride of course, but those feelings quickly became tangled with others – some of them not so pleasant. The strongest emotion was anger that took me back decades to "the great falling out."

I struggled to deal with my feelings. I wanted to push them down and out, but they were stubborn. You may recall that I went for a walk in the nearby trees, ostensibly to look for Phantom. The reason was I that wanted to deal with my emotions so that I could enjoy our time together.

During my walk in the ponderosas I was transported back to some of the interactions we have had in years past. I understand that you may not feel the need to "rehash the past," as you put it, so I needed find a way to deal with my own feelings.

Making this long trek, and struggling with the altitude here as you have, tells me how much you care. You really showed up for me. Thank you. I hope it warmed your heart also, to see how the seeds you planted so long ago have sprouted.

You taught me to work with my hands. And with that, I experienced the feeling of accomplishment that comes with creating. I received *many* gifts from you, but maybe the best gift was just delivered -- a way to find what I have been searching for here in Colorado. I call it my essential self. Part of me, maybe the essence of all human beings, may be summed up in all our creative efforts. Maybe, when we are creating, we *are* our essential selves.

As I near the end of this building project, I'm aware that I've recently been focusing on the finished form -- not the process. As I showed you and Greg around, a little voice in my head said, "Hey, look what *I* did, Dad!"

Over the last few years I have shared my trials and tribulations with you. My occasional calls and letters must have read like a soap opera. Looking back, I can see that I may have lost track of my core mission. But actually, I was *being* my essential self from the very first day I arrived. I didn't know this because I experienced so much fear, anger, stress, and anxiety along the way – the soap opera. I am also aware that these troubling feelings are not always there. They come and go, but I often choose to focus on what isn't working.

During the vast majority of the time here, I am happy and fulfilled. At times I thought the coming and going of negative feelings had something to do with how much money we had or didn't have. Programming. I thought my moods and emotions had to do with how our plans were progressing. Now I know better. There was, and is, something else that was coming and going, something inside of me.

When I experience peace and contentment, I am firmly rooted in the here and now. And when I am not experiencing peace and joy, I am in the past or future – emotionally and/or intellectually.

I know that you sometimes enjoy grapping with esoteric ideas. I would love to hear your musings. Maybe you can direct me to an author or book. I know your big library has been whittled down since you moved to your apartment, but you have a wealth of knowledge to share, and I welcome it.

Once again, thank you for coming to visit Sara and me. I am so thankful to Greg for bringing you here. My brother is a loving man, and his visit was a wonderful way to be loved. He brought you to my door and, in so doing, presented the opportunity for me to look back on our life together and drink in the love that is here for us now.

Love and blessings,

Coaching Principles & Practices

"I struggled to deal with my feelings. I wanted to push them down and out, but they remained."

When we encounter a strong emotion – in ourselves, or others we coach, we have two basic options; transform the emotional response into a new insight and lesson – work with it, or ignore it and move on.

In the past I sometimes suspended or stopped coaching sessions in the face of a highly emotional response because I felt it interfered with the rational thinking that I used to believe was required in coaching. Now I know that emotional responses open the door to deeper understanding and healing. Today I take advantage of the wonderful opportunity deep emotions offer when they present themselves. I have a specific approach I use to extract the richness residing within every strong emotion.

My approach is based upon the logical belief that the vast majority of emotional responses we feel in the present have their genesis in the past. There was some event or situation in our past that made an indelible imprint on our psyche. We bring this emotional experience with us as we continue through life. There may have been similar situations in our past that, taken together, elicit a particular feeling that shows up again and again in our current interactions and experience.

Based on this premise I use a process I recently learned from David Lesser, whose "whole being coaching" recently deepened my understanding of true listening. The approach can be captured in a simple sentence: *It's not so important what is happening, but who is experiencing it.* Another way to say this is, a past self is often present when we are feeling a residual emotion from an event that happened long ago. Maybe it was when you were seven years old and your father left you in the barbershop, and you felt abandoned and afraid. Maybe it was when your fiancé called off your engagement when you were twenty-one. In some ways the details don't matter because coaching is not therapy. As coaches it is not our responsibility to delve deeply into those events per se. We don't have to recount past events in detail to experience healing. What is necessary, in the present moment, is to recognize and "love the one" who was wounded.

Since my experience with David Lesser, I have had an opportunity to use this approach and process in my practice. It works like this. As a coach, I take a little time to explain the concept and process -- just as I did above. After that I engage a client with four simple questions:

[Stop the conversation when the emotion surfaces.]

- "What emotion are you experiencing right now?"
- "Can you recall a time in your past life when you had a response like this in a similar situation?"
- "When was that? "How old were you?"
- "Take a moment to imagine that person you were then. Now love that one."

While healing takes place in that moment, it may require addressing an old emotional response *many* times before the psychic imprint begins to fade. But with awareness and compassion, it will eventually lose its power to undermine one's experience of their True Nature. This process awakens self-love, a cornerstone of joy and fulfillment.

I was at my desk writing this section when the opportunity to use this tool "coincidentally" presented itself.

John was taking some vacation time with his son, his son's wife, and his new grandson. John's son is from a previous marriage and, until recently, they did not have a close relationship. Recently John has been working to change this.

I knew that his guests had just departed, so I decided to check in with him via email. He wrote back, "It was a great visit. Feeling kind of sad and a little lost at the moment." So, I wrote back and asked about his "feeling lost."

In his reply we described how painful the divorce was for him and, in particular the pain of being separated from his children for so long. Because I knew John was a conscious guy, I was able to send this short note:

"I know your love for your children is clear and present for them. Indeed, that is why they continue to seek, maintain and nurture your relationship. The love you recently shared with them is all that is important. And, remember to love the one that lost his family so many years ago. That's the one that feels lost, not John here and now."

John was familiar with this practice and this simple reminder transformed his feeling of aloneness, and feeling lost, into a bittersweet reality.

Establishing a habit of interrupting an automatic emotional response, in order to explore it, does two things: 1) It helps a person return and stay in the present moment, and 2) It prevents, or at least reduces, the likelihood that an individual will act solely from residual emotions. For example, if John had acted out of his emotion he might have impulsively reached out in a phone call to his kids seeking reassurance of their love, or acted in some way to try to change how he felt. While not necessarily bad, any outward action with its genesis in his "feeling lost" would not change this emotional experience. It was *his* feeling, and thus his to deal with internally.

This simple, beautiful process serves to remind us of the healing power of unconditional love. As I noted earlier, coaching is an expression of love and truth. That's what makes it so powerful. So, why not use love and truth more consciously, explicitly and directly. Hell, let's be really bold and say the word "love" out loud!

"Part of me, maybe the essence of all human beings, is summed up in all our creative efforts. Maybe, when we're creating, we are being our essential selves."

The idea that human beings are creative by nature and design is not a novel one. Indeed, coaching is usually focused on the need, or desire, to create something new and different. Coaching helps a person harness their innate ability to create.

In terms of creation, coaching operates on two levels: a practical, outwardly focused one, and an inner, psycho-emotional level. My recent experience as a human being and coach has shifted my attention to the psycho-emotional elements of coaching.

Some might label what I am doing as "spiritual coaching," and in a manner of speaking, it is. I am aware of being with clients in a different way than before. The shift in perception about who I am, that essential self that has called me on this journey, now facilitates a deeper connection with clients. The atmosphere of our sessions is more vibrant and authentic. The approach is holistic and not confined solely to problem solving. Yet it is the problem that opens the door to rediscovering our True Nature and a larger pool of inner resources. Within this fertile context of growing consciousness, clients discover their next steps.

And so we come back to the inquiry underpinning this book: What is the essential self?

I experience each one of us as an extension of the whole and ongoing creative process. The Natural world helps to cultivate this awareness. Mathematical cosmology suggests that we are all part of the big bang – the ongoing expansion and unfolding of the universe occurring moment to moment. Thus, in a very real and tangible sense, we are not only *part* of creation, but we are the creative process itself. We belong to the source of all creation. As my favorite mentor Tony DeMello might say, we are not dancing to the music of creation, "We are *being danced*."

Human beings are as much the manifestation of the spirit of creation as the planets of our solar system. That spirit is the source of *our* individual creative ability.

Beyond solving the initial problem that brought them to coaching, I hope clients experience the source of their own creative spirit. Facilitating this connection accomplishes four important things:

1) Clients operate from an elevated perspective and are better able to address the root cause of their problems and issues.
2) They experience fulfillment while in action, well before they achieve their goals, because their path forward is clearer.
3) Because clients' see themselves in a larger, richer context, what they create has deeper meaning to them.
4) What they create is enduring because it serves the bigger truth that underlies their life.

It is certainly possible for human beings to create things without understanding or consciously being in touch with the larger creative spirit. Many civilizations, including our current one, are built in the absence of such a foundation. This is why our current civilization is in peril. We frequently create beautiful forms that have little meaning or substance. At some level, humanity feels the emptiness and the futility of creating things in the absence of the True Spirit of creation.

These assertions are not religious dogma. They are not about beliefs. These assertions are about of awareness and identity.

Building a home and coaching center in the mountains of Colorado continues to reveal my sought-after essential self. But not in the manner I thought it would.

When I started the building project fourteen years ago, I believed that my essential self was covered up with thick layers of beliefs, assessments, judgments, ego-based facades, and the like. I hoped that the building process, like some "cosmic rasp," would shave off these dull layers of programming that were smothering me.

Instead what unfolded was the understanding that my essential self was *always* there. I simply did not see or recognize it. Now I can look back with amusement and love at that determined guy who drove all the way to the top of a mountain with his dog to build a home and find himself.

My identity is changed. I am a conscious part of ongoing creation-- a cosmic mirror enabling creation to experience itself. My essential-self was playing hide-and-seek within a mostly unconscious, self-centered, confused, middle-aged man.

All I can say now is, "Ollie ollie oxen free!"

"When I experience peace and contentment, I am firmly rooted in the hear-and-now. And, when I am <u>not</u> experiencing peace and joy, I am in the past or future – emotionally and/or intellectually."

Over and over again, my experiences draw me toward the need to cultivate present moment awareness. By now this mantra may seem monotonous. But as I pointed out at the beginning, one of my objectives is to deepen key distinctions we have around coaching. As you may recall, a distinction is a deep understanding, such that, your perception and behavior *automatically* change. Over many chapters I have been attempting to deepen your distinction for the present moment – what it is, how to achieve it, and why it is particularly important to us as coaches.

In exploring a letter to my late father, sent near the end of the building process, I was able to see how my experience led me to an inquiry that greatly contributed to my evolution as a coach, and human being. Once again, I was brought back to look, with new eyes, at this place called the-hear-and-now. Reaching out into the larger world for help and insight, I was introduced to the work of a fellow named Otto Rank.

Otto Rank was an Austrian psychoanalyst, writer, teacher and therapist. Born in Vienna, Austria in 1884, Rank was one of Sigmund Freud's closest colleagues. However, his psychoanalytical approach differed significantly from that of Freud.

Rank believed that our emotional life is rooted in the *present.* In <u>*Will Therapy*</u>, published in 1929, he used the term "here and now" for the first time in a psychological context. He offered a unique perspective on what he called "denied emotions" and how they can cause neurosis. This distinction, "*denied* emotions" versus Freud's "*repressed* emotions," represents a fundamental change. Rank said, "Freud made the repression historical, that is, misplaced it into the childhood of the individual, and then wanted to release it from there, while as a matter of fact the same tendency is working here and now."

In short, Otto Rank believed that we carry our traumatic emotions with us all the time. In this way, our emotions are experienced in the present and, in order to avoid feeling them, we tend to keep ourselves emotionally, and developmentally, in the *past* so we don't have to feel them. For Rank, "the neurotic lives too much in the past [and] to that extent, he actually does not live."

Rank's hypothesis resonates positively with me – especially in my experience. This explains, in part, why I have relegated my last book, *Leadership and the Art of Conversation*, to the old coaching paradigm.

As a culture we focus far too much energy on the future and the past. In particular, our obsession with the future might be called neurotic in that a majority of individuals in the western world report that, on a daily basis, they experience anxiety, sadness or depression, anger, irritability, low sense of self-worth, etc. – symptoms, according to DSM-IV (used to classify mental illnesses) of a neurosis.

Thinking of the future, while necessary to some degree, can easily become a neurotic obsession. Thinking about the past can be comforting, informative even, but it can also be a trap that shackles us to feelings of regret and futility. More importantly, thinking and focusing on the future and/or the past inhibits access to the-here-and-now – our only source of joy and peace.

I assist clients in learning to live here-and-now. *Here* is the unabated ability to be fully present to what is actually happening in and around us, without judgment. *Now* includes everything that exists, and the experience of being aware and present.

Coming into contact with the here-and-now, we give up emotional and intellectual control in order to achieve experiential inspiration. We respond to what is happening in this precise moment. In so doing, we operate in full alignment with Reality. This is wholeness. I believe this is living as it is intended to be, and not the schizophrenic feeling we have when what we are doing is not in response to what is unfolding around us.

I fall pray to this schizophrenic behavior all the time. Most recently when I was marketing my coaching and team building services in the midst of the recession that began in 2008. As I wrote and called past and potential clients to find work, I became increasingly angry, frustrated, anxious -- definitely NOT happy. I initially got caught up in the mass media mania, I projected my feelings on to bankers, politicians, network news personalities, etc. Why couldn't business leaders see that what I offered was desperately needed?

Only after collapsing under the futility of months-long efforts, and teetering on the edge of despondency, did I become aware of my reactionary behavior. I got quiet. I opened myself up to guidance and understanding – and it came. It came initially in the form of Sara (as it often does) who said to me, "The old paradigm is dying . . . why are you still serving it?" Now this was not the first time I had heard Sara say this, but until I was quiet and fully in the present moment, I never really felt the power of her statement.

I had been operating schizophrenically. It appears that the current world-wide socio-economic paradigm is falling apart. But my actions and activities were squarely focused on shoring it up and trying to maintain it. The moment I became fully aware of this reality, my negative emotions began to fade, as if magically. I found myself laughing at my own absurdity. My once heavy heart was lighter. I began writing transcendental poetry . . . look for my upcoming book of poems.

We are designed to be happy. And if we cannot be happy in the here-and-now, we will never be happy. This awareness has prompted me to discover tools and techniques for dealing with strong emotions that come up during a coaching session.

As noted earlier, deep emotions live in the present moment. Unless a client is able feel and deal with them, he or she will remain in a state of avoidance that keeps them operating from the past, or fleeing into the future. However, if clients can be in the here-and-now they are more likely to find inner resources for positive change. For some, the impulse to creative action may show up as a new idea or possibility. For others it may show up as insight or intuition. I would simply say that they are acting in alignment and agreement with the larger Reality that is unfolding within and around them.

Labels and conceptual frameworks are irrelevant. Please don't get hung up on terms and concepts. The practice of facilitating and keeping yourself, and those you coach, in the here-and-now is essential because action that flows from the hear-and-now will create something good, meaningful and lasting.

So, the future is not so much the result of a well communicated and executed plan, but the unfolding of the present moment. If there is any "magic" per se, in a future-focused conversation, it is that what we say flows from an awareness of what is unfolding inside and around us. Clients need not be aware of this philosophy and approach for it to work.

- *By cultivating present moment awareness in ourselves, clients are better able to experience being in the here-and-now.*
- *If we clarify a loving, non-judgmental intention within ourselves first, that intention will be palpable for those we coach.*
- *If Truth and Reality live in our present moment awareness, we will instinctively say and do the right thing during a coaching session.*

Everything in this book is simply intended to help us get to, and operate from, this fully integrated state of being.

So, the last letter has been "posted," and the last reflections shared. But this story continues in the pages to follow.

Construction Update

The letters ended in August of 2002, but the building process continued until September of 2008 with the installation of beautiful hand-built, cherry wood, kitchen cabinets. Before that the deck in 2003, the entrance, parking lot and entry walk in 2004, the raised garden beds in 2005, the rainwater-catchment system in 2006, and the high efficiency fireplace and majestic entry gates in 2007.

You can see pictures, including some constructions shots, and get more information about our home and center at one of two websites:

www.southwestmountainhome.com *or* www.coloradoretreat.org.

CONCLUSION

> *"The most strongly enforced of all known taboos, is the taboo against knowing who or what you really are behind the mask of your apparently separate, independent, and isolated ego."*
>
> Alan Watts

I have shared my personal journey with you as a way to gain deeper insight into how to accelerate human evolution – which is, for me, what coaching is about. When I use the term evolution, I am speaking about moving closer to a fuller realization of ourselves as wise, ingenious, interconnected creator beings that are an expression of the All.

Scientists tell us that in the last 100,000 years, we have evolved from ape-like creatures to homo sapiens sapiens – to wise, knowing creatures. However, there is contradictory evidence to this assertion.

I don't expect that all people in the coaching profession share my distinction for coaching – or what I feel it is the purpose of coaching. However, I see most any form of coaching as beneficial. Like human beings themselves, coaches and the coaching profession continue to evolve.

I recall that when I began my coaching practice over twenty-six years ago, I focused on what was then termed "behavioral coaching." I worked with clients to help them change how they act and show up. I drifted away from behavioral coaching because, more often that not, the change in behavior did not last. Change through willpower seldom works. It might modify behavior for a while, but not the person. Over time, most clients slipped back into their "normal," programmed way of operating in the world because their *perceptions* had not changed – particularly their perception of themselves -- their identity.

Behavior-focused coaching can be like asking a client to push around a "grocery cart of new behaviors" that has bent and wobbly wheels. They can do it, but it takes a lot of effort and energy as they move through their daily lives. They look and feel awkward, even though they may try to look nonchalant. Progress is slow. And even when they succeed, they do not enjoy the journey.

Focusing solely on behavior creates a negative context by contributing to self-dissatisfaction. By focusing mostly on what was wrong or missing in people, it felt like I was doing violence to their spirit

We need a new "grocery cart." For me that means two things: First, we must focus on cultivating and growing self-awareness. Second, we must invite what some call "the higher self" into the coaching process.

Cultivating Self-awareness

When you are aware of your behavior, and the causes of your behavior, change can be relatively easy and lasting. So, we need to cultivate awareness, in ourselves and our clients -- and not just awareness in reflection. Post action awareness is a starting point, and it can be expanded into awareness in the moment. As a coach you can accelerate this natural progression.

Even if a coaching goal is focused primarily on behavior change, it's helpful for clients to approach the need for change in a non-judgmental, loving manner. In other words, "I don't want you to *try* to change your behavior. I want you to become more aware of yourself and everything around you. Don't worry about trying to change. Change will happen as you become more self-aware."

You can continue to do awareness skill building by continually shining the light of awareness on feelings and reactions – yours and theirs -- during the coaching session. Again and again, "What is going on inside you/me right now?"

And finally, I encourage clients to develop healthy habits and practices that foster awareness – walks in Nature, watching sunsets, singing, gardening, journaling, and most any creative act.

Operating in this manner elevates coaching to a new, higher level. In addition to addressing the specific need that brings a client to us, we can leverage their coaching experience to make them happier and healthier human beings.

When we are aware, we minimize or eliminate the possibility for regret, guilt, and what many people call "mistakes." When we are aware, we are not limited or crippled by our emotions. When we are aware, we see with a clarity that inspires the perfect response most of the time.

Inviting the "higher self"

As human consciousness grows, individually and collectively, we begin to see ourselves, and our relationship with the universe, differently. This identify shift seems to be accelerating and showing up in science, technology, the arts, the mass media, and even some businesses. This identity shift has always been present in the coaching discipline, though not always explicitly. I can't imagine a coaching workshop that doesn't touch on using the "observer" as a tool. But few workshops I have attended go beyond this point. That is changing, and his book is part of that change.

It is not only "okay" to talk about human spirit, soul, or the divine intention driving ongoing evolution, it would seem to be *mandatory*. This is because coaching is centered in supporting individual and collective creation. Meaningful, wholesome, and lasting forms can only be created when they are an expression of our divine spirit.

You must find your own unique way to bring your divine and loving spirit into expression as an integral part of your coaching practice.

We do not need more information; we need greater self-awareness, and to bring our essential-selves into our coaching practice and the world. My experience in building a home and coaching center in the Sangre de Cristo Mountains put me in Nature and created challenges that helped me grow physically, emotionally and spiritually. I found my essential self. How will you find and bring forth your essential self?

My "Essential Self"

As I read the last letter to my Dad, written several years ago, I came face-to-face with the question that lurked in the background of the entire construction enterprise: "What is my "essential self?"

I attempted to put some of what I discovered in words, but more importantly, I *experienced* my essential self. Words can be limiting and clumsy at times. Describing my essential self is like trying to describe my first kiss. It is clear and perfect in my experience, yet there is no way for me to adequately describe it.

My experiences in the mountains of Colorado changed me. The Nature that surrounds me daily offers an ever-present glimpse of the Truth. I am embedded in that Truth. When I am in the Truth, I see my Self wherever I look. In this way, seeking knowledge of myself led me to knowing the Whole.

Unlearning and deprogramming continue. I am pulled more and more into the role of the observer. I find that the broader my perspective, the more perfect the universe appears. I pray that "the observer" is my Divine self and not the last refuge of my ego. Despite this concern, I no longer do battle with my ego. My ego and I are currently at a stalemate. I have learned that my ego serves a purpose, and I also know that it can and does limit my joy when I am not aware of it. For now it is enough for me to know that my ego is part of me and will likely always be there – which brings me to one last point that I need to share with you as a reader of this book.

A new awareness came to me as the last draft of this manuscript was completed. Setting down the manuscript, I felt a deep pride and accomplishment. I was aware that my ego was peeking around the corner, but I knew that the primary motivation for writing this book emanated from a deep love and respect for the discipline of coaching, and a desire to contribute to its continuing growth. However, this slight brush with my ego seemed to validate a recent decision Sara and I have made. We added one last thing to a decade-long "to do" list.

One More Task Remains

Sara and I recently decided to sell our home and center. There are several things motivating this decision, among them are the facts that I have grown too attached to the place, and it no longer makes sense ecologically, emotionally, spiritually, or economically.

Separating from any attachment can be painful, and I am sure we will experience some pain and sadness. However, holding on to it would be painful too, and it would limit us both. As we grow older, we want our lives to expand, not become smaller.

We have decided to sell our place without knowing exactly where we will go next, or what we will do. This lack of planning leaves room for inspiration, intuition and "cosmic serendipity." It will not only permit more possibilities in our lives, but most likely move us closer toward some new expression of our essential selves. Such a strategy goes against all my programming, so I suspect it is the right thing to do. One thing I have learned from this building process is that a known future offers less wonder and joy.

One idea that resonates deeply with Sara and me is the possibility of joining with a handful of like-minded people to contribute to a small, self-sustaining "family" or community, similar to the ecovillages that are sprouting up around the world. One possibility is Sunrise Ranch in Loveland Colorado. There are many aspects to such a venture that are attractive.

First, I resonate with Thomas Jefferson's notion that the more self-sufficient a human being is, the more personally free they feel . . . and are. I wish to leave behind a sophisticated lifestyle that inherently requires a high degree of dependency on others for my daily needs. Secondly, all my creative juices begin to flow as I contemplate contributing to the creation of a new cultural, economic and social infrastructure needed here on earth as our current socio-economic paradigm crumbles. If such a dream is to manifest, I suspect it will happen organically and naturally for us. We simply have to step into the flow of what is already emerging in the world today.

It is difficult to decide that most everything you have been taught, and everything you think you know, may not be the truth. What is worse, you suspect that much of what I have learned is 180-degrees from the truth. But somehow, in our hearts, we know that the truth of who we are will win out, whether we choose it or not. And if we choose the truth of who we are, life becomes infinitely more joy filled. We might as well put ourselves in harmony and accord with what is unfolding. Not just be okay with what is happening, but embrace it. And as we do we will find ourselves living within the very Truth we seek.

My most recent explorations have me reading David White's poetry, pioneering a tiny homestead and garden on the North Fork River near here, working with Sara to cultivate native plants on an estuary in La Penita Mexico, learning Spanish, becoming a student of the accordion -- and doing some coaching. In general, I am following my heart where it leads me. For the biggest choices I need to make are not intellectual ones.

Despite these myriad activities, I don't want to be called a writer, builder, gardener, linguist, accordionist, or even a coach. I reject all labels save one.

I am a human being.

CHAPTER SUMMARIES

Chapter I – A man and his dog . . . the journey begins - 1

Breakdowns and Emotions . . . The Coaching Process
Consequences of Consciousness . . . Silence in Coaching

Insights and Principles . . .

- Coaches have to be ready for the waves of fear, regret and other emotions that occur as a person commits to taking the road to an alternative new future.
- Consciousness does at least one significant thing: It gives us foresight that is both a blessing and a "curse." The "curse" is that consciousness and foresight allow us to know with certainty that we will die. The blessing is that it allows us to intentionally shape and change our future.
- In every moment of life, our biological and psychological characteristics and behaviors tend to be an expression of past experiences that have become incorporated into our body-mind. At the same time, we struggle against these constraints of determinism by using our innate ability to choose. "Man becomes truly human only at the time of decision." (Tillich)
- The ability to wisely choose a path forward can only happen when we are in touch with the values, beliefs and gifts that form the basis for our choices. A coach's first job is to facilitate *inner* exploration.
- Coaching reconnects us with our most important source of wisdom – our heart, our soul, and the Truth that seems to permeate the universe and everything in it.
- The use of silence may be one of the things that distinguishes a coaching conversation from day to day interactions – where silence is generally abhorred.
- Silence acts like a mirror. Ultimately, it allows us to peer deeply into our "inner waters" to a place where the truth of us lies. Coaching is a mirror too, encouraging silent reflection before, during and after the conversation.
- Silence facilitates self-awareness and taps the collective mind.

Models and Tools

THE COACHING PROCESS

It is easy to think of coaching as "a conversation," but verbal interaction is only part of the entire *process* we call coaching.

AUDIO JOURNALING

- Find a quiet place where you will not be disturbed for at least 20 to 30 minutes.
- Start with a question that focuses your initial comments, such as – What is the biggest barrier to my fulfillment? OR What's the single change would make the biggest difference in my life?
- Turn on the recorder and begin to answer that question.
- As you speak, let your conversation wander where it wants to. As thoughts and feelings bubble up, share them freely.
- You don't have to make sense or have a logical flow. Just keep speaking and sharing whatever comes to mind. One thought or phrase will inevitably lead to another.
- Go for at least 20 minutes or until you feel the energy dwindling, then stop the recorder.
- Put your recording away for at least 24 hours – a few days ideally.

- Then, get a pad of paper and pen in case you want to make notes.
- Rewind the your tape recording and play it back.
- Listen to yourself. Remember and make note of what you hear. Listen, not just to the words, but what is *behind* the words.
- Don't get so caught up in note taking that you aren't listening. If you feel compelled to scratch down more than a few words or a phrase, stop the recording and write. Then, continue again when you are finished writing.
- When the recording is over, sit quietly for a while and consider what you may have learned about yourself.

Chapter II – Stories, masks and too many questions - 11
Driven by Our Emotions . . . Rewriting Our Own Story
Wearing "Real" Masks

Insights and Principles . . .

- Many choices we make are driven more by emotion than reason, so it is necessary to gather emotional information during coaching conversations. Emotion mostly shows up in your client's body. Some people are better than others at concealing their emotions, but few can hide them completely.
- While coaching is a logical, intellectual, methodical process, by necessity it must tap into the deeper emotional body of a person where much of the truth for that individual lies. It is in revealing these emotions, exposing them to the light of awareness, that they take their rightful place in the learning and decision-making processes.
- Stories – particularly justifications – are often an intellectual rationalization for an emotionally driven action.
- Stories are at the heart of the human experience. Our seemingly unique ability, among all other creatures to consciously shape our future, depends on our ability to create, tell, hear and – yes -- live stories. We live in a constant interplay between the bigger story that we live within, and the one we are creating for ourselves.
- The ability and decision to become the primary author in our own story is the finest criterion for human beings. Supporting this process is the work of a coach.
- Coaches help others recreate a future. However, it is possible to create a future that is not only unfulfilling, but also sad and lonely. How does this happen? It happens when we let the world around us – our society and culture -- write most of our story. It is this dynamic that often brings clients to us.
- Part of the human transformation process often involves creating a *persona*. As we choose who we want to become, how we want to live, what values we want to express in our lives,

we have a natural tendency to take on the characteristics of what we want to become. It is not so much an attempt to deceive or hide, but an intermediary step to explore who we are seeking to become.

- Carefully choose where coaching conversations are held. It is helpful to remove the client from their office, meeting instead in a park or some place that supports protected introspection and a nurturing environment.

Chapter III – Not letting life "slip-slide" away - 19
Escaping Corporate Carousel . . . Language & Creation
Managing the Levels of Attention . . . the Magic Shop

Insights and Principles . . .

- When it comes to speaking and creation involving human beings, seven things must be present if language is going to give birth to creation.

  1) A clear *intention* and strong commitment within the speaker.
  2) The ability to say what is meant.
  3) A receiver (listener) who knows that the speaker is trying to communicate.
  4) Listening (message reception) by the receiver.
  5) A listener that knows and understands the *intention* behind the communication.
  6) A listener who understands the message itself.
  7) A shift in perspective and/or intention within the listener that leaves them poised to respond or act.

- Words carry meaning, but not power. Power lies in the intention, the commitment behind the words, and the context in which the words are used.

- Managing and shifting the focus of attention is key to the coaching process. *Focused attention* is when we are engaged emotionally and intellectually – fully sentient. The little censor in our heads, our voice of judgment, is fading into the background and we are fully present to the conversation. Ideally this is the level at which most coaching occurs. However, it is unlikely that any individual will remain in a state of focused attention for an entire coaching session. For that reason, a coach must be sensitive to his/her own attention level, *and* to that of the client, continually shifting the focus of attention to a higher state.

- There are times when you will want to get and keep someone in a focused state of attention, and then there are times when you will want to bring them to *interior attention* – the highest level of attention. In this state we are completely present to what's going on *inside* of us. We are more susceptible to suggestion in this state, and are able to take thoughts and ideas directly into our subconscious. Interior attention is helpful when you hit upon a critical insight and you want your feedback to register with you're client.

- There is a little "pundit" in our heads that does a running commentary on everything we think, see, feel and hear. As you know, a pundit is a critic of sorts, sometimes wise, and sometimes not – but always chattering away. It is difficult, if not impossible, to quiet the little pundit; but we can be aware of him. As a coach, one of the biggest challenges is managing your own listening.
- Focused listening is one of the biggest gifts you have to give. Focused listening is a manifestation of love and it powers coaching conversations.
- While illocutionary acts are useful to coaches, what John L. Austin calls perlocutionary acts are even more important. These are utterances that not only impact a listener's behavior, but actually change thoughts, beliefs, feelings, viewpoints, manner, mindset, position, etc. A perlocutionary act is doing something by saying something. It has to do with manifesting your intention *within* your speaking and being. For example, a coach typically asks many questions to elicit a response or action. These are *perlocutionary questions* – the kind that change a person in the moment they are uttered. An example is, "Is that the truth?"

Models and Tools

THE MAGIC SHOP

In the Magic Shop you create a deeply relaxed state by moving closer to the client. Lower your voice and speak slowly to signal a shift in the focus of attention. Tell them the story of a Magic Shop where people can go to get *anything* they want. The storeowner is a Magician who doesn't want or accept money. He likes to barter. The Magician is shrewd, but wants the trade to be fair for everyone. Then ask your client if she or he would like to visit the Magic Shop.

If they want to visit, ask them what they are shopping for – an attribute, a feeling, a goal, etc. Often the thing they seek relates to the issue they have brought to the coaching session.

Once they can clearly say what they want, ask them what they are willing to trade. At a deep level every person knows what he or she may have to give up for what they want. It may take some time for the client to articulate what that is. Remind them that the Magician will insist on a fair trade.

A coach may want to help a client avoid giving anything up. Do *not* intervene here because it is important that he or she wrestle with this trade-off. Doing so puts them firmly in touch with the commitment that is empowering them *and* the coaching process. Commitment is generated as the client gets in touch with what they really desire.

SHIFITNG THE FOCUS OF ATTENTION

Shifting the focus of attention is key in the coaching process. This ladder of distinctions for attention might be useful in coaching.

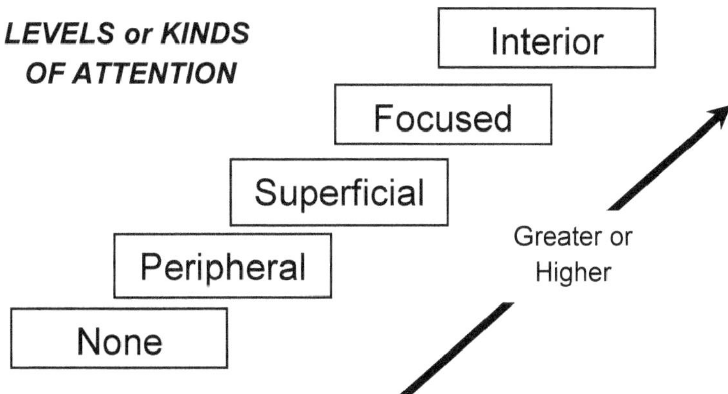

Chapter IV – Hard work . . .and the guy's night out - 35
Roles a Coach Plays . . . Exploring Coaching Tools
The Use of Will and Intention in Coaching

Insights and Principles . . .

Some of the many roles coach plays include:

Action generator – the client leaves every interaction committed to action. "Getting ready to act," even seeking more coaching before taking action, can be a stalling tactic.

Agent – sending the client-leader on a journey (e.g. The Magic Shop) to foster experiential learning.

Appreciator – communicating positive regard and acknowledging who the client is being and becoming.

Change manager – supporting the creation of a compelling vision by reducing the perceived cost of change, reflecting their dissatisfaction with current circumstances, and encouraging the first steps.

Clarifier – reducing confusion and chaos by separating real from imagined aspects of a situation – fact from opinion or fear.

Commitment generator – understanding that commitment can and must be generated, maintained and enlarged in order for actions to manifest powerfully.

Confronter – pointing out when a client is out of integrity, playing games, or may be lying to him or herself and/or others, etc.

Context Creator – creating a place and space to safely explore and try on a new persona, or explore new ideas and directions.

Distinction creator/explorer – using language to make the invisible visible. If we can "see it," we can acknowledge, manage, and use it to grow our awareness and mastery.

Edge finder – pointing out when the client hits the edge of their "box" or paradigm, and supporting exploration outside of it.

Explorer of limiting behavior and thinking patterns – these are our defenses against randomness and chaos that seem to facilitate our survival by creating the illusion of safety.

Giver of feedback / mirror – there is no growth, improvement or evolution without feedback.

Grower of awareness – increasing sensitivity to our inner selves, to those around us, and the world. Being more aware of what's going on in our bodies is a starting point.

Guide – encouraging exploration of new pathways, or sometimes modeling the "explorer spirit."

Perspective shifter – changing the point-of-view. A perspective is neither right nor wrong, but rather useful or not useful.

Point of accountability – a witness to promises and commitments made.

Seed planter – sharing useful notions, reactions, and observations with the understanding that nothing escapes the subconscious.

Shifter of time – moving out of the past to explore the future, and especially focusing on the present.

Trickster – provoking, prodding – e.g. intentionally incorrectly paraphrasing.

Models and Tools

COACHING TOOLS

Awareness – This is different than "attention." Attention is a focused presence, but *awareness* is more defused and expansive. It is possible to be paying attention to a person and, at the same time, be aware of others around you, or an energy shift in the room, and most importantly, of YOURSELF. As Anthony DeMello said, "Attention is a spotlight, and awareness is a flood light."

Compassion – *Feeling* compassion is critical because it tells you, and your client, that you are aware of your connection and are listening at a deep level. That said, there is a difference between feeling compassion and expressing it. You do not need to give voice to your compassion. If you feel it, it will be present for all.

Dialogue/Inquiry – This is one of the most useful forms of conversation in coaching and in all interactions. A coaching conversation is primarily an *exploration*. The purpose is greater clarity and understanding, not necessarily making a decision or acting on a solution.

Distinguishing – A distinction is a deep understanding of something such that, when present, it *automatically* and fundamentally changes perception, beliefs, values and/or behavior forever.

Intuition – This term comes from the Latin – *intueri*. It means the immediate apprehension of the senses, or coming into direct knowledge without reasoning or inference. If a coach is fully aware, intuition will be available for use. And it should be used.

Joy/Optimism – This is another great gift a coach can give their client. Clients come with issues and/or problems. You represent hope and possibility. Be just that. And when you are not hopeful or joyful, be aware that you are not.

Listening – A meta-tool tool for coaches. A coach must continually endeavor to build deeper distinctions for this amazing vibrational, cognitive and empathic connection.

Silence – Silence is underutilized – in life and especially in coaching. Silence creates the space wherein we can access awareness, intuition, our feelings, etc. Use it!

Will/Intention – This might be a new area to explore. We have the power to influence and change the world around us in unseen ways. Intention is, at its core, a focusing of energy. It brings our life force energies to a nexus. Our will is a mind-body force, an assertion of our being. From here our will amplifies this energy much like a magnifying glass does with the sun.

Before every coaching session I get in touch with my intention for my client. After the coaching session I align my own will with theirs as the session ends. In this manner, my coaching is congruent.

Chapter V – Two a.m. and the imps that dance in the night - 43
Facing Your Monsters . . . Keeping the Past in the Past
Self Forgiveness . . . Killing Snakey Doubts

Insights and Principles . . .

- Coaching is helping others break old patterns and cyclical themes to create a new future born of choice rather than conditioning.
- In each moment, the underlying desire and commitment of any person to be a better human being, makes a person perfect. They are only perfect in that moment, but that's the only moment that counts. This is important for coaches to remember. Our clients are all perfect in the moment. This knowledge makes it easy to offer unconditional regard.
- Forgiveness keeps the past in the past, and out of our present or future. People are not their past, but they tend to live as though they are. Coaches must facilitate the inner work that leads to forgiveness, completion and self-love. Only from that foundation is it possible to create a fundamentally new future.
- Doubt is a "gremlin" that coaches encounter on a regular basis. For, as any client considers new possibilities, you can expect that doubt is waiting in the shadows. Doubt is treacherous because it often masquerades as reason and sensibility.
- Doubt is triggered by incoherence and/or contradiction with our experience, and what we have come to believe. Doubt has its genesis in the past. So it stands to reason that the moment that clients break with the past, and begins creating a new self and a future, they can experience doubt.
- When a human being acts out of a deep commitment, the universe cannot resist lending a helping hand. Clients do not need to believe in this dynamic for it to work. They only have to identify and declare their commitments, and then take action to manifest those commitments. At that moment, help is on the way.

Models and Tools

COACHING MODEL

Forgiveness is what keeps the past in the past and out of our present and future. Our choice and our declarations grow from intention into being.

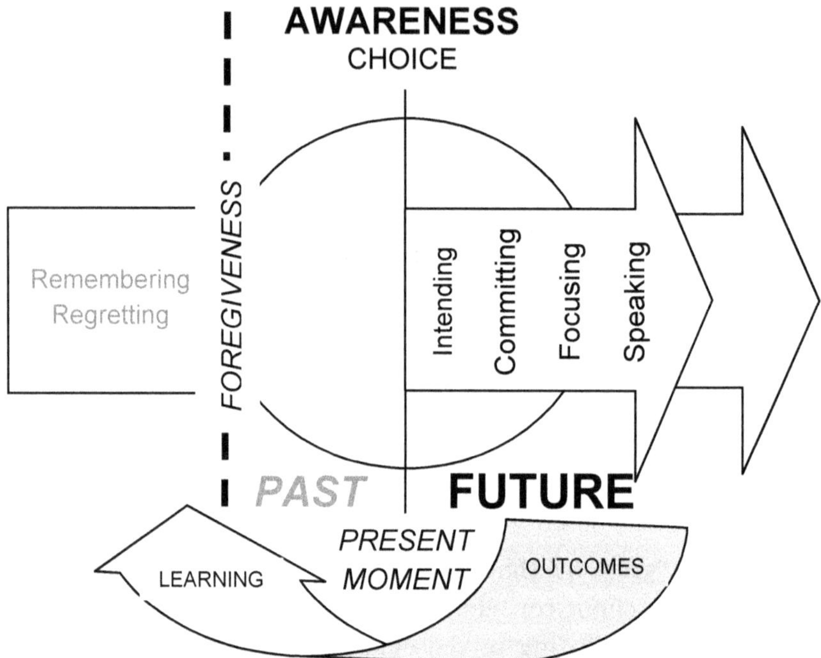

Commitment driven speaking and actions attract most of the people and resources necessary to manifest our intentions. When we create a result, the outcome, no matter what, provides *learning*, so there's no need for regret or recrimination. A coach not only needs to facilitate an exploration of the future, but also of the past.

ADDRESSING DOUBTS

Facilitating an exploration of doubts with a client requires three steps:

1) See and acknowledge doubts -- give voice to them, describe them – don't let them "hide in the shadows."

2) Find the proper tool. In the case of doubt, the tool is *truth* -- truth about who they are now, and are becoming. Truth also reveals what there actually is to fear, which is usually less than thought.

3) Then, act decisively going straight at it without hesitation. Be persistent in your inquiry. Doubt may linger in memory; but it will lose its power in the days ahead.

Chapter VI – It could only happen with guys - 53
The Other Side of Issues . . . Quality of Listening
Preparing to Receive and Listen to Your Client

Insights and Principles . . .

- When exploring any issue, it is important to deeply explore *all sides* of an issue before taking action. If we do not we often end up addressing the *symptoms* and not the cause.
- Usually we can say exactly what we mean. Other times we communicate *more* than words can without using language. We might lack the vocabulary, context, skill or internal awareness to share what is inside, but we can still communicate if there is deep listening present. That's because communication has its source in our being.
- Just as a client prepares for a coaching conversation, a coach does also. An important part of this preparation involves getting quiet, envisioning the client and appreciating who they are *being*. Often when this happens you will feel deep compassion. You are then ready to coach.
- Much of the power of coaching lies in listening. Deep listening allows for the truth to emerge. This is because the truth and the path forward is available to each person, but not always realized in the moment. A coach's job is to create both context and conversation that lets the Truth and the way emerge. Authentic and deep listening facilitates this nurturing context.

Models and Tools

This listening model is based in the belief that an individual communicates by speaking *and* through their being. Who a person is being is both conscious and unconscious. The conscious part has to do with the intention and commitment motivating their speaking. The unconscious part is the unique expression of awareness and presence that often shows up as empathy and compassion. This is what connects human beings. How much of both speaking and being are communicated depends upon the quality of our listening.

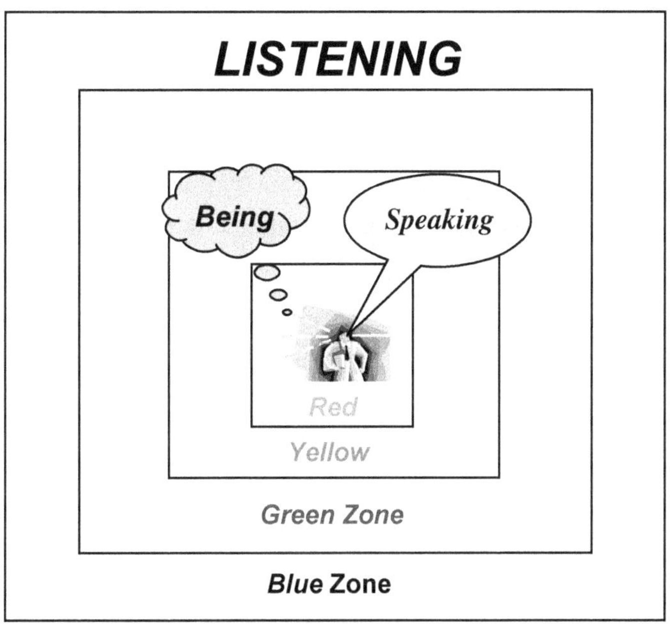

In the RED ZONE, words and sentences don't even get communicated. No aspects of being are communicated.

In the YELLOW ZONE we are able to hear and understand most of what is spoken. Being is felt, but is not fully present for us in our consciousness.

When we practice GREEN ZONE listening the communication process begins to shift from a one-way transaction to a two-way process. Our listening begins to impact the speaker and draws out the genius in them. Intentions and commitments are clear and present.

BLUE ZONE listening shows up as a collapse in boundaries between ideas, egos and individuals. Listening becomes reciprocal and a flow experience. Words and sentences fade into the background. What is communicated is almost totally *being*. We become agents in one another's awareness and growth. This is because blue-zone listening allows the bigger underlying Truth to emerge.

Chapter VII – A visit to Fred's Second-Hand store - 65
The Power of Language . . . Coaching for Creation
Breaking Out of "Our Box"

Insights and Principles . . .

- Coaching is a language-based process. Speaking is an act of creation. Language bridges thought and action to foster creation. Coaching then is "a conversation of creation."
- Conversation changes future options, but also mood, feelings, commitments, perceptions, understanding and even values and beliefs.
- Coaching, like most all communication, relays information, but not all information is equal. Information has the highest value when the ambiguity is the greatest. So, because clients seeking coaching are usually dealing with uncertainty and ambiguity, the information flowing from a coaching conversation has more potency than everyday conversations.
- Coaching, might appear like any serious conversation that one might have with a friend or colleague. However, coaching conversations differentiate themselves in the quality of listening, the elegance of the questions, and the fact that it is an *ongoing* conversation that includes preparation, reflection and integration.
- We can best come to know and understand ourselves in our interaction with another because every other human being has a different perspective, viewpoint and worldview. When we interact with another person, the differences in perspective are revealed. As that happens, we can see the "box" we live in. Until that happens we are trapped in a belief that "this is the way life is."

Models and Tools

LANGUAGE ATTITUDE AND ACTION EXERCISE

Write out a few depressing or negative sentences on some index cards and ask a person to read the card aloud, or a group read it in unison. The index card might read, for example:

My problems are impossible to solve.
I'm much too old and tired to be taking on this work now.
These problems may get worse, but there is nothing I can do about it.
There is nowhere to turn.
Even God does not care.

Hold silence for a moment, then ask the person/group what their mood is -- what they are feeling. They may be slow to respond. Be patient. Then go on to discuss what they just experienced -- the power of language. This exercise sets the stage for more conscious conversations.

COACHING AND CREATION MODEL

Most coaching relationships begin with an *intention* to make some kind of change, personal and/or professional. From there our conversations move through the next seven steps.

#1 – Intending
#2 – Committing
#3 – Focusing
#4 – Speaking
#5 – Doing
#6 – Attracting
#7 - Being
#8 - Manifesting

The first five steps are somewhat conventional in most approaches to coaching, but the last three deserve some explanation.

#6 - Attraction -- Once a client is in action, additional sources of help and support, both real and imagined, show up.

#7 - Being – It is possible for a human being to move from *having* and acting on a commitment, to *being* a commitment. Coaching may or may not be a vehicle for facilitating a shift to Being – which a state of fully aware and focused presence.

#8 - Manifesting – Our experience with manifesting – creation in the physical and material realm via thought and intention alone – is often discounted or denied because it doesn't fit in a modern cause-and-effect paradigm. I recognize manifestation as the ultimate creative force in our world. If nothing else, coaching can introduce human beings to this possibility.

INDICATORS OF A SHIFTING PARIDIGM

Here are some of the clues that indicate when clients are bumping into the walls or edges of their paradigm. They may display:

- Increasing indecision about next steps
- A visible emotional response to your conversation
- Feeling challenged or defensive
- Ambigious excitement about the future
- Unprovoked denial that they can change their life
- Reticence when possibilities are presented

Chapter VIII – Hustle the out-of-towner - 73
Coaching and Maslow's Hierarchy of Needs
Friction in Coaching and Human Development

Insights and Principles . . .

- The most important assessment a coach performs is assessing the client's willingness and ability to break from those aspects of the past that no longer serve. Future-focused conversations will fail if the person does not consciously choose to let go of the past.
- Patterns are a defense against the randomness that seems to threaten our survival. Patterns do not make us more secure, but create a powerful *illusion* of safety. These patterns show up in language, behavior, thinking, and ultimately, being.
- Old patterns have more power when people are at the lower end of Maslow's hierarchy of needs. A person in a physical or emotional survival mode will require a coaching process that will likely be more difficult and lengthy.
- The patterns that clients believe are protecting them are often superstitions. They work only because they believe they do. An opening for coaching occurs when patterns of thinking, acting, and believing are breaking down.
- Friction is a clash of perceptions and beliefs. The resistance caused by friction creates a momentary stop in action and (hopefully) opens the door to reflection, awareness, learning and change. All processes designed to facilitate personal growth have this in common.
- High quality coaching elevates a client's overall level of awareness and consciousness and equips them to more effectively deal with future issues and problems. This realization necessitates that as much energy and attention be placed on facilitating sustainable personal growth, as on problem solving.

Chapter IX – Cru-u-using with Eddie and Victor - 79
Invisible Prison Bars . . . Trapped my Our Culture
Questions are the Key to the Cell

Insights and Principles . . .

- A new way of seeing our circumstances and ourselves cannot take hold until a person gives up the old way of seeing. This is one of the basic tenants of coaching.
- Our prison bars are created, in part, by limiting beliefs, core assessments about life, and deep fears. It is the job of a coach to breach these walls and help people to escape. This is challenging work because most people do not realize that they are "in prison."
- A coach can help a client understand the root causes of many self-defeating behaviors and resulting unhappiness by exploring beliefs, attitudes, values, traditions, norms, expectations, cultural morays, ideals, principles, ideologies, etc.
- The consumer-culture teaches that we need to be something other than what we are to be happy. Driven by a sense of lack and scarcity we go after what we are told is *missing* and, when we attain it, we fear losing it. Add to this a belief that if we do not get what we need to be "happy" it is *our fault*, and it's a wonder anyone can be happy. All this creates layers of anxiety, guilt, despair, and anger.

Chapter X – Finally living on the land - 87

The God Within . . . Connecting with the Observer

Bringing Clients into the Present Moment

Insights and Principles . . .

- A classic coaching question is, "Who are you?" When you ask this, you are sending your client on a spiritual journey because you are asking them distinguish between who they *really* are, and who they currently *think* they are.
- Over time, clients will observe that their thoughts create a world. They initially think it is THE world. But by continually observing their thoughts they begin to see the difference. When you put someone in the observer role and ask them to observe themselves and their thoughts, you bring them closer to en theos – the God within.
- A coach must facilitate a balance between the present, the future and the past. A client must understand that while they might explore the past or future, but they can only experience joy in the present.

Models and Tools

A TECHNIQUE FOR COMING INTO THE PRESENT MOMENT

Calling on the *senses* of the client brings them into the present moment. For example, if you suspect the client is not present to what is happening in their body during a coaching conversation, you might ask (almost as an aside) "Are you comfortable?" or, "Are you too warm?" Such remarks bring them into in the present moment. Once there, they can more easily make contact with "the observer."

Chapter XI – A wild west way of life - 93
Power Dynamics . . . Distinctions for Leadership
Abuses of Power . . . Evolution of Awareness

Insights and Principles . . .

- Coaches can help clients distinguish power in a broader and more generative way, such as influencing the flow of energy and information in an organization.

- A new distinction for power, and increased consciousness around how we use power, can be the genesis of an organizational transformation.

- The mostly unconscious use of power and rank may be the root cause of many common organizational problems and workplace dysfunction.

- The common belief that power is controlling limited resources and directing people in order to achieve specific goals can lead to the conscious and unconscious *abuse* of power and rank.

- The term "leadership" implies someone to be lead. Immediately then, a dichotomy is created, a separation, a class distinction.

- According to Kipnis, the more power a manager has the more likely he or she is to devalue the workers they were supervising.

- If there is a belief that "I am fundamentally superior," then increasing the quality of listening, encouraging feedback, coaching, managing diversity and such, will have little lasting impact.

- The unconscious use and conscious abuse of power are often the root cause of:

- Diminished personal accountability and responsibility
- Restricted flow of information
- Competitive and adversarial relationships
- The presence of guilt and blame
- Less creativity and innovation
- Limited collaboration and teamwork
- Breakdowns in relationships
- Ineffective communication
- Undeclared problems
- Stifled commitment
- Increased turnover, absenteeism and illness
- Revenge
- Pseudo-loyalty

- Inquiries into personal and organizational power dynamics have a transformational effect because they are not simply conversations *about* power. Rather they are processes that reduce and, over time, eliminate abuses of power by making leaders more aware of how they tend to use it.

- Facilitating an inquiry into power dynamics should be a priority for coaches because individuals and organizations cannot fundamentally change until existing power patterns and structures change.

- Most behavior is deeply embedded in long standing *patterns* that makes it difficult to change. A benefit of coaching is that it makes people aware of these entrenched behavior patterns.

- Validation is a central task for coaches. When a client returns after a break from coaching it is useful to validate his/her interim progress and accomplishment.

Models and Tools

AWARNESS MODEL

Behavior change tends to be negatively reinforcing. That is, when an individual tries to change a behavior, they initially become aware of their troublesome behaviors AFTER they have acted. Coaching overcomes this barrier by acknowledging that awareness, even *after* the fact, is progress. This facilitates continued effort and awareness.

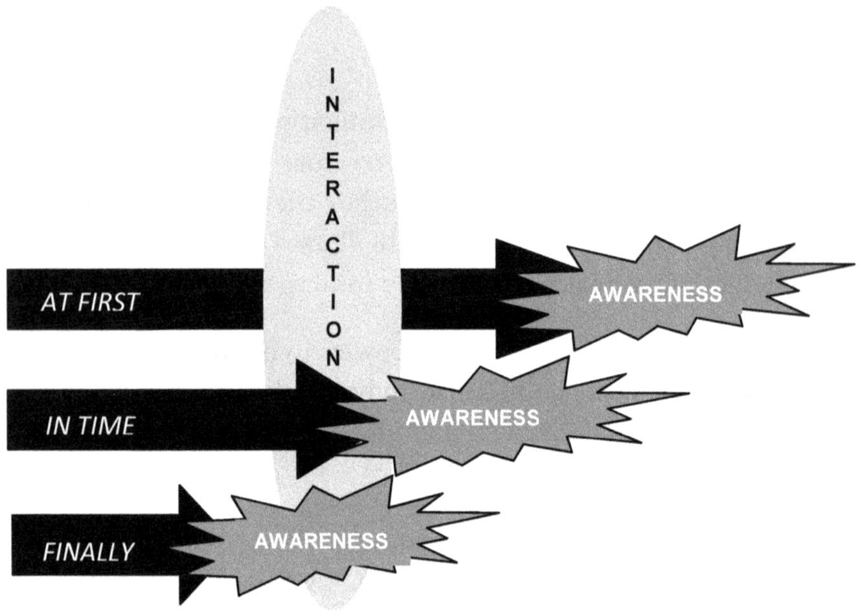

Chapter XII – Breaking the law . . . again - 103
Exploring a Client's Past . . . Dealing with Poor Choices
Managing the Risks in Coaching

Insights and Principles . . .

- Action always leads to learning, primarily because we will often make mistakes.
- When a client brings "mistakes" or failures to the coaching conversation, it is best to ask, "What prompted you to take this action?" – not "Why?" Why often implies judgment. Judgment is the antithesis of coaching. Not only does a good coach avoid judgment, but coaches must also help their clients avoid self-denigration that keeps them focused in the past.
- Observation can show that about eighty percent of our conversations are past-focused, and it would seem that at least one-half of our thoughts are as well. Most human beings spend a lot of time and energy on what is unfinished, on regret, and in sadness about the past.
- Forgiveness, particularly self-forgiveness, is absolutely necessary for happiness. Forgiveness does not mean condoning or pardoning. We can forgive ourselves while knowing that what we have done is not okay or right.
- You cannot focus solely on the individual and assume that what is best for the individual is best for all.
- Coaches must respond cautiously to requests for "dramatic change" from clients. You must assess a client's physical and emotional health, as well as their capacity for change given their current circumstances, relationships and responsibilities. You have a responsibility for the health of the entire "system" a client operates within.
- Risk always plays a role in change. Using thorough assessments, proper techniques and processes, coaches can *minimize* the risks associated with coaching, but we cannot totally eliminate them.

Models and Tools

EXPLORING PAST CHOICES

When a client brings a poor choice or failure to a session, a coach can facilitate self-forgiveness using six steps:

1) Remind the client that hindsight makes their choice appear poorer than it seemed at the time – they had diminished awareness in that moment.
2) At the same time, help the client take responsibility for the subsequent outcome. This is responsibility, not as blame, but as a simple fact. Even thinly veiled denial will make forgiveness difficult, if not impossible.
3) Extract the learning – What prompted them to make this choice and/or take this action? What do they better understand about themselves as a result of this event?
4) Ask them what they might they do today if faced with the same situation or circumstance? Point out that they have changed, grown and evolved since that time and that they are a fundamentally different person today.
5) Ask them to use this new perspective on themselves by holding that "old self" in their minds eye and then comfort and love that "old self." Point out that they are simply showing the same love for themselves that they would show another human being. They are not making themselves an exception.
6) Finally, reorient them to the future to keep them from squandering too much energy in the past. Remember the lesson, accept the love and compassion they are offering themselves, and move on. Remind them that this past event may surface again in their awareness, but they can, and will, dismiss it quickly.

Chapter XIII – An old fashioned 4th of July - 111

Problems and Commitments . . . Improvisational Conversation
Inner & Outer Creation Processes

Insights and Principles . . .

- Common commitments connect most people – not just problems. A good definition of "problem" is a perceived barrier to acting on a commitment or need. Clients often focus on problems because they don't see or share commitments readily.
- Focusing on generating action within a coaching conversation assumes that change happens as a consequence of actions taken *after* the coaching session. But, by focusing on the subject of *change* itself during the coaching conversation, that change actually begins to happen *within* the coaching conversation. The key is effective use of perlocutionary questions.
- External and internal processes *together* create change – not just external actions. The outer and inner elements of the clients' own processes must be in alignment in order to manifest a new creation.
- A shift in perception and attitude not only shows up bio-physically in our neuronets and glandular systems, but actually *changes* the physical structures of those systems.
- Coaches can move beyond working with externalized emotions when we offer the client an understanding of the role bio-physical processes play in emotion and therefore creation. This awareness leads us to appreciate the complexity of the processes that underlie a shift in *being*.

Models and Tools

THE FIVE RULES FOR IMPROVISATIONAL CONVERSATION

1) Hold no preconceived idea about what the scene is about or where it is going.
2) Pay attention to others.

3) Accept all "offers."

4) Always advance the action.

5) Support others in looking good.

THE HUMAN CREATION PROCESS

The power of conversation to create change, and consequently an alternate future, requires more than speaking. There is also an internal process simultaneously taking place throughout the processes of thinking, speaking and action.

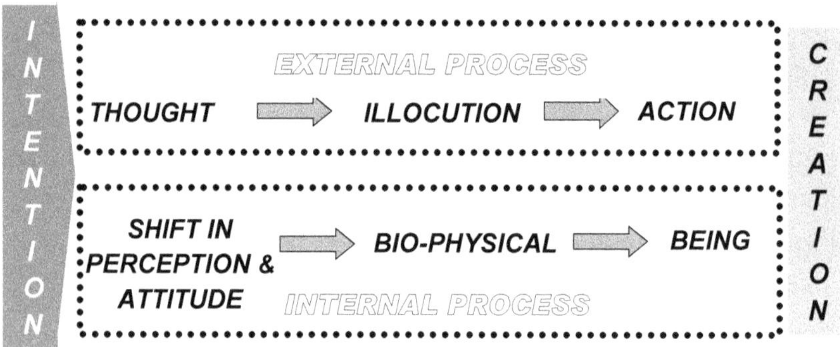

Chapter XIV – Missing intimacy - enter Sara stage left - 123
The Power of Witnessing . . . Creating a New Reality
Love is NOT Blind . . . Dealing with Secrets

Insights and Principles . . .

- We are continually presented with new ideas, possibilities and realities. Most people experience cognitive dissonance, when new ideas and possibilities contradict what they already "know" or believe. To a coach, cognitive dissonance is an ally.
- Validation of a client's process is part of coaching, but equally important is the fact that you are *witnessing* their journey. Most people, when confronted with the tug-of-war between the future and the status quo, do not explore a new idea, perceptual frame, or possibility. Instead they tend to seek refuge by revalidating their current reality. And so, they fail to respond to an invitation to grow and evolve.
- As much as possible, a coach sees their client as they are -- withholding expressing assessments and judgments. When we learn to be aware of our internal assessments and judgments, we can set them aside.
- When we see our clients as they really are, accepting them without assessment and judgment, we love them.
- Withholding judgment allows for spontaneous "ordinariness" from which client's can learn self-acceptance. They begin to trust and love themselves unconditionally.
- It is not *always* helpful for a client to share secrets with a coach – especially without preparation. Before a secret is revealed, try to determine how big and deep the secret is, and what the client's expectations are about sharing the secret. Then consider the consequences of delaying, or not sharing, the secret.
- The moment the secret comes up may not be the optimal moment to reveal it. More importantly, YOU – the coach – may not be the right person to deal with it. The client may need to seek help from other professionals or non-professionals.

Maintain the distinction between coaching and counseling or therapy.

Models and Tools

PREPARATION FOR REVEALING SECRETS

There are a series of questions you might ask any client before they reveal any secret(s).

Depth and Importance of the Secret

How long have you been keeping this secret?

Does this secret often surface in your consciousness? Do you think of it once a week?

How do you feel when you become aware of this secret?

Expected Responses

Have you ever told anyone else this secret? If so who? What was their response, etc.?

Why do you want to share your secret with me now?

What do you think my reaction might be? (Probe deeper here.)

What do you think your reaction will be after you tell me? How will you feel?

Impact of Delaying or Not Sharing with Coach

If you don't tell your secret to me now, what do you think might happen?

Why are you considering sharing this secret with me – your coach – rather than someone else? Who else might you explore this secret with?

If it is a "big secret" you must be prepared to spend some time exploring it. Indeed, it might change the whole direction and plan for coaching. You will want the client to, at least momentarily, consider the possibility of not sharing, or delaying the telling of a secret. This puts the choice clearly with them – where you want it to be.

Chapter XV – Christmas in Trinidad - 133
Awareness and Behavior Change . . . A New Paradigm
Coaches as Midwives to Human Evolution

Insights and Principles . . .

- Approaching behavior change in a logical manner can make both the coach and client oblivious to important dynamics and factors that need to be explored. One useful area of inquiry has to do with the fact that human *behavior* is most often directed by how a person *feels* rather than what they think. So, an exploration of the emotional underpinnings of decisions may necessarily be part of any inquiry. A useful question is, "What drove or motivated your decision?" All behavior change begins with awareness, and the broader and more complete one's awareness is, the greater the chance for lasting change.
- One of most useful distinctions we can create for a client is when coaching is needed. Begin creating this distinction in your first conversation with your client.
- The emergence of coaching in the last two decades has signaled an important shift from a paradigm where the individual is controlled, to one where an individuals is driven from their own heart and by their own commitments.
- Our current social, economic and political structures do not support the evolution of the human beings. Presently, personal growth must be systematically pursued. Coaching is a discipline that catalyzes and supports human evolution. So, as a coach, you are weaving the threads of transformation into the fabric of humanity.
- In-the-moment awareness that prompts a stop in action or thinking is not just a cornerstone of coaching, but the pathway to self-sufficiency. It is this process that will serve the client long after formal coaching ends. It is what prevents coaching from becoming co-dependent.

Models and Tools

THE COACHING SUPPORTED EVOLUTIONARY SHIFT

OLD FOCUS	***NEW FOCUS***
Goal is CONVENTIONALITY	Goal is CREATIVITY
COMPLIANCE	INVOLVEMENT
Seeking KNOWLEDGE	Seeking WISDOM
Attention to WHAT IS HAPPENING	Focus on WHAT COULD BE
Want to find ANSWERS	Want to explore POSSIBILITIES first
People are RESOURCES	People are THE MEANS

Chapter XVI – A life like a bad country western song - 143
Coaching in a World of Deficiency-motivated People
Success vs. Fulfillment . . . Getting Life's Messages

Insights and Principles . . .

- Abraham Maslow said, "All extrinsic goals and values are deficiency motivated." Thus, if people build their lives primarily on extrinsic needs and goals, they live with a constant feeling of deficiency. In this state, there is little possibility for lasting happiness.
- Usually, clients are focused on near-term happiness. As a coach, you help your clients to see the bigger, long-term picture. One way to do this is to initiate an inquiry by asking, "Are you happy?" When you ask this question, notice body language, as well as verbal responses.
- Success is defined *for* most people in the U.S. It is defined primarily in extrinsic terms – big office, nice car, home in a great neighborhood, financial investments, etc. This is part of the programming that begins almost the moment we are born. The primary focus of socialization and education is to make us productive workers, able to contribute the economy.
- All human beings are on a spiritual journey, if you define a spiritual journey as the evolution of human beings moving toward a higher level of consciousness that allows them to live within their true interconnected and interdependent nature.
- Almost every experience we have has a directional message within it. However, we do not always get Nature's GPS signals. If we're conscious at all, we recognize the message. We say, "I've been taught a lesson," or "I feel I'm headed in the right direction." However, if we do not get the message, life seems to intensify the negative feedback process.
- When a client brings a problem, one of the first questions to ask is, "Has anything like this happened before?" In other words, is there a pattern here? As a coach, you are there not just available to help someone solve a unique predicament, but

to see their problem in the context of a larger pattern. In this way, you help them receive the bigger message – the lesson.

- Pain is sometimes an indicator that a person is not pointed in a positive evolutionary direction. We cannot live without pain. However, we can avoid suffering – defined as being in pain longer than we need to be. A coach's job is not to help their client eliminate pain, but rather to avoid suffering. To do this, we must move beyond problem-solving into the deeper information that lies within the problem or issue.

Models and Tools

INITIATING AN INQUIRY INTO HAPPINESS

One way to initiate an inquiry into "happiness" is to ask clients to make a long list of what they want and need. After they are finished, look at the list and notice how many of the things on the list are *extrinsic*, and how many are *intrinsic*. If proportionally, there are far more extrinsic items, then it is likely that the individual is unhappy. If there are roughly equal parts of intrinsic and extrinsic items, then you may have to probe further by asking them to prioritize their list – identify the top four or five most important items. If the most important wants and needs are intrinsic then they have a good shot at happiness.

EXPLORING SUCCESS AND FULFILLMENT

As a coach you can use a simple graph to open a deeper inquire into the happiness and fulfillment:

Ask your client to put and X on each of two lines -- one on the success-failure line, the other along the fulfillment line. Then, point out that the ideal trajectory is to have success and fulfillment move in tandem. Combine their lines to make a graph to illustrate this point.

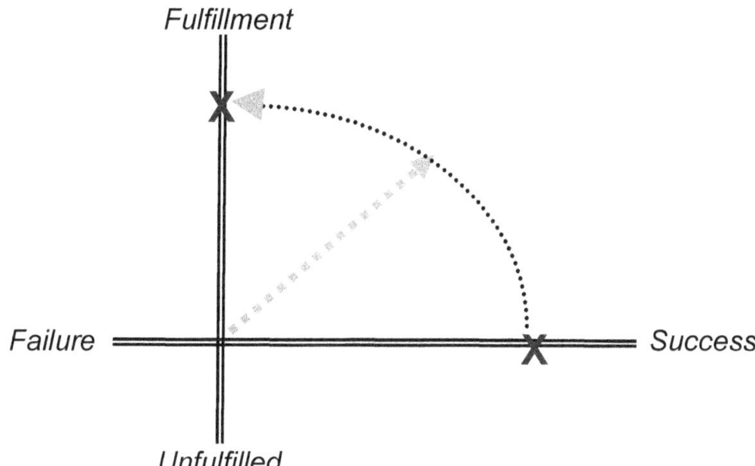

An obvious question usually comes to mind. "How can I get (or keep) success and fulfillment moving together in my life?"

Chapter XVII – Meet Sara . . . my Sara - 151
Getting in Touch with Our Authentic Selves
Using Different Roles to Gain Perspective . . . Nasty What-ifs

Insights and Principles . . .

- Human beings tend to habitually compensate for some real or perceived inadequacy by making themselves "special" in some way. By allowing ourselves to be "ordinary" and/or "average," we learn self-acceptance that leads to self-love.
- Clients come with a "problem" or need. Inquiring into a client's problem should begin with an exploration of the *need* behind the problem, before you take up a conversation intended to help them achieve their goal or solve a problem.
- Coaches should not share their personal assessments and prejudices within a coaching conversation. What enables you to do this is *awareness* of your assessments and opinions in the moment. By being aware of what is going in inside you, you can make choices about how to speak, listen, and show-up.
- Your degree of self-awareness in the moment, is what distinguishes good coaches from great coaches.

Models and Tools

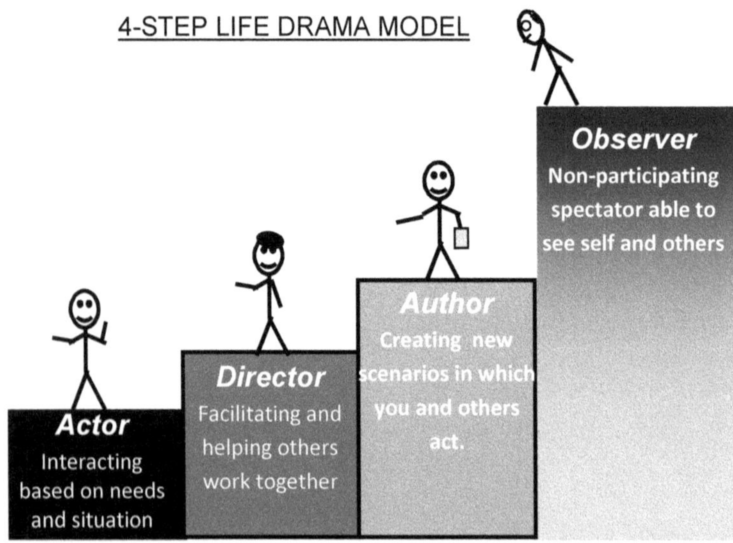

You can use a simple 4-step model in your coaching practice to help your clients gain helpful perspectives on their “problems” and circumstances.

Draw a simplified version of 4-step model on a piece of paper and point to the “writer” for example, and ask if they could rewrite the “scene” how would they do that? The most powerful place to stand is in the place of the *observer* or spectator.

Chapter XVIII – Cursing the wind – a metaphor - 161
The Status of Coach and Client . . . New Perspectives
Questions that Provide Elevation

Insights and Principles . . .

- One of the ways coaching can be distinguished from therapy is that a coach operates as a completely equal partner with the client. Equal status is necessary in order to create a context for greater self-disclosure, higher self-esteem on the part of the client and, most importantly, client responsibility for outcomes.
- Remember that the mostly unconscious use of power and rank is one of the root causes for many breakdowns in relationships and/or dysfunction within organizations.
- How effective a coach is depends, to a large degree, on the quality and creativity of the questions asked of the client.
- The genesis of human transformation is a shift in perspective. This shift can be triggered by the questions a coach asks.

Models and Tools

QUESTIONS THAT SHIFT PERSPECTIVE

You can facilitate a change in perspective or a larger view, by asking well designed questions. Examples of "larger view questions include:

What is the larger issue of which this is only a part?

Is this situation a problem of the system? If so, how might you bypass it?

You can change perspective by facilitating a deeper, less superficial, look. Examples of this type of question are:

What does the person creating this situation really want?

What might be the root cause of this situation?

One of the most interesting ways to shift perspective is a 180-degree turn. Here you get in touch with the underlying assessment and reverse it. Examples of this include:

> *What would happen if this situation meant exactly the opposite of what you think it means?*

> *What would you do if this problem were an opportunity? What would make it an opportunity?*

Then there are my personal favorite ways to facilitate a shift in perspective – off-the-wall questions:

> *If this situation were funny, what would we be laughing at?*

> *How would you resolve this problem if you were 20 years younger?*

Chapter XIX – Trapped between success and failure - 169
Managing Your Own Internal Emotions as a Coach . . .
Exploring the Limits of Language . . . Plan ≠ Future

Insights and Principles . . .

- Language influences and shapes our *thoughts* and *emotions*. It is important to bring feelings into the light of awareness as part of the coaching process.
- It is important to create a neutral emotional context for your clients. Be positive and affirming without "cheering." This is a line coaches need to walk.
- Coaches know better than to give advice, yet we do so when we non-verbally react to a client. This requires being aware of your emotional state and accompanying body language. If you are having an emotional reaction to something a client shares, that's a clue that *your* "stuff" is coming up. Beware.
- If you are not aware of what is going on inside you, then emotions control you. If you are aware of what is going on inside you, then you can manage your emotions. The same is true for our clients.
- Observing our interactions with others offers the greatest opportunities to know and understand ourselves.
- Coaching allows the imagined self to stand next to the real self. This fact is one of the things that gives coaching its power.
- Coaching is less about creating a new future, and more about creating a *change in perception* that leads to a new reality. When you can fully appreciate that difference, you will find yourself operating at a whole new level – personally and professionally.
- Since language is the coach's primarily tool, it is important to understand that language can limit one's ability to fully perceive. For example, language is filled with duality – up-down, right-wrong, in-out, you-me, etc. This not only creates polarized thinking, but it also keeps us from true Reality.

- Another way to overcome the limitations of language is to "redistinguish" an existing word or term to give it new, deeper meaning.
- If we redistinguish "the future" as the place I will be as a consequence of my choices *now*, then I am in the heart of the future. Present moment awareness of myself and the choices I am making, shifts the focus to the here and now – the only domain of time to which we have access.

Models and Tools

THE FIVE RULES OF IMPROVISATION REDUX

The actor's rules of improvisation can help coaches maintain a truly generative interaction.

1) Hold no preconceived ideas about what this is about or where it is going.
2) Accept all offers.
3) Pay attention to others.
4) Always advance the action.
5) Support others in looking good.

Chapter XX – Back against the wall – down to my last cent - 177
Trapped in the Past . . . 3 Step-Coaching Conversation
Inner Work for Coaches

Insights and Principles . . .

- A good coach understands and honors the relationship between the past, the present and the future.
- Helping someone to imagine a new future, a new option, is relatively easy. The harder part, for anyone, is letting go of the past.
- In my experience, people spend at least one-half of their time thinking about the past. In order to help someone move forward, we often have to assist him or her delve into the past. This process includes helping a client develop and generate compassion for themselves and others.
- Forgiveness is, at its core, a choice. We simply choose to let understanding and compassion take the place of anger and regret. Forgiveness is one of the purest forms of love.
- Explorations of the past are a catalyst for "inner work." The client must do the inner work. A coach can only stimulate the need and desire to do it and provide support. I believe that no human being can achieve fundamental and lasting change in the world – their outer life -- without doing their inner work.
- If we only focus on a client's outer work, we are deluding ourselves. We may be able to bring momentary emotional relief, but client will likely be in a similar situation in the near future.

Models and Tools

COACHING AND TIME-TRAVEL

A typical coaching conversation typically touches all three areas of time within one interaction. As the diagram on the next page indicates, a coaching conversation is a balanced one -- beginning in the past, moving to the future, and ending in the present:

3 STEPS IN THE COACHING CONVERSATION

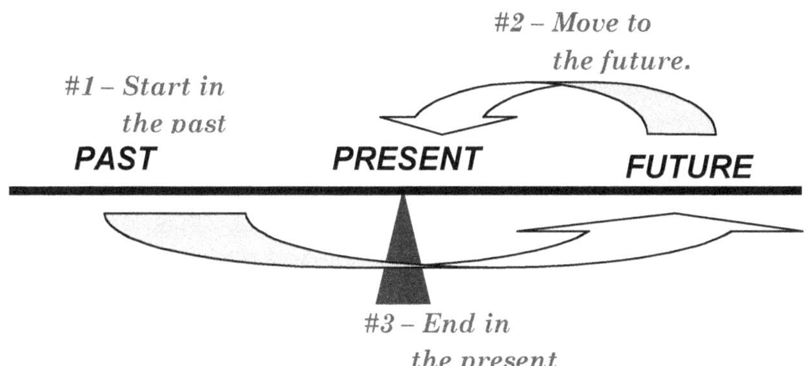

A HELPFUL COACHING MODEL

	PAST		PRESENT		FUTURE
		FEELINGS		INTENTIONS	
DOMAIN:	Spirit		Heart		Head
PROCESSES:	Remembering		Being		Creating
	Reflecting		Choosing		Exploring
FOCUS:	Cyclical Themes		Listening		Possibilities

INNER WORK ***OUTER WORK***

Chapter XXI – The angels have arrived - 185
Choice and Change . . . Attitudes and Behavior
Unconscious Action in the Modern World

Insights and Principles . . .

- Any action or inaction contains a risk. The familiar doesn't look risky, but that assessment is based upon a primordial feeling, not logical thinking.
- Patterns are a defense against randomness that our animal brains believes threatens our survival. A coach must expect emotional resistance as their clients begin to explore out-of-the-ordinary possibilities and actions.
- Fear and comfort keep us trapped in old patterns – the past. Once these barriers are identified, two things happen: First, the pattern loses its' emotional power. Second, it opens the door to exploration.
- Attitudes determine our behavior and the way we interact with others. The way we interact with others determines how they listen and respond to us. And the way they respond to us ultimately determines the possibilities and results we are able to create. It's a chain reaction that begins with being aware of your thoughts and attitude.
- If you could only be aware of one thing – your thoughts might be it.

Models and Tools

OVERCOMING RESISTANCE AND BREAKING PATTERNS

Exploring fears lessens emotions and resistance that keeps old behavioral patterns in place. It allows for a more rational decisions leading to change.

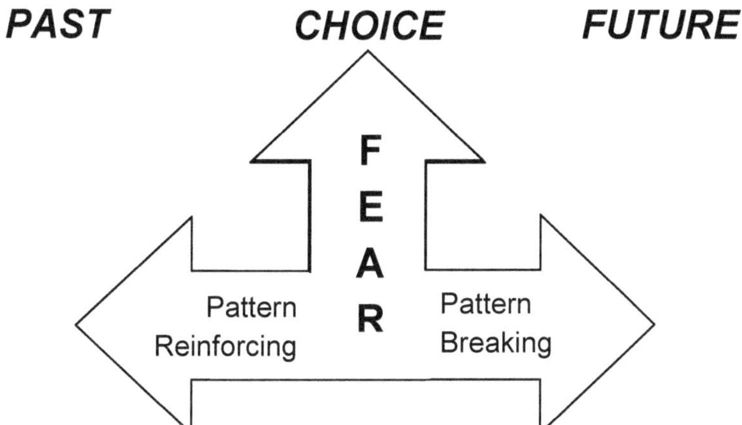
PAST
CHOICE
FUTURE
FEAR
Pattern Reinforcing
Pattern Breaking

Chapter XXII – Who am I if I'm not my stuff? - 195
Problems and Opportunities . . . Closing the Gap
A Universal Model for Coaching

Insights and Principles . . .

- Use whatever term the client uses to describe a problem, then redistinguish problems in a new way. For example, note that you hear commitment as they describe the problem. Of course, this is true because there cannot be a problem without a commitment behind it. Coaching is commitment driven – so problems might even be seen as a good thing.
- The distance between what someone needs/wants, and their assessment of where they are with regard to getting what they want (the gap), determines how big the problem is. As a coach your job is to close the gap, or at least make is smaller.
- A coach's job is to identify, support and strengthen the commitment behind the problem or need. Human commitment provides the energy that is needed to act and change. Some call this motivation.

Models and Tools

PICTURE OF A PROBLEM

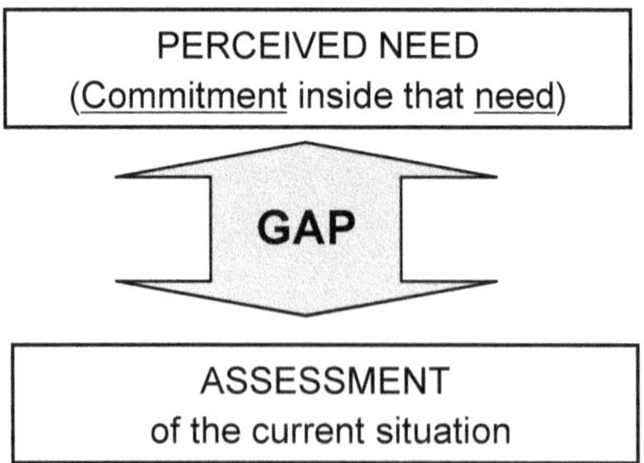

A coach works both ends of this model by helping a client clarify their need, and by exploring the validity of their assessment.

Most initial assessments human beings make are limited because we rely primarily on past experience for possibilities. The coaching objective is to generate new options and opportunities to move forward and leave the client poised to act.

Once someone is in action to meet his or her need, the emotion behind the problem diminishes. This is because the oppression felt from problems is mostly generated within an individual's *interpretation* of their circumstances. What is more, the problem itself is easier to explore and resolve once the emotions around it subside.

Chapter XXIII – Still in search of my essential self - 203
Coach as Context Creator . . .
Creating a Caring Nurturing Coaching Environment

Insights and Principles . . .

- One important role of a coach is that of a context creator. A coach creates a caring, non-judgmental environment wherein an individual can safely explore.
- When a client pauses as they are speaking, they are sometimes lost in thought, but sometimes they are censoring themselves. If your intuition suggests they are censoring, you can use those occasions to build trust and a more nurturing context.
- For many people, a coaching session is the only place they feel free to express themselves without regard to how they will be judged. Providing an open, accepting and compassionate context is as important as anything a coach says or does.

Chapter XXIV – Spring . . . Easter . . . and renewal - 209
Coaching as a Rollercoaster Ride . . . Exploring Worry
The Need for Periodic Renewal

Insights and Principles . . .

- Be aware that the original issue that motivated the request for coaching does not magically vanish when the client identifies a new possible pathway and is poised to act. The emotional content within that breakdown must be addressed during the coaching session and often later on.
- A coach's job might seem complete once a client commits to action, but in the space between seeing and choosing a new path and taking action, there is at least one more "emotional speed-bump." Expressed in words it's, "Uh-oh, what have I committed to here!" At these and other junctures a coach's continuing and supportive presence is critical because the client's "post commitment" journey can become a roaster coaster ride.
- A coach must be aware that the processing of the emotional content within any issue often resurfaces again . . . and again.
- Since people's behavior is often driven by their emotions, you must employ pragmatic ways to bring emotions into the coaching conversation. This process starts with awareness. A coach needs to shine the light of awareness on a client's feelings and create a safe place for them to explore the emotions present.
- Whether or not a client is totally, partially, or not in any way, responsible for a troublesome situation, it is critical that they take *full responsibility* for addressing it.
- Awareness eventually diminishes the intensity of the emotion. Negative emotions -- fear, anger, sadness, guilt, etc. – should not be allowed to determine one's choices in life. To do so could be considered irresponsible.
- Renewal is something sorely missing in our culture. A coach can offer this gift of renewal, at challenging junctures in a

client's life. Renewal happens when human beings are solidly in touch with, and in action on, those things that are most important to them.

Models and Tools

EMOTIONAL AFTERSHOCKS

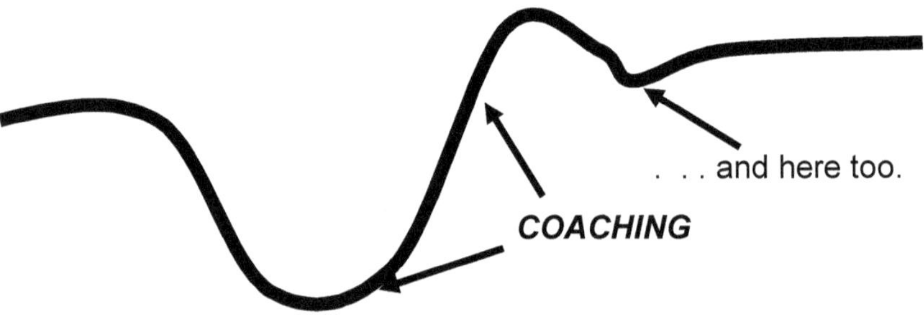

A coach must be aware that the original breakdown that created the request for coaching does not magically vanish when the client identifies a new possible pathway and is poised to take action. Emotions resurface again . . . and again.

Chapter XXV – Making possibilities real . . . tangible - 217
The Flow Experience . . . Not Out-There, but In-Here
Leveraging your Life: The A-B-C Work Model

<u>Insights and Principles . . .</u>

- The handful of basic truths about human beings, and how to live a rich and fulfilling life, has to be dusted off and "repackaged" for each generation. The evolution of language, and emergence of new cultural perspectives, requires that each culture, and each generation, must be reintroduced to Truth and Wisdom.
- At the core of ancient wisdom lies the assertion that the key to joyful living is found in the present moment. Mihaly Csikszentmihalyi identified the conditions that seem to create a flow (present moment) experience:
  - » You know clearly what you have to do.
  - » You know every movement, and are focused on the *movement* not the goal.
  - » The challenges perfectly match your skills.
  - » There is a gentle focus on what you are doing.
  - » You feel totally in control of life.
  - » You are unselfconscious.
  - » Time seems non-existent.

  Summing it up, being and doing collapse and merge. A flow experience gives us a glimpse of a life without awareness of the past or the future.
- Finding and using our innate gifts enabling us to live a present-perfect existence.
- When you get an invitation from a potential client, don't be surprised if it is couched in a request to fix it someone or something "out there." Your coaching can help them shift their perspective, initially focusing on "it," and later focusing "right here" -- on themselves. It is only by focusing on oneself that lasting change can manifest.

Models and Tools

OUT THERE – IN HERE MODEL

I don't expect leaders or clients to immediately focus on themselves. *Out There – In Here* is an ontological dynamic that represents the innate reaction most human beings have to problems or calls to change.

Initially there is denial. But when you finally get an invitation to address an issue or problem from a potential client, don't be surprised if it is couched in a manner that puts the blame on something, or someone else. For greater and lasting effectiveness, shift their perspective and focus on the role *they play* with regard to the issue or problem.

A-B-C WORK MODEL

The A-B-C Work model that follows illustrates how to think and operate in more highly leveraged ways. The progression is from A-work to C-Work. The optimal place from which to operate is where B and C work is naturally incorporated into all A-work.

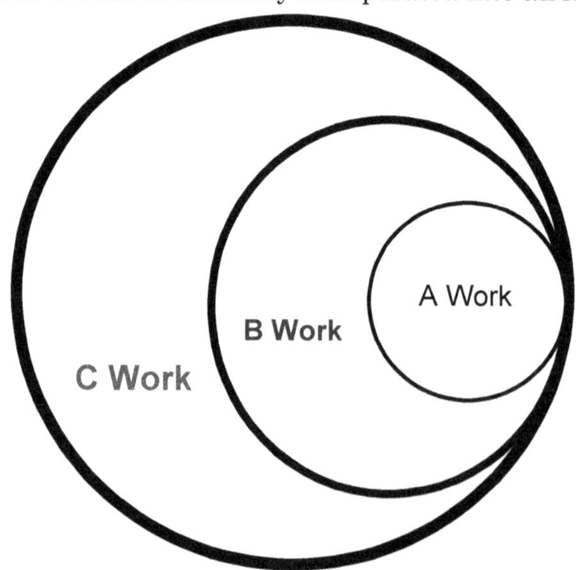

This model is useful, not only for coaching clients, but for coaches, because when we have greater perspective and operate at a higher level of thinking, we are more likely to generate fundamental and lasting change.

A Work – Includes all work that meets day-to-day, quarter-to-quarter personal and stakeholder needs.

B Work – Includes all work *intended* to improve the quality, effectiveness and/or efficiency of A-Work.

C Work – Includes all work *intended* to improve the quality, effectiveness and/or efficiency of A-Work by focusing on the *type*, *choices*, *nature* and/or *effectiveness* of B-Work.

This mental model suggests that a greater amount of time and energy be directed at B and C work. The caveat is that *poor quality* B and C work can quickly and dramatically *reduce* organizational and personal effectiveness. If a coach shifts the conversation from an A-level to B or C-level, there has to be a simultaneous elevation in the quality of the coaching and thinking.

Chapter XXVI – Coaching hat off, tool belt on - 229
Breaking Out of the Box . . . Emotions of Change
How Thoughts Become Reality

Insights and Principles . . .

- Everyone lives in a box created by his or her beliefs, values, education, fears, experience, etc. We think, "This is the way it is." But the box can grow bigger. When we begin to question our beliefs, values, judgments, and what we have been taught -- especially their assessment of ourselves -- the box expands.
- Coaching is about helping clients get out of the box. A coach can do this because she or he stands outside of a client's box and thus has the advantage of a clear perspective. A coach can see the edges of a client's box.
- If you use the term "edge" with clients, first distinguish this term. Then, when you notice a client hits an edge, quietly note it – "I think we may have hit an edge here." Leave it to *them* to determine if they want to explore it or not.
- Indicators that we are banging against the edges of our box include: fear, feeling attacked, defensiveness, unnatural excitement, quiet caution, quick denial, physical disengagement, anger, etc.
- Breaking out of the box does not always happen suddenly and dramatically. Sometimes a client can simply feel a "stretch." This often shows up in subtle, less emotional ways such as indecision, a momentary lapse where they cannot think clearly, or nervous laughter.
- A client's willingness to explore the self-imposed boundaries of their world will depend the degree of trust they have in you as a coach. An individual must be willing to be wrong. As we all know, the need to be right is one of the most powerful imperatives within the human psyche.
- Language is first and foremost a thinking tool. Our thoughts show-up in words – an internal dialogue (thinking), and/or a conversation.

- Even when not using forms of speaking designed to create action, speaking often changes people's minds. The point is that speaking and words create a change, a new reality – internally and sometimes externally. Upon this simple fact rests the coaching discipline.
- Coaching primarily intervenes in the thought-to-reality process between thoughts and words. This is the boundary between the individual and the world around them.
- Our efforts are but drops of water in the ocean of consciousness in which we all swim. And, drops of water eventually hollow out a stone.

Models and Tools

PERCEPTUAL STRETCH ZONE

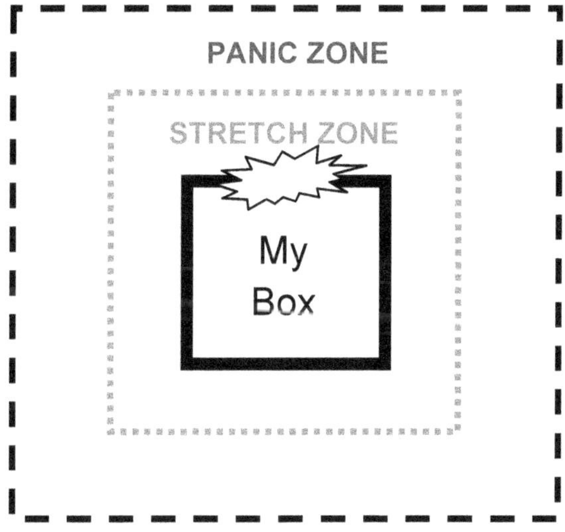

As a person begins to explore outside their box you may become aware of how far out they are beyond their boundaries by the intensity of their emotions. The farther out a client is, the greater the discomfort, stress and anxiety.

Your job as a coach is one of support . . . do not *push* them beyond their current perceptual limits.

THOUGHTS TO ACTION MODEL

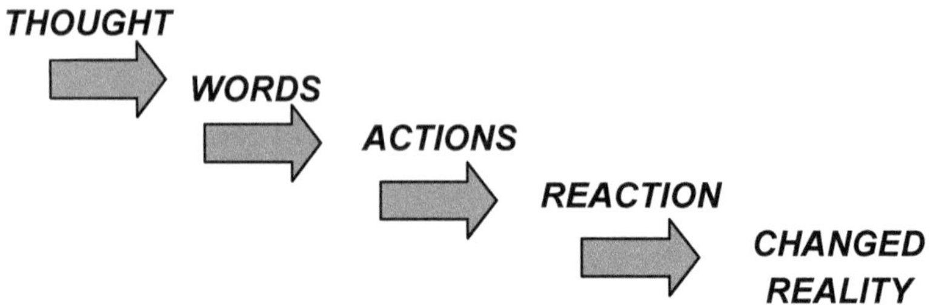

Thoughts ultimately create a "world" – a reality.

Chapter XXVII – A milestone – the occupancy certificate - 241
Exploring What is Real and What is Not Real . . .
Swinging the Great Sword of Freedom - Doubt

Insights and Principles . . .

- Words – conversations -- are the tools of a coach. The spoken word is magical. It is an act of creation. Words can be white magic or black magic.
- A word is a way to describe a thing, but it is not the thing. This seems obvious, yet people often confuse words with the things they represent.
- The words that point to concrete things don't cause the biggest problems when compared to the words that represent concepts or ideas.
- When a client speaks, be aware of what they are focusing on. Is it concrete or conceptual? If it is conceptual, then your first task is point this out.
- If your coaching flows from your ongoing exploration into your own True Nature, then it has the potential to touch the True Nature of your clients.
- Doubt is the great sword of freedom. With it you are able to cut through everything you have been taught -- what your culture demands of you, your attachments, fears, desires, and even your current beliefs.
- This book is an exploration of what a coach might be and become. It is intended to stimulate *your* thinking, to deepen *your* distinctions around coaching, and to support a discipline that has the potential to reveal one's True Nature.

Insights and Principles . . .

- Suspending or ending coaching sessions in the face of a highly emotional responses is not necessary for an experienced coach. Emotions open the door to deeper understanding and healing.
- Exploring an emotional response as the client is in the experience of it, does two things: 1) It puts the client in the present moment, and 2) It prevents or reduces the likelihood that an individual will act solely from their residual emotions.
- Coaching helps a person harness their innate ability to create by operating on two levels: a practical, outwardly focused one, and an inner, psycho-emotional level. Including and focusing on inner, psycho-emotional dimensions facilitates a positive evolutionary shift.
- We are not only *part* of creation, but the creative process itself.
- Moving beyond just solving problems to helping clients discover the source of their own creative spirit, accomplishes four important things:
  1) Clients operate from an elevated perspective and are better able to address the root cause of their problems and issues.
  2) They experience fulfillment while in action, well before they achieve their goals, because their path forward is clearer.
  3) Because clients' see themselves in a larger, richer context, what they create has deeper meaning to them.
  4) Finally, what they create is enduring because it serves the bigger truth that underlies their life.
- Otto Rank believed that we carry our traumatic past emotions with us all the time. In this way, our deeper emotions exist in the present moment and can be accessed from there. In order to avoid feeling their residual emotions, clients often escape to the past, or flee into the future.

- We focus far too much energy on the future and the past in our western culture. Our obsession with the future might be called neurotic.
- We can assist our clients in living in the here-and-now. Coming into contact with the hear-and-now enables clients to give up emotional and intellectual control in return for experiential inspiration.
- When clients are in the here-and-now they are more likely to find inner resources for positive change. For some, the impulse to creative action may show up as a new idea or possibility. For others it may show up as insight or intuition. Either way, they are acting in alignment and agreement with the larger Reality that is unfolding within and around them.
- The future is not so much the result of a well communicated and executed plan, but the unfolding of the present moment. If there is any "magic" per se, in a future-focused conversation, it is that what we say flows from an awareness of what is unfolding inside and around us.
- By cultivating present moment awareness in ourselves, clients are better able to experience being in the here-and-now.
- If we clarify a loving, non-judgmental intention within ourselves first, that intention will be palpable for those we coach.
- If Truth and Reality live in our present moment awareness, we will instinctively say and do the right thing during a coaching session.
- We are designed to be happy. If we cannot be happy in the here-and-now, we will never be happy.

Models and Tools

DEALING WITH AN EMOTIONAL REACTION

When a client feels and exhibits a strong emotional response, you can transform the situation into a learning and healing experience by facilitating the following process:

Stop the conversation when the emotion surfaces and ask:

- "What emotion are you experiencing right now?"
- "Can you recall a time in your past life when you had a response like this – maybe in a similar situation?"
- "When was that? "How old were you?"
- "Take a moment to imagine that person you were then. Now love that one."

ABOUT THE AUTHOR

Kim Krisco founded Transition Technologies in 1990 to focus on organizational change management. This mission evolved to include leadership development, business communication, coaching and team development programs. In recent years he has focused on sabbatical and work-life balance programs for leaders and their spouses. His continually metamorphosing mission has him now focusing on ways to leverage the discipline of coaching as a tool for accelerating human consciousness. In this same context, he is also exploring the use of transcendental poetry with coaching clients as a vehicle for deeper inner exploration.

Transition Technologies develops and delivers customized organizational and personal transformation programs that use coaching as a key component. Kim's approach to is based upon the belief that our personal power is a product of our in-the-moment awareness that is reflected within our interactions with ourself and others. By being embedded in an awareness of what is happening inside and around us, and how we speak, listen and interact, we can naturally and easily improve our effectiveness and the quality of our experience. More importantly, this approach ensures that the outcomes from our thoughts, actions and interactions serve both the individual and the greater good.

Krisco's diverse career has helped prepare him for his new focus. He has taught college; managed instructional media and distance learning programs, written and directed TV and films; and served in corporate communications, human resources and training functions. He is currently being educated by Nature and his work is more and more focused on serving non-profits.

Krisco has worked with both for-profit and nonprofit organizations from NASA to Merck. His most recent clientele includes AARP, the Lakota Nation, FDIC, YMCA, United Methodist Church, and the Mt. Carmel Health Wellness and Community Center.

In addition to this book, Kim has written and published *Leadership & the Art of Conversation*, *Leadership Your Way: Play the Hand You're Dealt and Win*, and *Aikido Leadership*. After *Talking to Trees*, Kim will focus on poetry.

With their own hands (and a lot of help), Kim and his "wife" Sara Ferguson built a straw-bale home and coaching center in south-central Colorado. The decade long process of building this center – along with what it taught Kim about coaching -- is shared in this book. They are now moving on deeper into Nature to create (as much as possible) a self-sufficient lifestyle.

Kim holds graduate and undergraduate degrees and is in the process of sorting through this "education" for useful bits.

His website is: www.kimkrisco.com.

www.ingramcontent.com/pod-product-compliance
Lightning Source LLC
Chambersburg PA
CBHW051939090426
42741CB00008B/1200

* 9 7 8 0 9 8 4 8 1 3 5 0 6 *